I0644908

Praise for

FASHION, MODERNITY, AND MATERIALITY IN FRANCE

"The book's strengths lie in its interdisciplinarity, along with the deep knowledge and impressive scholarship of the contributors. Their specialist knowledge and their care in what they are writing shines through."

— Malcolm Barnard, author of *Fashion Theory: An Introduction*

"The essays in this collection establish a constellation of strong and rich French fashion notes in modern history, and together constitute a dynamic that resonates with recurring and related imagery and ideas. The fact that it's conceptually sophisticated and philosophical doesn't get in the way of it being a good read."

— Brian Seitz, author of *Intersubjectivity and the Double: Troubled Matters*

FASHION, MODERNITY, AND MATERIALITY IN FRANCE

FASHION, MODERNITY, AND MATERIALITY IN FRANCE

FROM ROUSSEAU TO ART DECO

EDITED BY

HEIDI BREVIK-ZENDER

STATE UNIVERSITY OF NEW YORK PRESS

Cover art: Claude Monet, *The Beach at Trouville*, 1870. ©The National Gallery, London.

Generous support for this volume was granted by
the Borchard Foundation Center on International Education.

Published by
State University of New York Press, Albany

Printed in the United States of America

For information, contact
State University of New York Press, Albany, NY
www.sunypress.edu

Library of Congress Cataloging-in-Publication Data

Names: Brevik-Zender, Heidi, [date], editor.
Title: Fashion, modernity, and materiality in France : from Rousseau to art deco / edited by Heidi Brevik-Zender.
Description: Albany : State University of New York, [2018] | Includes bibliographical references and index.
Identifiers: LCCN 2018000359| ISBN 9781438472355 (hardcover : alk. paper) | ISBN 9781438472362 (e-book)
Subjects: LCSH: Clothing and dress—France—History. | Fashion—France—History. | Clothing and dress in literature. | Fashion in literature. | Modernism (Literature)—France. | Materialism—France. | French literature—History and criticism.
Classification: LCC GT853 .F38 2018 | DDC 391.00944—dc23
LC record available at https://lccn.loc.gov/2018000359

10 9 8 7 6 5 4 3 2 1

CONTENTS

ILLUSTRATIONS

INTRODUCTION

Heidi Brevik-Zender

Once appreciated merely for its glamorous allure and regularly dismissed as frivolous and shallow, fashion is now thriving as a subject of serious academic inquiry that has attracted scholars working across a range of fields to explore dress in relation to culture, history, politics, and identity.[1] As Elizabeth Wilson has influentially observed, fashion is "a cultural phenomenon" and "an aesthetic medium for the expression of ideas, desires and beliefs circulating in society" (9). "Fashion may then be understood as ideological," she continues, "its function to resolve formally, at the imaginary level, social contradictions that cannot be resolved" (9). Both the ideological functions of fashion and its power as an aesthetic medium are evidenced by the fact that, over the last several decades, dress has emerged as a dynamic catalyst for new approaches to literature, art, design, and related forms of representation. In the French context in particular, scholars have productively linked fashion to expressions of what is often described as "modernity," a term that evokes rupture, a break with the past, whether actual or perceived.[2] Accordingly, the present volume

1. Currently design colleges and museums are spearheading academic efforts to interrogate fashion's myriad ideological, social, and historical functions. The Museum at the Fashion Institute of Technology in New York, for instance, has organized recent colloquia and published excellent exhibition catalogs on fashion's intersections with queerness, black identity, and the environment, among other important and timely subjects.

2. The body of scholarship on fashion and French modernity is robust and reflects a wide range of disciplinary perspectives and ideological concerns. For reasons of space, the following list of relevant titles is limited to book-length studies only (full references given at the end of this introduction): Elizabeth Amann, *Dandyism in the Age of Revolution*; Heidi Brevik-Zender, *Fashioning Spaces*; Kimberly Chrisman-Campbell, *Fashion Victims*; Alison Matthews David, *Fashion Victims*; Mary E. Davis, *Ballets Russes Style* and *Classic Chic*; Rhonda K. Garelick, *Rising Star*; Gloria Groom (ed.), *Impressionism, Fashion, and Modernity*; Susan Hiner, *Accessories to Modernity*; Simon Kelly and Esther Bell (eds.), *Degas, Impressionism, and the Paris Millinery Trade*; Marni Reva Kessler, *Sheer Presence*; Ulrich Lehmann, *Tigersprung*; Michael B. Miller, *The Bon Marché*; Philippe Perrot, *Fashioning the Bourgeoisie*; Mary Lynn Stewart, *Dressing Modern Frenchwomen*; Hannah Thompson, *Naturalism Redressed*; Nancy J. Troy, *Couture Culture*; Caroline Weber, *Queen of Fashion*. Of note is Valerie Steele's *Paris*

situates modernity as the era beginning with the philosophical interventions of the Enlightenment and lasting through the postwar 1920s, a span of years that were marked in France by radical social changes and transformations of thought that those living through the period, as well as those reflecting upon it later, often associated with the newness—the modernness—that fashion evokes and embodies.

Fashion, Modernity, and Materiality in France: From Rousseau to Art Deco mines the complexities of fashion—its artistic appeal, its problematic associations with superficiality and hypocrisy, its relationships to affective and corporeal human experience, to name a few—to create an intellectually significant interchange that uses dress to inspire new ways of thinking about the history of modernity, the body, material culture, and how they were represented in France during this period. Nine chapters illuminate reciprocal relationships between fashion and a range of media, including literary fiction, poetry, paintings, moral treatises, decorative arts, satirical literature, fashion magazines, mass-circulating newspapers, popular theatrical works, advertisements, and material objects. The research presented here revolves around a specific constellation of themes—fashion, modernity, and materiality from the eighteenth to the early twentieth centuries—offering historical coherence and depth of focus. At the same time, the chapters adopt a range of approaches, drawing on a variety of theoretical viewpoints including deconstruction, psychoanalysis, phenomenology, sociology, and gender theory. The book examines garments in connection to an array of subjects, from the performance of sexual identity to the trauma of war and efforts at post-war recovery, from the blurring of class distinctions to the gendering of different forms of labor, from evolving technologies of printing to modern techniques of painting and narrating. Several key questions framing this collection remain relevant today: What separates and connects clothing and the lived body? How do garments hold traces of the past and activate memories of human experience? What roles do clothing and adornment play in expressing gender identity? How does fashion help to define what it meant and what it means to be modern?

As the book's title indicates, the following chapters address in various ways fashion's *materiality*, that is, the fact that objects of dress are "things," as Bill Brown might term them, that are endowed with a physical, material presence. Recent scholarship in material culture studies has examined how people engage with objects to help situate themselves in society and also as a part of the formation of collective cultural memory. There is a reciprocal relationship between experience and objects in that, as has been argued, "matter (objects) can act upon subjects (people) through material and sensorial engagement as much as people can change and act upon matter" (Witcomb 44). In studying the impact of clothing on how individuals come into contact with the world, sociologist Joanne Entwistle (2000) understands

---

Fashion, a landmark in the scholarly treatment of fashion, now in its third edition. See also the pioneering special issue of the journal *L'Esprit Créateur* entitled *Fashion and Fashionability in French and Francophone Culture* (1997).

the dressed body as "a discursive and phenomenological field" (326). For her, "the body and dress operate dialectically: dress works on the body, imbuing it with social meaning, while the body is a dynamic field that gives life and fullness to dress" (327). Linking the sociological with the historical and the art historical in her examination of the nineteenth-century crinoline, Lynda Nead (2013) writes that "time, history and memory are all folded into the meaning of clothes" and, following Entwistle, argues that clothed bodies "can evoke memories and the past, as much as the constant change of the present" (502). Dress is a trigger for memory in part because it is a material instantiation of the past.

As the present volume argues, the fact that certain fashions during the historical period in question were as familiar to cultural producers and consumers as the clothes on their backs contributed to fashion's efficacy in invoking generalizable concerns. Accordingly, some chapters emphasize single items of dress that, during these years, would have been commonly encountered as a part of everyday life: chapter 2 is concerned with hats, chapter 3 examines gloves, chapter 6 explores veils, and chapter 7 considers military uniforms. In other essays particular dress items are highlighted as emblematic of specific forms of sexual, gendered, class, and racial identities, including the fop's wigs and toiletries (chapter 1), spinning skirts and bonnet ribbons (chapter 4), garments made of cotton from overseas colonies (chapter 5), servants' neo-aristocratic-age livery (chapter 7), and the modernist fedora (chapter 9). If the scholars in this collection understand items of attire in symbolic terms and approach them through literary, art historical, design, and cultural critique, they also draw on studies that focus on textile and garment manufacturing practices, as well as on historical developments in methods of production. Linking the material histories of clothing objects to their textual and pictorial depictions in art and culture, this book thereby forms a bridge between the important work accomplished by those who research material garments and those who take representations of them in novels, artworks, exhibitions, and plays as their primary areas of investigation.

The following chapters recognize fashion's historical associations with luxury, with aristocratic and high-society lifestyles, and with elegance, pleasure, and beauty, but they are also attentive to the array of sobering concerns equally ingrained in this epoch of France's past. If this was an exhilarating period characterized by thrilling forms of entertainment, advancements in technologies of communication and circulation, and creative revolutions, it was also a volatile time of labor and class struggle, gender and sexual discrimination, violent conflict, and national trauma. Against this backdrop, haute couture and the ready-to-wear clothing industries emerged as important markets and cultural exports just as their transforming production and consumption processes embedded themselves in France's evolving habits, its relationships to its own history, and its emergent performances of gendered, sexual, and class identities. In her groundbreaking analysis theorizing an intersection of race and fashion at what she calls the "second skin," Anne Anlin Cheng (2011) declares that "it may not be too much of an overstatement to say that the material and metaphysical boundary of the human body—and, by implication, what constitutes the human—forms one of the central philosophical concerns of the twentieth century" (8). If Cheng's study focuses on style and racial sexualization in relation to the (un)clothed body of Josephine Baker and is thus interested primarily with the period of modernism between the two World Wars, the present volume suggests that the philosophical concerns that Cheng cites had antecedents prior to modernism. As the authors in this volume show, the presence of dress in both demarcating and troubling categories of the human—as citizen, as man or woman, as living or uncanny, for example—were already informing the cultural production of modernity, when garments were called upon to conjure embodied anxieties, desires, and fantasies of the nation.

Practices and functions of dress, then as now, were far from standardized, given that fashions have diverse meanings that can be layered, shifting, ambiguous, and even contradictory. For instance, in chapter 8 by Áine Larkin, the form-fitting, buttoned, and braided livery donned by footmen in Marcel Proust's magnum opus *À la recherche du temps perdu* emphasizes the ornamental but socially subordinate role played by these attractive male servants in early twentieth-century moneyed Parisian circles. At the same time, as Nicholas White reveals in chapter 7, similar types of decorated men's garments, namely military uniforms, took on a radically different set of ominous, violent, and, as he terms it, "polymorphous" social and sexual connotations when worn by soldiers marching into battle, as depicted in the popular illustrated press, in Émile Zola's 1892 war novel *La Débâcle*, and in paintings and mass-produced lithography. Pointing to discursive connections between servant and military uniforms, these chapters illuminate how two turn-of-the-century, tailored masculine fashion items with comparable ornamented appearances could in fact enact a number of contrasting modern concerns.

Another subject brought to the fore throughout this volume might be called "traces of the (in)human," or instances where slippage occurs across the not-so-fixed categories of the living and the nonliving. Chapter 5 and Cary Hollinshead-Strick's chapter 4 both perform close readings of fictional works that center on uncanny figures including beautifully attired corpses and mummies. These two chapters, examining Gustave Flaubert's *Madame Bovary* and Théophile Gautier's *Le Roman de la momie*, respectively, illustrate how representations in novels of human residue left on worn garments reveal an authorial attentiveness to tensions between the animate and the inanimate. They join Marni Reva Kessler's discussion in chapter 6 of the spectral qualities of the veil and the unexpected way it may function simultaneously as both a presence and an absence; Susan Hiner's examination in chapter 2 of *marottes*, artificial yet realistic-looking mannequin heads used in the creation of ladies' hats; and Anne Green's chapter 3 study of gloves as objects that, for some writers, caused hands to resemble statues and troubled boundaries between flesh and fabric. Pierre Saint-Amand's opening chapter on the extravagantly dressed eighteenth-century petit-maître fop shows that through his hypercivility, this paragon of male fashion was likened less to a man than to a kind of mechanized puppet. As Saint-Amand reveals, the petit-maître's distinctive, exaggerated physical gestures of self-beautification and identity performance led some contemporaries to compare him to a marionette, an automaton, and even a mechanical being from another world. Collectively these analyses suggest the ways in which conceptions of the organic and the inorganic had come to overlap in this period, reflecting preoccupations of an age informed by rising technologies that seemed increasingly to confuse distinctions between human and nonhuman, between (wo)man and machine.

Following welcome trends in scholarship to provide a balanced gendered perspective on fashion, an additional feature of this volume is its substantive treatment of both female and male attire.[3] In the case of the former, Marni Reva Kessler's analysis of Impressionist Claude Monet's painting *The Beach at Trouville* focuses on the veil, offering a detailed reading of the materiality of both veil and pigment in this image of the artist's wife Camille and her female companion. Kessler illuminates how Monet played with interchanges among skin, fabric, and shadow, and argues that representing this ladies' accessory and its effects was key to the artist's developing a hybrid haptic-visual expression in his feminocentric beach scene. Also concerned with womenswear, Susan Hiner concentrates on the figure of the *modiste*, or female hatmaker, a popular character on the vaudeville stage and in mass-circulating fashion imagery. Exposing the ubiquity of the *modiste* as a polyvalent symbol of modernity, Hiner's chapter teases out links between representations of hats and the women who wore and constructed them, calling attention to the overlooked *modiste* and demonstrating her relevance to the scholarship of both women's history and material culture.

Focusing on masculine attire, Pierre Saint-Amand examines the social anxieties provoked by confusions of gender and sexual identity performed by the petit-maître, a precursor to later elegant male types such as the Italian *macaroni* and the Directory-era *incroyable*. For the Enlightenment philosopher Jean-Jacques Rousseau and other moralizing authors of the period, this proto-dandy figure represented a disquieting intermingling of feminine and masculine traits. On stage, in literature, and in satirical texts the petit-maître thereby came to be targeted as the embodiment of larger perceived threats, not just to modern virtue but also to the nation-state itself. Nicholas White, in his essay on military uniforms, turns toward displays of masculine identity that emerged against the tense backdrop of the Franco-Prussian War of 1870. Taking inspiration from theoretical writings on homosociality by Eve Kosofsky Sedgwick and on homoeroticism by Sharon Marcus, White explores a range of textual and pictorial examples of male soldiers, wherein nationalistic ideologies are complicated by homoerotic undertones that communicate deep fissures in the politics of Republican fraternity during the first decades of the Third Republic. In chapter 9, focusing on the Art Deco period, John Potvin calls attention

3. Recent groundbreaking work by Rachel Mesch to examine clothing's relation to transgender identity in nineteenth-century France promises to enrich future research on connections between gender and dress.

to displays of menswear at the 1925 and 1928 World Expositions, examining the turn toward industrialism and rationalism in France's national restoration efforts following World War I. These efforts, Potvin reveals, drew on attempts to increase consumption of French-made men's fashions, whereby objects of masculine attire, such as the iconic fedora, came to represent in material form France's presumed cultural preeminence as well as its postwar ambitions for economic expansionism.

The labor of fashion is another theme considered by multiple chapters in this collection. Susan Hiner's discussion of the *marotte*, a *modiste*'s essential tool of production, concentrates on the liminal status of the female laborers who were the primary manufacturers of hats but were also those most subject to commodification by a fashion system that simultaneously employed and objectified them. Anne Green's chapter examining gloves as material objects and as symbolic items in literature includes a discussion of the evolution of glove construction and its impact on the demographics of work. Green traces how an explosive rise in consumer demand for gloves throughout the 1800s provoked a range of changes, including glove-manufacturing jobs for provincial women, a nationwide need for more leather (and thus livestock farming), and the fabrication of new inventions such as glove sizing, cutting, and folding machines. The history of glove making, which was predominantly artisanal before the nineteenth century and became one of mass production in the following era, represents trends occurring more generally to social labor practices in the increasingly industrialized French economy.

In her chapter, Cary Hollinshead-Strick links work to literary creation, examining how fashion served as a longstanding leitmotif in Théophile Gautier's reflections about the transforming labor of writing. As a journalist Gautier profited firsthand from innovations such as the rotary printing press, a technology adopted from the fabric-decorating industry that enabled increased production of inexpensive mass-circulation newspapers. The recurrence of fashionable spinning women in Gautier's fiction and poetry echoes the whirl of the industrial printing press, a trope through which Hollinshead-Strick tracks the author's ambivalence about ever-blurring lines between "high-art" literary production and what he viewed as the nonaesthetic business of commercial journalism. For Áine Larkin, tensions between the labors of art and of domestic service are central to Marcel Proust's fashion-laden representation of alternately rigid and shifting social stratifications in *À la recherche du temps perdu*. Citing social theory by Proust's contemporary Thorstein Veblen and expanding the concept of work across gender lines and to include different categories of laborers such as the high-class prostitute, footman, cook, and maid, Larkin uncovers the ways in which Proust's nostalgic anxieties about social instabilities manifest in classed spaces—vertical staircases and horizontal railway platforms—and through outfits that both democratize and reinforce social and economic privilege. In his chapter John Potvin underscores the work of Parisian tailors to produce elegant garments for the modern man of the 1920s and to position themselves as leading manufactures of menswear against the dominance that had traditionally been held by British suit makers. By capitalizing on the rational, stabilizing, industrialized aesthetics of masculine fashion following the war, Potvin demonstrates, French government officials, journalists, and tailors sought to tap into the male garment industry in an attempt to enlarge their cultural and commercial predominance in national and international markets.

Questions of race and ethnicity in relationship to spectacle, performance, and the fashioned body are also central to this volume's organization. These overlapping issues, here termed "ideologies of color" with a nod to the volume's sartorial subject matter, were informed by global encounters that took place as international travel for pleasure and its criminal twin, colonization, soared to unprecedented levels during this period of French empire building and border crossing. Under these conditions dress increasingly operated to bring issues of race and ethnicity to the fore. They come into play, as the chapter by Pierre Saint-Amand demonstrates, in Michel-Étienne Descourtilz's travel narrative *Voyage d'un naturaliste* (1809) featuring the Haitian petit-maître Joseph, whose black skin further destabilizes the opulently dressed fop's already ambiguous sexual identity. They are seen, Susan Hiner indicates, on the vaudeville stage, in the upending presence of a blackface (and cross-dressed) actor in *L'Art de ne pas monter sa garde*, a nineteenth-century farce set in a milliner's studio. They are alluded to, Cary Hollinshead-Strick submits, in racially essentializing caricatures of Chinese visitors to the 1867 Paris Exposition, which connect by way of a popular hairstyle to modish Parisian women and illuminate links between Gautier's orientalist fiction and his writings on modern fashion. And they are present, chapter 5 shows, in George Sand's 1832 novel *Indiana*, in which the title character's creole maid dons her white mistress's dress, wearing it "incorrectly" and then suffering a tragic end portended by the incompatibility between her racially coded body and her borrowed ball gown. The fact that ideologies of color emerge across this volume rather than appearing in a single isolated chapter demonstrates both their cultural presence during the period in history that the book examines and their broad inclusion in current academic discussions.

Finally, several chapters explore the notion of representation itself, delving into the ways that fashion served as a potent catalyst for period reflections on the very processes by which literature and art were imagined and executed. How did authors and artists conceptualize the methods by which they produced their works? Where in the final creation might the writer or painter leave evidence of his or her own aesthetic engagement and concerns? Marni Reva Kessler cites Sigmund Freud's concept of the contranym to unravel Monet's depiction of the veil as both a material item and an absence, as a garment as well as its own ineffable shadow. In this way, Kessler shows, Camille's veil captures Monet's interrogation of the art of painting itself, a form of visual expression that on one hand comprises physical substances such as pigment and stretched fabric and, on the other hand, materializes an endlessly signifying set of meanings for painter and viewer about the subjects that the work concomitantly represents. Chapter 5 draws on Jacques Derrida and Walter Benjamin to examine "the fashion trace" in novels by George Sand, Gustave Flaubert, and Guy de Maupassant. This work explores how depictions of marks on dress were used to embed storytellers into their stories, suggesting a practice on the part of nineteenth-century novelists to use clothing less to achieve Baudelairean ephemerality and more to access the eternalness available in realist narration. In Anne Green's chapter, the force of the literary metaphor itself is made evident in the striking evolution of symbolic meaning that gloves undergo throughout the 1800s. If fiction writers first depended on gloves to suggest distinction, propriety, and honesty, by the end of the century the same accessories conveyed fears of violence, political unrest, and moral degeneration, amounting to what Green terms a "dystopian vision" of modern society. As writers of the period understood, it was the special potency of the figurative, the very symbolizing impetus of artistic expression itself, which enabled the articulation of their powerful social commentaries.

Invoking fashion's innovative spirit, this volume provides a new forum on dress in French modernity. As such it seeks to inspire future cross-disciplinary conversations in the scholarly study of dress that will continue to build on fashion's exceptional position at the junction of modernity and materiality.

Works Cited

Amann, Elizabeth. *Dandyism in the Age of Revolution: The Art of the Cut.* U of Chicago P, 2015.

Brevik-Zender, Heidi. *Fashioning Spaces:* Mode *and Modernity in Late-Nineteenth-Century Paris.* U of Toronto P, 2015.

Brown, Bill. "Thing Theory." *Critical Inquiry*, vol. 28, no.1, 2001, pp. 1–22.

Cheng, Anne Anlin. *Second Skin: Josephine Baker and the Modern Surface.* Oxford UP, 2011.

Chrisman-Campbell, Kimberly. *Fashion Victims: Dress at the Court of Louis XVI and Marie-Antoinette.* Yale UP, 2015.

David, Alison Matthews. *Fashion Victims: The Dangers of Dress Past and Present.* Bloomsbury, 2015.

Davis, Mary E. *Ballets Russes Style: Diaghilev's Dancers and Paris Fashion.* Reaktion, 2010.

———. *Classic Chic: Music, Fashion, and Modernism.* U of California P, 2008.

Entwistle, Joanne. "Fashion and the Fleshy Body: Dress as Embodied Practice." *Fashion Theory*, vol. 4, no. 3, 2000, pp. 323–48.

Garelick, Rhonda K. *Rising Star: Dandyism, Gender, and Performance in the Fin de Siècle.* Princeton UP, 1998.

Green, Anne. *Changing France: Literature and Material Culture in the Second Empire.* Anthem, 2011.

Groom, Gloria, editor. *Impressionism, Fashion, and Modernity.* Yale UP, 2012.

Hiner, Susan. *Accessories to Modernity: Fashion and the Feminine in Nineteenth-Century France.* U of Pennsylvania P, 2010.

Kelly, Simon, and Esther Bell, editors. *Degas, Impressionism, and the Paris Millinery Trade.* Prestel, 2017.

Kessler, Marni Reva. *Sheer Presence: The Veil in Manet's Paris.* U of Minnesota P, 2006.

Lehmann, Ulrich. *Tigersprung: Fashion in Modernity.* MIT P, 2000.

Miller, Michael B. *The Bon Marché: Bourgeois Culture and the Department Store, 1869–1920.* Princeton UP, 1981.

Nead, Lynda. "The Layering of Pleasure: Women, Fashionable Dress and Visual Culture in the mid-Nineteenth Century." *Nineteenth-Century Contexts*, vol. 35, no. 5, 2013, pp. 489–509.

Perrot, Philippe. *Fashioning the Bourgeoisie: A History of Clothing in the Nineteenth-Century*, translated by Richard Bienvenu. Princeton UP, 1994.

Steele, Valerie. *Paris Fashion: A Cultural History*. Berg, 1998.

Stewart, Mary Lynn. *Dressing Modern Frenchwomen: Marketing Haute Couture, 1919–1939.* Johns Hopkins UP, 2008.

Thompson, Hannah. *Naturalism Redressed: Identity and Clothing in the Novels of Emile Zola.* Legenda, 2004.

Troy, Nancy J. *Couture Culture: A Study in Modern Art and Fashion*. MIT P, 2003.

Weber, Caroline. *Queen of Fashion: What Marie Antoinette Wore to the Revolution*. Picador, 2007.

Wilson, Elizabeth. *Adorned in Dreams: Fashion and Modernity*. Rutgers UP, 2003.

Witcomb, Andrea. "Using Souvenirs to Rethink How We Tell Histories of Migration: Some Thoughts." In *Narrating Objects, Collecting Stories*, edited by Sandra H. Dudley, Amy Jane Barnes, Jennifer Binnie, Julia Petrov, and Jennifer Walklate. Routledge, 2012, pp. 36–50.

CHAPTER 1

PETITS-MAÎTRES AND FOPS IN THE EIGHTEENTH CENTURY

Pierre Saint-Amand
(Translated by Jennifer Curtiss Gage)

The Great Masquerade

Montesquieu's *Persian Letters*, in a discussion of Parisian conversation with all its excess and notorious grandiloquence, paints a portrait of the petit-maître as someone whose clothing has become his primary instrument of communication, the proxy for his representation in society. Rica showcases these "little talents" raised to the level of great art, on a par with the fop's dazzling eloquence: "There are others I know who have hit upon the happy idea of introducing inanimate objects into the conversation, and letting their embroidered coat, their blonde wig, their snuffbox, cane, and gloves speak for them" (*Persian* 112–13).[1] It is this figure, the paragon of fashion in the eighteenth century, that I wish to trace through its many literary and sociological representations. To begin with, he is the star of the libertine stage. Patrice Bollon, who has studied trends and revolutions in style and appearances, identifies the petit-maître as a proto-dandy phenomenon and describes the ironic sociological evolution of this class of young men who flamboyantly parade their aristocratic swag:

> [T]hese wayward aristocrats, disciples of debauchery galore, are beyond the pale in their behavior. . . . Their wigs are taller, more convoluted than their peers'; their heels are high and red, impractical and baroque; their faces are powdered and caked, highlighted with beauty spots, and

1. "petits talents"; "J'en connais d'autres, qui se sont trouvés d'introduire dans les conversations des choses inanimées et d'y faire parler leur habit brodé, leur perruque blonde, leur tabatière, leur canne et leurs gants" (175). The literature of the period weaves countless variations on these "inanimate objects" that constitute the accoutrements of the petit-maître.

FIGURE 1.1 "Habit de drap galonné à la financiere avec un galon large." French, 1779. *Gallerie des modes et costumes français, 20e : Cahier de costumes français, 14e suite d'habillemens à la mode en 1779.* U.118 Photograph © 2018 Museum of Fine Arts, Boston.

FIGURE 1.2 "Jeune Elégant vêtu d'un habit brodé avec une veste du plus nouveau goût." French, 1787. *Gallerie des modes et costumes français, 53e : Cahier de costumes français, 47e suite d'habillemens à la mode en 1787.* iii.336 Photograph © 2018 Museum of Fine Arts, Boston.

> the silk of their stockings is as finely spun as spiderwebs: they stretch their aristocratic essence to the point where, exposed in all its absurdity, it vanishes. (261)[2]

The petits-maîtres help foment the famous "revolution of appearances" identified by historian Daniel Roche, along with a new concern for hygiene; in fact, they escalate the "struggles of representation" engendered by new patterns of consumption (*Enlightenment* 555).[3] They are, in short, the advocates and the practitioners of an immoral economy, the addicts in a burgeoning new culture of materiality, desiring an array of futile objects.

Such fops can be found in a midcentury novel by the Chevalier de La Morlière, *Angola* (1746), which recounts the title character's education. Angola is presented with a superlative model in the person of Almaïr, "a young man of the highest birth and one of the most fashionable courtiers" (399).[4] La Morlière sets his petits-maîtres in motion at the theater and the opera, in the customary spaces of representation. Endowed by the novelist with a sophisticated theatricality, the tribe is placed from the outset within the cult of visibility revered by these insolent young men. La Morlière takes care to illumine them by the glow of candlelight: "Most of them were there to display their charms in the half-light of the stage, that distant reflection of candles that is so kind to features past their prime" (433).[5] La Morlière emphatically denounces their noisy parade. The petits-maîtres exploit every available prop, using the embellishments of costume as weapons of charm, instruments of seduction. The portrait painted by the author shows a full-dress spectacle of self, a quasi-masturbatory masquerade of auto-reflection, a dizzying display of superficial signs. Various accessories (lorgnette, bouquet, watch) are diverted from their usual functions and serve only to enhance the spectacular aspect of the wearer:

> Reclining provocatively rather than propped against the stage, they flaunted their seductive charms, constantly *brandishing* their lorgnette, *caressing their cravat*, nuzzling their bouquet. . . . they were awaiting the

---

2. "ces aristocrates dévoyés, adeptes de toutes les débauches, outrent leurs comportements. . . . Leurs perruques sont plus hautes, plus tarabiscotées que celles de leurs pairs ; leurs talons sont hauts et rouges, impraticables et baroques ; leur visage est poudré et fardé, rehaussé par les mouches, et la soie de leurs bas d'une minceur arachnéenne : ils portent leur essence d'aristocrates au point où, en se révélant dans toute son absurdité, elle s'évanouit." (Quotations translated by Jennifer Curtiss Gage, except where otherwise indicated). On men's fashion in the eighteenth century, see Delpierre, *Se vêtir au XVIIIe siècle* (37–43) and *Dress in France in the Eighteenth Century* (23–28).

3. See Roche, *La France des Lumières* (505); trans. *France in the Enlightenment* (555).

4. "jeune homme de la plus haute naissance et un des seigneurs de la cour le plus à la mode." Further citations will be supplied in parentheses.

5. "Le plus grand nombre était là pour étaler leurs charmes dans le demi-jour de spectacle, dans cette réflexion éloignée des bougies si favorables aux attraits surannés."

> moment for the most interesting place to cross the stage while consulting their watch, distracting the actors . . . (433, original emphasis)[6]

La Morlière couches this version of masculine youth in terms of the companionship and promiscuity of women, blurring the lines of sexual identity in his portrait: the lexicon he uses for these petits-maîtres belong equally to a feminine register, and indeed the petits-maîtres share with the women who admire them the same coquetry, their habitual *minauderies* (simpering) (433). In fact, they rival the other sex in exhausting "all the commonplaces of a coquetry that would have been fitting in the most feminine of women" (433).[7]

Louis de Boissy stages this exhibition of the gentleman of fashion in his play *Le Français à Londres* (1727), with its portrayal of a certain marquis de Polinville, an indecent petit-maître, an artist of self-satisfaction and self-promotion. Like La Morlière's heroes, Polinville promotes outrageous exhibitionism: "He flings himself into a chair, crosses his legs, taps his foot, hums a tune, twiddles his jabot with one hand, and with the other strokes his chin" (194).[8] Polinville confides to a young English lord the secret of the petit-maître's grand masquerade—a fluid repertoire of body language, a special code of etiquette, a ridiculous hypercivility: "A shake of the head, a shrug of the shoulder, a gesture, a smile, a look, an expression, a tone of voice; the way one sits down, stands up, holds his hat, takes snuff, uses a handkerchief, spits" (191).[9]

This particular pantomime leads Elisabeth Bourguinat to describe the petits-maîtres in mechanical terms. Echoing the marquis Louis-Antoine de Caraccioli, she compares them to *pantins* (marionettes), wooden figures operated by strings. Bourguinat mentions their self-proclaimed appropriation of mechanized movements as a sort of perverse asceticism that raises these figures to the stature of prototypes, of creators of fashion: "their peculiar gestures and especially their habit of pirouetting on one heel, combined with an excess of makeup and ornament, often earns them comparison to automata or marionettes" (140).[10] Bourguinat cites a satirical journal of the period, *Le Courrier des planètes*, which describes the

6. "Couchés immodestement plutôt qu'appuyés sur le théâtre, ils étalaient leurs charmes séducteurs, *braquaient* continuellement leur lorgnette, *caressaient leurs jabots*, badinaient avec un bouquet. . . . ils attendaient le moment de l'endroit le plus intéressant pour traverser le théâtre en regardant leur montre, dérangeaient les acteurs . . ."

7. "tous les lieux communs d'une coquetterie qui aurait paru décente dans les femmes les plus décidées."

8. "Il se précipite dans un fauteuil, une jambe sur l'autre, tape du pied, marmotte un air, joue d'une main avec son jabot et se caresse le menton de l'autre."

9. "Un coup de tête, un air d'épaule, un geste, un souris, un regard, une expression, une inflexion de voix ; la façon de s'asseoir, de se lever, de tenir son chapeau, de prendre du tabac, de se moucher, de cracher."

10. "leur gestuelle particulière et notamment l'habitude qu'ils ont de pirouetter sur un talon, jointe à l'abus du fard et de la parure, les font souvent comparer à des automates ou à des marionnettes."

petits-maîtres as strange creatures, machine-men from another planet. They stand out as kings of curls and scent: "It seems that the creator said to these creatures: 'Be powdered, curlicued, perfumed; admire yourself in the mirror. . . . eat, drink, sleep, be insolent, and strut your stuff: that is all I ask of you to fulfill your destiny; for that alone I have created you'" (cited in Bourguinat 140).[11] But for the same Caraccioli, the petits-maîtres' mechanization means the mastery of a set of gestures, a refined extension of their bodies' function: "They must be completely automated, moved only by springs, with no soul apart from eyes, tongue, and fingers, flashing diamonds, flourishing two or three snuffboxes in succession, whipping out first an English watch and then a Parisian one" (35).[12]

The definition of petit-maître given in the *Encyclopédie* of Diderot and d'Alembert covers the various attributes noted so far, the narcissism and obsession with transitory fashion: "name given to youth intoxicated with self-love, boastful in speech, affected in manners, and refined in the cut of their clothes. Someone has defined the petit-maître as a gossamer insect that glitters in its evanescent finery, flits about, and flutters its powdered wings" ("Petit-maître," *Encyclopédie*).[13] If the humanity of these creatures seems to be in question, given the mechanical attributes repeatedly evoked, here they metamorphose into insects. But what appears truly problematic is their masculine identity as *vir*, belonging to the masculine gender. The *Encyclopédie* article also raises suspicion as to the female company they frequent: "Let us add that everywhere this sort of man is tolerated, there are also flighty, vain, capricious, self-serving women, in love with their looks. . . . Thus the term petit-maître is extended to the sex tainted with the same defects, who are called petites-maîtresses."[14] The *Encyclopédie* notes this genealogical transfer, this

---

11. "Il semble que le créateur ait dit à ces êtres-là : 'Sois poudré, frisé, ambré ; regarde-toi dans un miroir . . . mange, bois, dors, fais l'insolent, et promène-toi : voilà tout ce que je demande de toi, tu auras rempli ta destination ; je ne t'ai créé que pour cela.'"

12. "Il faut être tout automate, n'agir que par ressorts, ne connaître d'âme que ses yeux, sa langue et ses doigts, étaler des diamants, promener successivement deux ou trois tabatières entre ses mains, tirer tantôt une montre anglaise et tantôt une de Paris."

13. "nom qu'on donne à la jeunesse ivre de l'amour de soi-même, avantageuse dans ses propos, affectée dans ses manières et recherchée dans son ajustement. Quelqu'un a défini le petit-maître, un insecte léger qui brille dans sa parure éphémère, papillonne, et secoue ses ailes poudrées." The article was perhaps authored by Diderot, who knows the subject well, and, in his novel *Les Bijoux indiscrets* (1748), depicts petits-maîtres with a combination of entomological caricature and pneumatic metaphor: "toward the end of the salon fluttered about two petits-maîtres and a young magistrate full of airs, blowing on his ruffles, incessantly adjusting his peruke, visiting his mouth, and complimenting himself in the glass that his paint held on so well. Except these three butterflies, all the company was in profound veneration . . ." (*Indiscreet Toys* 202); ("sur le fond de la salle voltigeaient deux petits maîtres un jeune magistrat rempli d'airs, soufflant sur ses manchettes, sans cesse rajustant sa perruque, visitant sa bouche et se félicitant dans les glaces de ce que son rouge allait bien : excepté ses trois papillons, le reste de la compagnie . . ." Diderot, *Œuvres* [193]).

14. "Ajoutons que partout où l'on tolère ces sortes d'hommes, on y trouve aussi des

strange transmigration of the sexes. But it must be noted that here the prototype for the feminine is the man, tricked out from head to toe (the author of the article recalls examples of petits-maîtres going back to ancient Rome). The history of fashion is often preoccupied with the feminine copy of the petit-maître's model, to the point of ignoring the original.[15] It behooves us to restore this precedence of makeup and artifice within the male. A companion *Encyclopédie* article by Joseph-François Desmahis, on the topic *Fat* (Fop), also provides a portrait of this original species that keeps aloof from the world while making a spectacle of himself within it. The fop, that impossible blend of flaws turned into virtues, observes only "the time of the embroiderer and the jeweler."[16] Envisioning his character's ultimate subjection, his total domination by fashion, Desmahis continues: "He looks to fashion for his quirks and his clothing alike, for both his ailments and his carriages, for his doctor as well as his tailor."[17] Desmahis concludes with the figure's histrionics, his continual alteration through a succession of roles: "to see him you would think he is wearing a mask; to hear him you would think he is playing a role."[18]

Louis-Antoine de Caraccioli, a prolific and inspired writer who made the petit-maître the star of his appropriately titled *Livre à la mode* (1759), also addressed the confusion of gender, the transfer of this obsession with appearances to the sphere of men, as a sort of transgression against the original inclination of the species:

> Attire that one would never dream could suit anyone but a woman became at the beginning of this century indispensable furnishing for men of style. . . . and in Paris there was such fanaticism for frippery that soon the sexes became indistinguishable. The cavalier looked as effeminate as women themselves, and like the latter he had his powders, beauty spots, perfumes, and his cosmetics. (91)[19]

---

femmes changeantes, vaines, capricieuses, intéressées, amoureuses de leur figure. . . . Aussi le nom de petit-maître est-il étendu jusqu'au sexe taché des mêmes défauts, et qu'on nomme petites-maîtresses."

15. This applies even to the recent book by Kimberly Chrisman-Campbell, *Fashion Victims: Dress at the Court of Louis XVI and Marie-Antoinette*, which devotes a chapter to the *petite-maîtresse* while only briefly mentioning the original.

16. "l'heure du brodeur et du bijoutier."

17. "Il consulte la mode pour ses travers comme pour ses habits, pour ses indispositions comme pour ses voitures, pour son médecin comme pour son tailleur."

18. "à le voir vous croiriez qu'il a un masque ; à l'entendre vous diriez qu'il joue un rôle."

19. "Les toilettes qu'on ne soupçonnait pas pouvoir convenir à personne qu'à des femmes, devinrent au commencement de ce siècle un meuble indispensable pour les hommes du bel air. . . . et ce fut dans Paris un tel fanatisme pour les toilettes qu'on y confondit bientôt les deux sexes. Le cavalier parut aussi efféminé que les dames même, et comme elles, il eut ses poudres, ses mouches, ses odeurs et ses fards . . ." In the *Encyclopédie* article "Toilette (Modes)," Louis de Jaucourt notes an anthropological mutation, a confusion of genders: "The term toilette is also applied to hangings of silk or other luxurious fabrics, lace-edged or fringed, that are draped above the mirrors adorning women's dressing tables, or even men's, since the

FIGURE 1.3 "Petit Maitre en chenille Fraque de couleur à la mode." French, 1781. *Gallerie des modes et costumes français, 35e : Cahier de costumes français, 27e suite d'habillemens à la mode en 1781.* II.201(bis) Photograph © 2018 Museum of Fine Arts, Boston.

For Caraccioli, the petit-maître is the product of a unique anthropological evolution, first through differentiation from the animal kingdom, and then within the scale of humans themselves. Through assorted adornment and accessories, the petit-maître achieves an impossible but unique hypercivility: "we have become pretty little puppets who mince and bat their eyelashes and wave their hands, who powder and perfume themselves" (33).[20] The aim is to reach the height of prettiness, the supreme level of excellence and taste, of absolute refinement. Caraccioli also imposes the imperative of "dematerializing" oneself (33). Even if the petit-maître is drawn to excessive consumption in response to the relentless cycle of novelty, his expenditure is somehow sublimated, swept up in the volatility of the ephemeral, the exactions of appearance. He blasts through sartorial routine, blows open wardrobes: "You must get the first new fabric of the year from Lyon, you must look askance at any outfit that is not equally cutting-edge, continually fuss with your laces and know how to show them off, wave around a handkerchief doused in perfumes, and use it with simultaneous grace and force" (35).[21] This last gesture requires a peculiar and virtually impossible choreography. Caraccioli's version of politeness is an inversion of ancestral violence, of ancient rusticism: "Every day we are taught to kill one another, which never strikes us as the least bit strange: is it not more reasonable to show one another how to live prettily and to make ourselves agreeable?" (40).[22] This politeness is in fact stunningly modern, representing an evolution of civility, the universalization of the pretty (joli): "make the world wholly marvelous and wholly pretty" (40).[23]

Jean-Jacques Rousseau, whose works contain many scathing attacks on the petit-maître, portrays the figure in an early comedy, *Narcisse ou l'amant de soi-même* (1752), where already we see the confusion of gender that fascinates Rousseau above all else. Valère, blind to the effect of his airs, is depicted with feminine attributes, adorned with *fleurs* and *pompons* (*OC* 2: 985) ("Flowers! Tassels!" *Narcissist* 239). He is caught grooming himself, preoccupied with his "jewel box," obsessed with "the

---

latter have turned into women" ("On appelle pareillement toilettes, les tapis de soie, ou autres riches étoffes, bordés de dentelle ou de frange, et qu'on étend au-dessus du miroir qui orne la toilette des dames, ou même des hommes qui de nos jours sont devenus femmes").

20. "nous sommes maintenant de jolies petites marionnettes qui faisons des mines, qui jouons de la prunelle, qui remuons des mains, qui nous poudrons, qui nous parfumons."

21. "Il faut avoir la première étoffe qui se fabrique chaque année à Lyon, jeter un œil de mépris sur tout habit qui n'est pas aussi neuf, arranger souvent des dentelles et savoir les mettre en ostentation, étaler un ample mouchoir baigné dans des eaux de senteur, et se moucher avec grâce et force en même temps." The petit-maître's life must be regulated by a set of rules: the arrogation of frivolity, membership in a like-minded community, the life of *style* that Caraccioli advocates as "living prettily" (*vivre joliment*) (40).

22. "On nous apprend tous les jours à nous tuer, et cela ne nous paraît point étrange : n'est-il pas plus raisonnable de nous montrer à vivre joliment et à nous rendre aimables ?"

23. "rendre le monde tout merveilleux et tout joli."

use of makeup" (238).[24] Surprising him in the act, his father Lisimon scolds Valère for wasting time ("Do you need all this to tie your hair and put on a coat?") and for "pirouetting in front of a mirror" (243).[25]

Later in the play, Rousseau alters his character's sex, through a portrait that disguises him as a woman. Thus, Valère metamorphoses from "the handsomest young man" (233) into a "[female] beauty" (240) before his very own blind and enchanted eyes.[26] His valet Frontin finishes off the portrait, making the identity switch explicit: "Just a little coquette, very empty-headed, and very vain without having any reason to be: in a word a female petit-maître" (240).[27] Clearly, Rousseau wished to conceive masculine vanity as a radical transposition of feminine attributes. The prototype of the fop is none other than the woman, as if male vanity made sense only as a borrowing from her "unbearably vain [nature]" (252).[28] The petit-maître is a perfect mimic of the other sex: "Valère, with his delicate manner and affected elegance of dress, is really a kind of woman hidden in a man's clothing; and this portrait seems less to disguise him than to reveal him in his natural state" (233).[29] The effeminacy of Valère is understood here, as elsewhere in Rousseau's work, as the contamination of one sex by the other. He designates fashion as the generator of this generalized travesty, as the grand equalizer of differences. For Rousseau, fashion is what brings about this perverse intermingling, this promiscuity that blurs the two sexes, effacing their distinctness.

In *Narcisse*, the gender confusion reverts back onto language itself. Frontin, the servant, finds himself confronting the unnameable: his description of this transvestite portrait descends into "gibberish" (256): "It's my master, a young woman . . ." (257).[30] Later there is a medley of muddled pronouns: "it's he! Who? He? You mean 'she'!" (265).[31] The restoration of order at the conclusion of *Narcisse* allows Valère to regain his manhood again only through the renunciation, the total loss, of his feminine borrowings, and through a true discovery of the other sex. He must sacrifice homosexual narcissism and demonstrate a definitive tropism toward woman as sole love object. Thus is Narcissus corrected.

If in the person of Valère Rousseau raises the question of the original and the copy from the perspective of male or female gender, it cannot be ignored that

24. "boîte à mouches"; "l'usage du rouge" (983).

25. "Faut-il tant d'appareil pour nouer des cheveux et mettre un habit ?"; "faire la roue devant un miroir" (990).

26. "plus joli homme" (977); "belle" (986).

27. "Une petite personne bien coquette, bien minaudière, bien vaine sans grand sujet de l'être : en un mot, un vrai petit-maître femelle" (986).

28. "vanité insupportable" (1001).

29. "Valère est, par sa délicatesse et par l'affectation de sa parure, une espèce de femme cachée sous des habits d'homme, et ce portrait ainsi travesti, semble moins le déguiser que le rendre à son état naturel" (977).

30. "galimatias" (1005); "c'est mon maître, c'est une fille . . ." (1006).

31. "c'est lui . . ."—"Dites donc, elle" (1015).

Rousseau's literary character is himself a copy of multiple models that emerge in the theater of the period. Valère belongs to a celebrated lineage of petits-maîtres, from Damis in Voltaire's *L'Indiscret* (1725) to Marivaux's better-known *Petit-maître corrigé* (1739).

In *La Nouvelle Héloïse* (1761), Rousseau's critique of the theater reveals his anxiety vis-à-vis the chiasmic inversion of the two sexes. The danger of unbridled circulation of the sexes is for Rousseau a communicative contagion that erases the boundaries between identities. Saint-Preux observes in his letters on Paris: "One can hardly conceive whence come enough men to spread themselves everywhere. . . . and men like money seem to multiply by circulating. So that is where a woman learns to speak, act, and think like them, and they like her" (*New Heloise* 221).[32] Castigating the French stage for its foolishness, Saint-Preux singles out those he designates as the grotesque descendants of Molière's various Marquis, the "petits-maîtres bourgeois." They are the prime targets of his attack on topocentrism in the Parisian theater, and Rousseau simultaneously condemns the bourgeoisie's appropriation of ridiculous aristocratic extravagance. Saint-Preux writes:

> The theater exists for them alone. They appear both as represented in the middle of the stage and representing on the two sides; they are characters on the stage and comedians on the benches. . . . so it is that the modern stage never sheds its boring dignity. They know only how to show people in gilt clothing. (207)[33]

The French theater, abandoning the convention of illusion, produces actors transformed into drawing-room fashion dummies. The incursion of theater into the public sphere makes men and women alike into creatures of display, devoted to wholesale ostentation. Soon we see "Cato powdered in white, and Brutus in a pannier"; "They paste French fashion over the Roman costume" (208).[34] The two sexes reflect images of one another in the disguises they project. Possessing a repertoire of artifices, each is a "simulacrum of fashion" (223).[35] The disfigurement of the two sexes is activated by the fashion machine: powder, hoopskirts, rouge . . . Such are the magic ingredients of artifice.[36]

---

32. "On a peine à concevoir d'où tant d'hommes peuvent se répandre partout . . . et les hommes semblent, comme les espèces, se multiplier par la circulation. C'est donc là qu'une femme apprend à parler, agir et penser comme eux, et eux comme elle" (*Julie* 192).

33. "C'est pour eux uniquement que sont faits les spectacles ; ils s'y montrent à la fois comme représentés au milieu du théâtre, et comme représentants aux deux côtés ; ils sont personnages sur la scène, et comédiens sur les bancs. . . . c'est ainsi que la scène moderne ne quitte plus son ennuyeuse dignité : on n'y sait plus montrer les hommes qu'en habit doré" (179–80).

34. "Caton poudré au blanc, et Brutus en panier"; "Ils calquent, remarque encore Saint-Preux, les modes françaises sur l'habit romain" (181).

35. "simulacre de la mode" (195).

36. In *L'Homme dissonant au dix-huitième siècle*, Caroline Jacot Grapa discusses these

FIGURE 1.4 "La Petite Loge," *Troisième suite d'estampes pour servir à l'histoire des modes et du costume en France dans le XVIIIe siècle.* Bibliothèque nationale de France, Paris.

---

pages on the petit-maître in terms of Rousseau's dread of the effeminate man. Recalling Rousseau's dream of perfectly delineated sexes, she writes : "The petit-maître is the powdered and beribboned featherbrain, the flightiness of sexual confusion made flesh. . . . His borrowing of feminine traits . . . earns him Rousseau's vehement condemnation : 'A perfect woman and a perfect man must be no more alike in soul than in countenance ; such vain imitations between the sexes are the height of unreason ; they make the wise man laugh and cupids

Inspired by Rousseau's critique, Fougeret de Monbron evokes the distortion of sexual identities in similar terms in *La Capitale des Gaules* (1759). Observing the process of rivalry engendered by fashion, he describes the mimetic behavior of young men. Like Rousseau, Monbron sees the woman as the original model to be emulated: "Young men see fine clothes; they covet similar ones. Everything makes an impression on them, everything awakens their desires. What is false in everything is what excites them the most. Nothing is more prized by them than dealings with a fashionable girl, an actress at the Opera, or a comedienne" (172).[37] They are thus caught up in an economy of speculation, debts, and consumption of mimetic objects. Monbron goes further than Rousseau in proclaiming his disgust for the confusion of the sexes: for the former it is a sign of advanced decadence that vitiates genealogy itself, undermining the ancestral race. Observing modern man sapped by softness, he is nostalgic for ancient times when men brandished their virility unflinchingly. In Monbron's view, salons are designed to corrupt men. In order to regain their potency, they should return to cabarets and taverns: "The only things that set apart the sexes today are the cap and the hat, skirt and britches. Apart from these, men are the same as women. They require adornment, perfume, and thrice-ruffled cuffs. In the closet they need contraptions that even Sybarites would not recognize" (184).[38]

This reproach of decadence is tinged with a graver hue that shadows the petit-maître and concerns no less than the nation itself. The petit-maître is a perfect distillation of French defects, a most fitting representation of France herself. Boissy's previously cited play *Le Français à Londres* clearly illuminates this aspect, which the satirical literature of the century revisits ad infinitum. Polinville is French in all his splendor, "a petit-maître of France" (181)[39] par excellence, and his character presents a threat to his host nation. In fact, he represents a doubly corruptive threat expressed simultaneously in the realm of civility (his hyperbolically exaggerated manners) and sexuality (his ambiguous sexual orientation). In an original family

---

flee'" ("Le petit-maître, c'est le frivole poudré et enrubanné, c'est toute l'inconséquence faite chair du mélange des sexes. . . . L'emprunt des traits féminins . . . suscite les condamnations les plus vives de la part de Rousseau : 'Une femme parfaite et un homme parfait ne doivent pas plus se ressembler d'âme que de visage ; ces vaines imitations de sexe sont le comble de la déraison ; elles font rire le sage et fuir les amours,'" 354; Rousseau, *Julie*, part 1, Letter XLVI [from Julie], 105).

37. "Les jeunes gens voient de beaux habits ; ils veulent en avoir de semblables. Tout les frappe ; tout leur donne des désirs. Le faux sur toute chose est ce qui les touche le plus. Rien ne leur paraît au-dessus du commerce d'une fille à la mode, d'une actrice d'Opéra ou d'une comédienne."

38. "Il n'y a tout au plus aujourd'hui que la cornette et le chapeau, la jupe et la culotte qui distinguent les deux sexes. A cela près, les hommes sont des femmes. Il leur faut une toilette, des eaux de senteur et des manchettes à trois rangs. Il leur faut dans la garde-robe de ces meubles dont les Sybarites ont ignoré l'usage."

39. "petit-maître de France."

drama, he succeeds in seducing two of Lord Craff's children. The English father is confronted with a twofold menace to his children: a daughter (Eliante) to be remarried and a son (Lord Houzey) to be extricated from a compromising friendship, a seduction. Indeed, for Houzey, Polinville is "the most congenial, most gracious young man" (178).[40] Later, the young Englishman expresses the effect of dazzled subjugation that he feels in the presence of the marquis, who has become his sole object of desire: "I count as lost every moment passed without the pleasure of your company." Or again: "Teach me, I beg you! how you manage to be so agreeable. It is a mystery that eludes us, that I cannot express" (190).[41]

In satirical texts, the English aristocrat is often contrasted with the French petit-maître. The former resists effeminization and the seductions of fashion and succeeds in observing properly virile behavior, upholding the nobiliary genealogy long lost to his French counterpart. Kimberly Chrisman-Campbell cites contemporary English writings on the subject in her book *Fashion Victims*. They highlight the pressure to consume experienced by visitors to Paris, where the seasonal requirements of fashion reigned supreme. She points to a statement by John Adams: "The first thing to be done, in Paris, is always to send for a Taylor, a Peruke maker and Shoemaker, for this nation has established such a domination over the Fashion, that neither Cloaths, Wigs nor Shoes made in any other place will do in Paris" (75). In similar terms, the Scottish writer Tobias Smollett describes the strange situation of the English traveler who must shed his native dress in an instant metamorphosis:

> When an Englishman comes to Paris, he cannot appear until he has undergone a total metamorphosis. At his first arrival he finds it necessary to send for the taylor, perukier, hatter, shoemaker, and every other tradesman concerned in the equipment of the human body. . . . on his return to his own country all this frippery is useless. He cannot appear in London until he has undergone another thorough metamorphosis." (Cited in Chrisman-Campbell 75–76)

The Many Worlds of the Petit-maître

The satirical literature of the eighteenth century was captivated by these petits-maîtres, at once victims and agents of fashion. In *Le Livre des quatre couleurs* (1759 or 1760), a companion booklet to his earlier *Livre à la mode*, the Marquis de Caraccioli again turns to the latest fashions, the most current tastes of the day, and here too the petit-maître is front and center. Caraccioli begins with a portrait of this contradictory, flighty figure:

---

40. "le garçon le plus aimable, le plus gracieux !"

41. "Je compte pour perdus tous les moments que je n'ai pas le bonheur d'être avec vous"; "Enseignez-moi, de grâce ! comment vous faites pour être si aimable. C'est un je ne sais quoi qui nous manque, que je ne puis exprimer."

> A perpetual preacher of variety, he flaunts it in his clothing, his expressions, his gestures, his postures, his gait, his beliefs and in his language. . . . he is ecstatic at the sight of a new fabric, and no sooner is it cut than he rejects it; every day he summons new wigmakers, and new tailors, and every day he sports a coiffure and an ensemble of extraordinary taste; . . . he can no longer stand ambergris and he orders it by the shop full; he calls for his carriage, and goes to bed; he wants to write, and he continually goes walking; in a word, one eye is laughing while the other cries; his forehead relaxes and his eyebrow frowns; he disguises his face every which way, and he gives an impression of being a marionette, a chameleon, a monkey, or Proteus himself. (77)[42]

These attributes are later embodied in the person of Caraccioli's Chevalier de Muscoloris, whose last will and testament are presented. In this posthumous text, Caraccioli details the character's biography. Muscoloris (whose name substantiates the figure's blend of perfume and colors) was born in the midst of a ball, a veritable "pleasure-child" (99).[43] His youth realizes the promise of this extraordinary birth: "The grace he lent to a ribbon, a purse, a cuff, was beyond imagining. His adornment and his gestures endlessly turned the heads of our young women" (99).[44] Fast becoming a "fashion doll" (99)[45] modeling the latest fashions, ambassador at large for Parisian purveyors of fashion, perfume, and flowers, he is also their faithful client, a rabid consumer of these prized wares.[46] Returning to Paris, he is named Grand

42. "Prédicateur perpétuel de la variété, il l'affiche sur ses habits, dans ses regards, dans ses gestes, dans ses postures, dans sa démarche, dans sa croyance et dans son langage . . . il s'extasie à la vue d'une nouvelle étoffe et à peine est-elle coupée, qu'il la rejette ; il fait appeler chaque jour de nouveaux perruquiers et de nouveaux tailleurs, et chaque jour, il arbore une frisure et un habit d'un goût tout à fait extraordinaire ; . . . il ne peut plus souffrir l'ambre et il s'en fait apporter des magasins ; il fait atteler, et il se met au lit ; il veut écrire, et il ne cesse de se promener ; en un mot, il rit d'un œil, et pleure de l'autre ; il épanouit le front, et il fronce le sourcil ; il travestit son visage de toutes manières, et il laisse douter s'il est pantin, caméléon, singe ou Protée lui-même." Chantal Thomas quotes Louis Sébastien Mercier's comment on the practice of curling as an active process of cultural emasculation: "Two centuries ago we had the weakness of imitating women in the art of curling, which effeminizes and denatures us" ("Il y a deux siècles que nous avons eu la faiblesse d'imiter les femmes dans cet art de la frisure qui nous efféminе et nous dénature," 36).

43. "enfant de la volupté."

44. "On ne peut imaginer toutes les grâces qu'il donnait à un ruban, à une bourse, à une manchette. Sa parure et ses gestes tournèrent mille fois la tête à nos plus jeunes femmes."

45. "poupée."

46. History confirms that conspicuous consumption was never far from Caraccioli's imagination. Daniel Roche evokes "the costlier brilliance" (136) of the nobility's wardrobe. See "The transformation of men's clothes" in *The Culture of Clothing: Dress and Fashion in the Ancien Régime* (134–41). Regarding the effeminacy of petits-maîtres, Morag Martin offers a perspective that takes into account the consumption of cosmetics; see *Selling Beauty:*

FIGURE 1.5 "La Toilette du petit maître," *Monument du costume physique et morale de la fin du dix-huitième siècle ou tableaux de la vie.* Smith College Museum of Art, Northampton, Massachusetts.

Petit-Maître in "the Order of Frivolity" (100).[47] His entry into the Order is marked by an accession to excellence: "His graceful way of presiding over the chapter meetings, when they debated the proper manner of taking snuff, of using a handkerchief, or of spitting, was a sight to see. He was the first to introduce embroidered pumps, which are now worn to such high praise" (102).[48] The Chevalier's death is entirely in character, an end befitting his potential: struck down as it were by the ephemeral, he dies to be reunited with the volatile matter of which he was the most splendiferous incarnation:

> The too obliging Muscoloris was stricken with his deadly illness while chasing a butterfly that was flitting from flower to flower. Several ladies, admiring his agility, and taking pleasure in urging him on in this entertainment, caused him to become overheated. A dewy efflorescence appeared, pleurisy ensued, and all at once our Adonis wilted, dropping like a tender jasmine uprooted by the wind. (102)

Muscoloris's will in *Le Livre des quatre couleurs* leads us to another text that strikes a resonant chord. This is a booklet addressed expressly to petits-maîtres, *La Bibliothèque des petits-maîtres* (1762) by François-Charles Gaudet, who showcases an array of striking portraits. I will focus here on that of the Abbé de Pouponville. Gaudet intends his portrait of this "effeminate creature" as part of an ambitious plan to establish "an exact parallel between ancient and modern petits-maîtres" (2, 3).[49] But the project is soon abandoned because it is "out of style." In a document that once again takes the form of a will, Gaudet presents the biography of a man whom he calls "the pearl of petits-maîtres" (155).[50] The son of an "opera doll and of the famous Chevalier de Muscoloris, Seigneur de Pomador, Ambresée et autres lieux" (155),[51] Pouponville will become a trendsetter: "It is from him that our young priests have inherited the fine manners that set them apart: the custom of wearing double and triple rows of curls, of using perfume to fill the hall with their pleasant scent" (155).[52] If the Abbé is destined for elegance, he adheres to a strict asceticism, a discipline of manners.

Cosmetics, Commerce, and French Society (82–85).

47. "l'Ordre de la Frivolité."

48. "Il fallait voir avec quelle grâce il présidait aux chapitres de l'ordre, lorsqu'on y délibérait sur la manière de prendre du tabac, de se moucher et de cracher. Ce fut lui qui proposa le premier l'introduction des souliers brodés, dont on se sert aujourd'hui avec tant d'applaudissement."

49. "être féminisé"; "parallèle exact des petits-maîtres anciens avec les Modernes."

50. "hors de mode"; "la perle des petits-maîtres."

51. "pouponne de l'Opéra et du célèbre Chevalier de Muscoloris, Lord of Pomador, Ambresée and other domains."

52. "C'est de lui que nos jeunes abbés ont hérité des belles manières qui les distinguent : la coutume de se faire coëffer à double et triple rang de boucles, de se parfumer pour remplir l'auditoire de leur bonne odeur."

Pouponville dies from a simple gust of wind, a fatal collapse, a flaw inherent in his ethereal constitution. His last wish at the moment of death concerns the details of his outfit: "his embroidered pumps, his gold-tasseled belt, and the latest fashion in beauty spots which he had ordered from Du Lack" (160–61).[53] A postmortem anatomical note reveals the character's fundamental fragility, his precarious matter: "his blood was like rosewater, and his tender, delicate skin like the stuff of zephyrs" (161).[54] The Abbé de Pouponville leaves behind him a library of literary curiosities and technical treatises whose imaginary titles include: *L'Encyclopédie perruquière* (*The Encyclopedia of Wigs*), *Le Traité des perruques* (*Treaty on Wigs*), *Les Étrennes de 1759 ou les Mouches Garnies de Brillants* (*New Year's Gifts of 1759 or Bejeweled Beauty Spots*), *Les Berloques ou les Grelots de la Folie* (*Baubles or Bells of Folly*) (163–64)—all of which sheathe the character in a cocoon of vanity, a jewel box of frivolity. But most notable is the mausoleum erected to Pouponville's memory, a monument to the fleeting glory of this shining hero, the essential furnishing for this petit-maître and his motley assemblage, a whole universe of cosmetic objects serving as a counter–memento mori, in stubborn obeisance to defunct vanity. Gaudet enumerates them: "there was a dressing table, richly laid and most elegantly decorated with candlesticks, mirrors, boxes, jewels, creams, perfumes, rouge, white makeup, sponges, toilet water, etc." (161–62).[55] The will adds that the funeral bier was lined with "scented cotton" (161).[56]

Petits-maîtres were even exported to the colonies. Dominique Harcourt Lamiral, a slaveholding colonist, distinguishes from the other "Negroes of America" those who are *candiots*, a term he applies to "the petits-maîtres or the refined" with special attention to their clothing: "they wear white linen, impeccably clean jackets and britches, fancy handkerchiefs on the head or draped across the body" (231).[57] But it is Michel-Étienne Descourtilz, in his *Voyage d'un naturaliste*, who best describes the unforgettable figure cut by these candiots as they appear in Saint-Domingue, now Haiti. Descourtilz singles out one of these *nègres créoles* (i.e., those born in Saint-Domingue), named Joseph, whom he designates in the chapter heading as a *dandy nègre*. In this portrait, the European observer piles on the absurdities associated with the petit-maître (even if the latter is transplanted to a well-known valley in Saint-Domingue):

---

53. "ses souliers brodés, sa ceinture à glands d'or, et la nouvelle façon de mouches qu'il avait fait commander chez Du Lack."

54. "son sang ressemblait à l'eau de rose, et sa chair était tendre et délicate comme la substance des zéphirs."

55. "c'était une table de toilette richement garnie et très élégamment décorée de bougeoirs, de miroirs, de boîtes, de bijoux, de pâtes, de parfums, de rouge, de blanc, d'éponges, d'eaux de senteur, etc."

56. "coton parfumé."

57. "les petits-maîtres ou les élégants"; "ils ont du linge blanc, des vestes et des culottes fort propres et des mouchoirs de prix à la tête ou en écharpe autour du corps."

> Our guide to the cotton mills was one Joseph, a petit-maître renowned throughout Artibonite, whose caricature pleased me so much that I painted him in full regalia, ready for riding. . . . I will provide a more precise description. . . . I saw my man, his large hands covered in a pair of white women's gloves, which he had found who knows where, and which, insufficiently elastic to fit his fingers, were torn all over, and covered them only halfway; an extremely high hat in his hand; his head waxed and powdered white in the back, and his hair in front black and naturally kinky; long earrings deflected by the bulk of the cravat that buried him up to the eyes, above which were layered three necklaces; a nankeen vest that did not belong to him, was much too short and exposed his two black forearms, contrasting with the whiteness of his gloves, dimity britches destined to be soaked with the valiant rider's sweat; and finally boots, from who knows which century, for I do not believe I have ever seen their like: thus was he decked out! (192–94)[58]

Descourtilz dresses his tropical dandy in a mismatched hodgepodge of an outfit: Joseph has the look of a grotesque puppet. The naturalist underlines the combination of nature and artifice (powder and naturally kinked hair); there is also the mix of white (the color of his gloves) and black (his skin), and both men's and women's items of clothing, conveying sexual ambiguity. This secondhand ensemble does not detract from Joseph's powers of seduction, confirmed in his female conquests: "he was in demand by all his women; for these negroes are boastful ladies' men" (193).[59] Joseph momentarily transcends his servile condition for a class act.[60]

---

58. Nous avions pour conducteur des moulinières à coton un nommé Joseph, petit-maître réputé dans toute l'Artibonite, et dont la caricature m'avait tant plu, que je le peignis en son costume, prêt à monter à cheval . . . je vais y suppléer par une description exacte. . . . Je vis mon homme, ayant ses larges mains revêtues d'une paire de gants blancs de femme, qu'il avait trouvée je ne sais où, et qui n'ayant pu se prêter, par leur élasticité, à la grosseur de ses doigts, étaient déchirés de toute part, et n'en recouvraient que les phalanges ; un chapeau à la main, d'une forme très haute, la tête suifée et poudrée à blanc par derrière, et les cheveux du devant noirs et naturellement crépus, de longues boucles d'oreilles ayant peine à suivre le contour de sa cravate qui l'engonçait jusqu'aux yeux, et par dessus lesquels étaient trois rangs de colliers ; une veste de nankin qui ne lui appartenant pas, lui était de beaucoup trop courte et laissait voir deux avant-bras noirs, contrastant avec la blancheur de ses gants, un pantalon de basin, destiné à être imbibé de la sueur du valeureux coursier qu'il devait éprouver ; enfin des bottes, je ne sais de quel siècle, car je ne crois pas jamais en avoir vu de pareille forme : voilà son costume !" Deborah Jenson's examination of this figure mentions his association with libertinage. He operates in the realm of sensual pleasures and is linked with mimeticism. See *Beyond the Slave Narrative: Politics, Sex, and Narrative in the Haitian Revolution* (254–55).

59. "il était désiré par toutes ses *commères* ; car ces nègres sont avantageux et fort prévenus en leur faveur."

60. Regarding the African diaspora in eighteenth-century London, Monica L. Miller studies the case of Mango Macaroni, a black character originating in the theater and depicted in

Transporting him across the Atlantic, the century's satirical gaze imposes another crossing on the petit-maître: that of race. He is subjected to a further confusion, an ultimate scandal. The petit-maître compounds differences. In both Europe and America, he effects the same ambiguous seduction. Propelled by the currents of fashion, he is a creature of changing and unstable identities, exposed to the flash of the evanescent.

Works Cited

Boissy, Louis de. *Le Français à Londres: Répertoire du théâtre français*, vol. 21. Foucault, 1818.

Bollon, Patrice. *Morale du masque: merveilleux, zazous, dandys, punks, etc.* Seuil, 1990.

Bourguinat, Elisabeth. *Le Siècle du persiflage*. PUF, 1998.

Caraccioli, Louis-Antoine de. *Le Livre à la mode*. Presses de l'Université de Saint-Étienne, 2005.

Chrisman-Campbell, Kimberly. *Fashion Victims: Dress at the Court of Louis XVI and Marie-Antoinette*. Yale UP, 2015.

Delpierre, Madeleine. *Dress in France in the Eighteenth Century, translated by Caroline Beamish*. Yale UP, 1997.

———. *Se vêtir au XVIIIe siècle*. Adam Biro, 1996.

Desmahis, Joseph-François. "Fop." *Encyclopédie*, t. VI, 1756.

Descourtilz, Michel-Étienne. *Voyage d'un naturaliste*, vol. 3. Dufart, 1809.

Diderot, Denis. *Les Bijoux indiscrets: or, The Indiscreet Toys*. 1749. Translation anon., vol. 2.

———. *Œuvres romanesques*. Garnier Frères, 1962.

Diderot, Denis, and Jean le Rond d'Alembert. "Petit-maître." *Encyclopédie*, t. XII, 1765.

Gaudet, François-Charles. *La Bibliothèque des petits-maîtres. Ou, Mémoires pour servir à l'histoire du bon ton & de l'extrêmement bonne compagnie*, Au Palais-Royal, chez la petite Lolo, Marchande de Galanteries, à la Frivolité, Préface.

Jacot Grapa, Caroline. *L'Homme dissonant au dix-huitième siècle*. Voltaire Foundation, SVEC, 1997.

Jaucourt, Louis de. "Toilette (Modes)." *Encyclopédie*, vol. XVI, 1765.

Jenson, Deborah. *Beyond the Slave Narrative: Politics, Sex, and Narrative in the Haitian Revolution*. Liverpool UP, 2011.

Lamiral, Dominique Harcourt. *L'Afrique et le peuple affriquain, considéré sous tous leurs rapports avec notre commerce et nos colonies*. Dessène, 1789.

La Morlière, Jacques Rochette de. *Angola, Romans libertins du XVIIIe siècle*. Laffont, 1993.

---

caricature, known for the quality of his attire. But she also devotes particular attention to a certain "Julius Soubise," an opulent household slave, a fop among fops, whose unusual story she recounts as a vestimentary conquest by the former slave from Jamaica. Drawing on contemporary memoirs, Miller analyzes the complex reception of Soubise's evolving image in the English imaginary, as well as investigating its appropriation in satirical literature. See *Slaves to Fashion: Black Dandyism and the Styling of Black Diaspora Identity*, chapter 1.

Martin, Morag. *Selling Beauty: Cosmetics, Commerce, and French Society*. Johns Hopkins UP, 2009.

Miller, Monica L. *Slaves to Fashion: Black Dandyism and the Styling of Black Diaspora Identity*. Duke UP, 2009.

Monbron, Louis Charles Fougeret de. *La Capitale des Gaules ou La Nouvelle Babylone*. Ducros, 1970.

Montesquieu. *Lettres persanes*. GF Flammarion, 1995.

———. Persian Letters, translated by Margaret Mauldon. Oxford UP, 2008.

Roche, Daniel. *The Culture of Clothing: Dress and Fashion in the Ancien Régime*, translated by Jean Birrill. Cambridge UP, 1994.

———. *La France des Lumières*. Fayard, 1993.

———. *France in the Enlightenment*, translated by Arthur Goldhammer. Harvard UP, 1998.

Rousseau, Jean-Jacques. *Julie, or, The New Heloise*, translated by Philip Stewart and Jean Vaché. *The Collected Writings of Rousseau*, series edited by Roger D. Masters and Christopher Kelly. UP New England for Dartmouth, 1997.

———. *Julie ou La Nouvelle Héloïse*. Garnier-Flammarion, 1967.

———. *The Narcissist: A Comedy*, translated by Alan Orenstein. In *Trent Rousseau Papers: Proceedings of the Rousseau Bicentennial Congress, Trent University, June 1978*, edited by Jim Macadam, Michael Neumann, and Guy LaFrance. U of Ottawa P, 1980.

———. *Œuvres Complètes*, vol. 2. Gallimard-Bibliothèque de la Pléiade, 1964.

Thomas, Chantal. "La Sphère mouvante des modes." *Louis Sébastien Mercier: un hérétique en littérature*, edited by Jean-Claude Bonnet. Mercure de France, 1995.

CHAPTER 2

FASHION ANIMATION

Heads, Hats, and the Uncanny Work of Fashion

Susan Hiner

> Here it's the Mannequin that becomes the master's teacher.
> —Isn't it always so, in its pleasing dumbness.
>
> —Octave Uzanne, "Les Femmes dociles"[1*]

In the well-known opening sequence of Zola's 1883 "department store" novel *Au bonheur des dames*, set in the late 1860s, the provincial heroine Denise Baudu and her two young brothers arrive in Paris and are wonderstruck by the extravagant displays of women's clothing in the vitrines of Octave Mouret's *grand magasin*. The visual rush that was modernity is epitomized by Zola's lengthy and galloping description of delicate laces and silk gowns, fur-trimmed velvet coats, feathered capes, and cashmere evening wraps artfully combined in tableaux in the window, ending in the jolt of the most arresting image: headless mannequins dressed to the nines with price tags where their *têtes* should be.[2] Although headless dressmakers' dummies had existed since the 1830s, and had come to be used for display purposes by the time in which Zola's novel is set, the effect of their appearance before these provincial spectators here signals the potential for the inanimate object, a simulacrum of a woman, to slip into animation. The consequence, of course, is to cast doubt onto the status of the original—real, animate women.[3] This experience constitutes what German psychologist Ernst Jentsch in 1906 termed the "uncanny effect" that arises out of a "doubt as to whether an apparently living being really is animate and,

1. *"C'est ici le Mannequin qui devient le professeur du maître.

—Ne l'est-il pas toujours d'ailleurs, dans son complaisant mutisme."

Uzanne, "Les Femmes dociles," 12–13, preface to Riotor (9–16). All translations are mine unless otherwise indicated.

2. Brown, "Thing Theory."

3. See Evans and Park. My discussions of the *marotte* here are indebted to the work of these two scholars.

conversely, doubt as to whether a lifeless object may not in fact be animate" (8). For Marx, commodities themselves are inherently uncanny, or "mysterious" as he describes them, because as they enter the marketplace they seem to assume a human capacity for social relations.[4]

While Zola's powerfully symbolic headless bodies pointedly suggest the de-animating powers of capitalism and modernity in the Second Empire and beyond, in this essay I wish to consider the missing part—the absent presence of the head—that the dummies cannot help but conjure. For what is missing from these simulacra of women is the seat of both reason and subjectivity, an apt image for a novel that wishes to showcase the increased mechanization of modern life and the dehumanizing effects of consumption through women's seduction by fashion. But it also quite simply implies that women, too, and not just their simulacra, are severed from reason, an obvious prerequisite for their objectification.[5]

What of the absent head, then? Where did it go? And what do its separation from the body, so commonplace in fashion illustration and advertisement, and frequent recurrence in nineteenth-century popular visual and literary representations inspired by fashion reveal about fashion's commodification of women's bodies? Here I wish to defamiliarize this common trope of fashion imagery to get at what I am calling the "uncanny work of fashion," that is, the marketing of objects and images that depends on a certain violence to or erasure of women's bodies. If the mannequin was one instrument of this process, the *marotte* (or headform) was another. They were also visual and material reminders both of fashion's objectification of women as consumers, which I will explore in the first part of this chapter, and of fashion's erasure of women as producers, which I take up in its second part.

Têtes à poupée or *marottes* were headforms on which *modistes* (milliners) from the earliest decades of the nineteenth century worked to embellish hats and which stood in for the heads of female consumers. Like the headless mannequins of the department store windows, or dressmakers' dummies, these objects were also, to cite the brilliant title of Jane Munro's 2015 exhibition and catalog, "silent partners" in fashion's most elite industry in nineteenth-century Paris—ladies' hat making. The "silence" of this partnership opens onto endless narrative possibilities, and, like the doll, the fashion plate model, and the mannequin, the *marotte* belongs to a family of feminine doppelgangers.

---

4. This essay draws on Marx's discussion of "commodity fetishism" in *Capital*. While Marx famously used the example of a table to illustrate his theory, nineteenth-century ladies' fashion provides a vast field in which to explore the mechanism of the commodity fetish, which is, as I argue here, precisely the uncanny animation of products. Freud's theory of the uncanny (in which he cites Jentsch) is a spectral presence here as well. It is no coincidence that his seminal essay of 1919 is primarily focused on E. T. A. Hoffmann's fantastic tale "The Sandman," which features the dangerous animation of a female automaton.

5. For productive analyses of this scene, see Ross, "Introduction" to the 1992 English translation of *The Ladies' Paradise*, and Brown, *A Sense of Things*, 32.

Along with their evident practical function in the processes of fabrication and display, thus serving fashion's inseparable objectives of production and marketing, *marottes* were also powerful symbolic visual props in the construction of an artificial femininity in which bourgeois respectability existed largely in distinction to its disreputable counterpart. The *marotte* has a rich genealogy, but it is also visually linked to the advertisements routinely found in the fashion press throughout the nineteenth century, in whose pages, typically, headgear was advertised via a series of "head shots," that is, heads and shoulders of painted models arranged in groups on a single page (fig. 2.1). Furthermore, the *marotte* was closely tied to the luxury product it was designed as a tool to serve—the lady's hat—a fashion object that was also frequently displayed in the fashion press in illustrations that dissociated it from the living bodies for which it was destined. Finally, the *marotte* doubles her less-silent partner, the *modiste* herself, whose nimble fingers work their magic on its artificial head, poking and gluing, sewing and tying, to create "this magical object (which) had the power to idealize face and makeup and to dramatize the slightest gesture; lifting one's veil, smoking, drinking, smiling, every movement took on an aura of mystery" (Demornex 7).[6]

The *marotte* appeared in many popular visual, textual, and theatrical representations of the *modiste*, creating a kind of material shorthand for the magical processes of fashion production and consumption. Although in his analysis of capital Marx discusses neither hats nor *marottes*, the hat becomes a way to tease out Marx's theory of the commodity. The *marotte*, an object that participates in the *production* of the commodity, also plays a role in the human side of production: made to look lifelike, a *marotte* stands in for the female consumer who will herself become objectified by the fashion system. Indeed, objects such as *marottes* worked paradoxically both to obscure and enhance the actual labor of these most elite Parisian fashion workers. If the final product itself (the hat) was fetishized as the very essence of fashionability, the tool on which it was created (the *marotte*) uncannily duplicated in inert form both the woman who created it and the woman who purchased it. Both worker and consumer are thus dehumanized before the power of the *poupée* to supplant them.

By examining several representative prints and vaudeville plays of the mid-nineteenth century in conversation with each other, I will consider here the ways in which heads and hats were represented in popular media and how their uncanny powers of animation and verisimilitude both underpinned and troubled fashion's work. After tracing the history of the *marotte* and placing it within the context of fashion and popular culture, I will turn to the lady's hat—that super-accessory—and its promotion and status as a particular kind of commodity fetish. Finally, I will gesture toward an understanding of fashion's "uncanny" work.

---

6. "cet objet magique [qui] avait le pouvoir d'idéaliser visage et maquillage et de théâtraliser le moindre geste : relever sa voilette, fumer, boire, sourire, chaque mouvement s'auréolait de mystère."

FIGURE 2.1 Winter hats in *Magasin des demoiselles* from Paris, France, 1878. University of Washington Libraries, Special Collections, UW 38849.

Uncanny Heads

The terms that identify the headform tie it to a family of similar tools and objects of fashion used over the course of several centuries to simulate a woman: *marotte* and *tête à poupée*, or sometimes, just *tête*. In etymology the word *marotte* originates with the Virgin Mary in the fifteenth century, and it may have been linked to the statues of the virgin used in ceremonies and festivals: this is also the source of the word *marionnette*, whose use originated in early mystery plays. But the term was also simultaneously linked to the fool's scepter, a long stick capped with a head and hat, garnished with dangling bells. This *marotte* thus became symbolic of folly. In the *marotte* as headform, we find both the strangeness, even alienation, connected to folly and the solemn idolatry of woman.

Marottes were one of many three-dimensional simulations of woman useful to the production of fashion, beginning with the *poupée de mode* popularized in the eighteenth century and enduring with the live fashion model of today's industry. Although in existence since the fifteenth century, fashion dolls were created in France and widely used in Europe in the eighteenth century, demonstrating the increasing power of the *marchandes de modes* (who would become milliners) to shape and commodify fashion. Before the rise of the fashion press in the late eighteenth and early nineteenth centuries, when printed plates could circulate more easily, the fashion doll traveled around the world and served to prescribe, disseminate, and unify ideas about appropriate femininity. "Before fashion models existed, French dressmakers promoted their work internationally by sending dolls, fashionably dressed in the latest modes, around Europe. . . . They were known in England as 'babies' or 'jointed babies' and in France variously as *courriers de la mode*, *Grande Pandores*, *Petites Pandores*, *poupées*, *grandes poupées*, *dolls à la mode*, and *mannequins*" (Evans 12). This doll was both a marketing tool, offering a visual and material example of potential goods for purchase, and a mirror of the would-be female consumer, sparking her imagination and promoting the principle of substitutability that fashion plates would eventually assume. The fashion doll thus enjoyed a double function, vital to both production and consumption of fashionable products and the behaviors that accompanied them. As Juliette Peers has remarked in her study of the fashion doll across centuries, "the doll was an essential part of the emergence of fashion as both a social trend and a creative genre" serving, as she puts it, as an "interlocutor between fashion and the consumer" (18, 20). Ever the silent partner, the fashion doll communicated visually and materially, and her interlocution involved a shared language of signs—fabrics, ornaments, colors, and cuts.

In her remarkable study of objects and subjectivity in eighteenth-century England, Julie Park traces the psychic and cultural connections between women and dolls by focusing in part on the fashion doll. She argues that the Enlightenment's fascination with dolls and their many variations offered a way to "stabilize the uncertainty generated by the real woman" (84). The doll, and her cousins—waxworks, automata, mannequins—served as models for femininity and were, simultaneously, directly modeled on the feminine; the doll remained, however, safely inanimate, "a lifeless object that is already a simulacrum of 'life itself'—not the woman" (86). Fashion dolls served as advertising tools and were thus intimately linked to the commodification of women through fashion, but they also "produced charged encounters between the natural and the artificial, the original and the copy, and the human and the inhuman" (104). Dolls, Park concludes, literalize "the uncanny condition of femininity," which I interpret as the conscious object status of women, made more acute through her relation to fashion (225). Frequently pictured in popular prints of the nineteenth century, the *marotte*, the severed head of the dressmaker's dummy or mannequin, is the missing piece of the whole body, ironically restoring subjectivity to the woman as object, yet reobjectifying her through its unmistakable resemblance to the represented woman at her side and its lifeless, vacant stare.

The *modiste* with her uncertain social and moral status in many ways best illustrates the instability that Park identifies as the root source of the doll's popularity and, indeed, urgency. Inhabiting the liminal space between respectable lady, whom she resembles and aspires to, and streetwalking prostitute, with whom she is associated, as she swings her hatbox on the Paris boulevards or sits behind the shop's vitrine, ostensibly arranging a hat before the lustful eyes of the flaneur, the *modiste* incarnated in the French imaginary the moral dangers of women more broadly (Clayson; Higonnet 147). *Modistes* were widely depicted in popular prints from the nineteenth century, and, very frequently, they were portrayed "at work" with a *marotte* by their side, hands busy with the tools of hat making and ornamentation (fig 2.2).[7] Like the hatbox, the *marotte* is a visual clue to the subject's métier in this and many similar images—but it is more than simply a sign of work identity. Akin to a doll, a headform, like a mannequin, is an idealizing mirror, an inanimate double, and in many nineteenth-century visual representations, often resembled the *modiste* herself, who was frequently portrayed as harboring aspirations of becoming a bourgeois consumer. In figure 2.2 from the 1830s, we find a *modiste* at work on a model head that allows her to produce her deluxe *chapeau*.

This *tête à poupée* is made up and lifelike, and, indeed, the artist has taken pains to make *modiste* and *marotte* nearly identical: the inanimate head replicates the "live" fashion worker depicted next to it. The *tête à poupée* is oriented in the same direction as the *modiste*'s own head, further emphasizing the doubling of the living *modiste* and the inanimate head. Another striking feature of this image is that while the *modiste* is clearly engaged in work, her hands busy with elaborate ribbon trimmings for the hat, she does not look at the object she is creating. Instead, she gazes beyond the frame of the image, perhaps at a spectator. Images like this one exemplify the pioneering thesis of John Berger in his seminal and still pertinent study of gender in representation, *Ways of Seeing*: "Women watch themselves being looked at. This determines most relations between men and women but also the relation of women to themselves. The surveyor of woman in herself is male: the

7. I am currently at work on a more detailed treatment of the *modiste* in my new book in progress, "Behind the Seams: Women, Fashion, and Work in Nineteenth-Century France."

Figure 2.2 "Modiste," 1830s. Photograph © Trustees of the British Museum.

surveyed female. Thus she turns herself into an object—and most particularly an object of vision: a sight" (Berger 47). The doubling effect of the *marotte* exaggerates the objectification already implicit in representations of women.

The *modiste* is engaged in luxury production, and, although wearing the traditional black apron commonly designating a fashion worker, she is also quite fashionably turned out—which contributes to one of the principal elements of the myth of the *modiste*: that she is dangerously similar to the bourgeois consumer herself. This mirroring between *modiste* and *tête à poupée* is further proof of the commodification of the *modiste*; yet it also proposes that the *modiste* controls the shaping of her own image, inasmuch as she is pictured literally shaping her double. The slight tilt to the *modiste*'s head is the only indication that she might be less inert than her headform double, and this sliver of doubt is the crack through which the uncanny slips.

We also find this kind of duplication in an image created by the celebrated caricaturist and fashion illustrator Numa, who here portrays the morning rise of the *modistes*, with its predictably erotic overtones and shabby-chic intimate interior (fig. 2.3). The details of this image are familiar to a nineteenth-century public: peeling wallpaper and cracks in the walls, a cashmere shawl serving as blanket, hatbox functioning as night table, and hat decorations strewn about the floor. The casual mixing of luxury and poverty is an important hallmark of the representation of the nineteenth-century female fashion worker, as is the eroticization of "private" dormitory scenes—the *dortoir*, by the way, very often resembles a ramshackle variation on the atelier, which was also a popular subject for prints, as well as a setting for vaudeville plays, as we shall shortly see.

Here, one semi-clad *modiste* watches from bed as the other dresses her hair in the mirror, her reflection just visible over the wide brim of an elaborately decorated hat worn by a *marotte* that is perched on the dressing table. This fancy creation might belong to one of the *modistes* but, as she expected to work from home, trimming a client's hat in the evening and returning it to the atelier when completed, the hat is more likely the property of the *maîtresse-modiste* and is being prepared for a client. Work at home is further substantiated by the remnants of hat decorations littering the floor; these could also be present, however, merely to assert the love of finery that these fashion workers stereotypically possess—claiming little scraps from the atelier to bring home and use to concoct their very own hats. In any case, the indeterminate ownership of the hat works to destabilize the figure of the *modiste*—she is both a producer and an aspiring consumer of fashion.

The composition of the illustration and the curious placement of the *marotte* call attention to the blurring of animate and inanimate so often latent in fashion illustration. And this slippage is essential to fashion's success, for the consumer needs to be able to conceive of herself as an object in order to imagine herself in new hats and dresses.[8] In Numa's illustration, the head clones the reflection in the mirror, already a double, and the *marotte*'s sightless gaze serves as a pendant to that of the "living," reclining girl on the bed. We might say that there are really four heads in the image, and a network of eyes and gazes (including the spectators') are all working both to posit and to expose the false "seamlessness" of femininity in a staging of what Park aptly refers to as the "cultural production of femininity" (202).[9] At the same time, the headform and the multiplication process in which it

8. For more on the female gaze in nineteenth-century fashion plates, see Marcus.

9. On the wall in the upper-right corner hangs a print depicting a human figure holding a hat; there are actually five heads in the image.

Figure 2.3 "Le Lever des modistes." Photograph © Trustees of the British Museum.

participates once again evoke the slippage between animate and inanimate upon which fashion discourse and illustration rely for their powers of suggestion, their marketing of desire. For the lifeless gaze of the *marotte* implies the object status of the woman she replicates; Numa's illustration makes this confusion clear because the nubile fashion workers are objects to behold, nearly indistinguishable from the headform on the dressing table.

It is no surprise that the multiplication of female heads that we find in popular visual representations of *modistes* should also occur on the vaudeville stage. The *modiste*'s workroom was a common stage set for a number of vaudeville plays, the *modiste* herself a stock character, and the audience of vaudeville very likely included *modistes* and other working people. By definition, the theater provides a setting that trades in disguise, fantasy, and improbabilities. In an 1832 play first performed at the Théâtre des Variétés, *L'Art de ne pas monter sa garde*, stage directions help to situate and define the principal character, Henriette, who is a *modiste*: "The scene depicts an attic; to the right, a window, a trunk; to the left a workroom, a worktable, on which we see thread, needles, artificial flowers and *a mannequin head* wearing a lady's hat. In the back, next to the entry door, a fireplace with a mirror; a family portrait, several chairs" (my emphasis).[10]

This play recounts the attempts of Victor (who in the play is an actor) to conceal his identity from the police, tracking him for military service. Much like the illustrator Numa discussed above, Victor hides out in a *modiste*'s garret, where, naturally, he finds all he needs to disguise himself (improbably) as . . . a *négresse*. The illustration that accompanied the print version of the play offers a bridge between popular visual and dramatic representation (fig 2.4). To the right, we see an appropriate couple, and to the left, an entirely inappropriate one—a visual contrast that encapsulates the questions of identity and problems with coupling on which the play turns. The buffoonery resulting from mistaken identity and disguise characteristic of vaudeville reaches its climax in scene 10, which is depicted in the illustration on the title page of the printed edition of the play pictured here. In this scene we interrupt a fake lovers' triangle and multiple intersecting plots. The national guardsman, also a grocer's assistant and the *modiste* Henriette's suitor (on the far right), is "exposed" by Victor (on the far left), the actor disguised as the *négresse* who lives on the third floor, as having relations with "her"—the *négresse*. This false revelation shocks the *modiste* and creates so much consternation for the guardsman-suitor that Victor (as *négresse*) seems bound to escape military conscription. We see also the telltale *haut-de-forme*, with the name "Victor" inscribed inside the brim, and this discovery now throws *Henriette's* honor into question.

Behind the *haut-de-forme*, however, at the center of the worktable, most importantly for us, sits a *marotte*, wearing the *capote*, or poke-bonnet, that Henriette has brought home to complete. This *tête à poupée*, signaled as a mere prop legitimizing the stage setting, gazes out at the disguised Victor and does three things at once: first, it makes a visual connection with the spectators, who also silently observe the

10. "Le théâtre représente une mansarde ; à droite, une croisée, une malle ; à gauche, un cabinet, une petite table à ouvrage, sur laquelle on aperçoit du fil, des aiguilles, des fleurs artificielles et *une tête à poupée* coiffée d'un chapeau de femme. Dans le fond, à côté de la porte d'entrée, une cheminée ornée d'un miroir ; un grand portrait de famille, plusieurs chaises" (Barthélemy et Lhérie 3; my emphasis).

SCÈNE X.

L'ART DE NE PAS MONTER SA GARDE,

VAUDEVILLE EN UN ACTE,

par MM. Barthélemy et Lhérie,

REPRÉSENTÉ, POUR LA PREMIÈRE FOIS, A PARIS, SUR LE THÉATRE DES VARIÉTÉS.

PERSONNAGES.	*ACTEURS.*
M. VINCENT, épicier et sergent-major dans la garde nationale. . .	M. Cazot.
SYMPHORIEN, premier garçon épicier chez M. Vincent.	M. Dubourjal.
ANATOLE, commis en nouveautés.	M. Astruc.
VICTOR, artiste dramatique. . . .	M. Lhérie.
UN COMMISSAIRE DE POLICE.	M. Charlet.
HENRIETTE, jeune modiste, cousine d'Anatole.	Mlle Jolivet.
Deux Gardes municipaux.	
Un Portier.	
Un Ramoneur.	

La scène se passe à Paris, dans la maison de M. Vincent.

Le théâtre représente une mansarde ; à droite, une croisée, une malle ; à gauche, un cabinet, une petite table à ouvrage, sur laquelle on aperçoit du fil, des aiguilles, des fleurs artificielles et une tête à poupée coiffée d'un chapeau de femme. Dans le fond, à côté de la porte d'entrée, une cheminée ornée d'un miroir ; un grand portrait de famille, plusieurs chaises.

SCENE PREMIERE.

HENRIETTE, ANATOLE, *entrant.*

HENRIETTE, *assise auprès d'une petite table, occupée à travailler.*

Tiens! c'est vous, mon cousin... Vous le voyez, je suis bientôt prête... Je viens de terminer le chapeau que Mme Vincent m'a donné à arranger.

ANATOLE.

Ouf! je suis tout essoufflé! comme le cœur me bat!... ça me fait toujours cet effet-là quand je suis auprès de vous, et que j'ai monté vos cinq étages.

HENRIETTE.

Eh bien! m'apportez-vous mon billet?

ANATOLE.

Le voici : avec ça, vous serez placée au Champ-de-Mars, dans une tribune réservée.

HENRIETTE.

C'est gentil, une revue de la garde nationale... Comme je vais m'amuser!

ANATOLE.

Dimanche prochain vous vous amuserez bien

XXVI. 7

Figure 2.4 From Barthélemy et Lhérie, *L'Art de ne pas monter sa garde.* Bibliothèque nationale de France, Paris.

action; second, it parallels the *modiste*, whom the *tête* most resembles; and finally, it has a troubling correspondence with the *négresse*, who can be used, like an absent yet present object, to conceal *and* reveal troubling, if comically rendered, cultural truths. The object status of the ex-slave is recalled in the literal object of the *marotte*, whose fixed, lifeless stare seems both to accuse the shirking actor and to remind viewers that women and, certainly more brutally, former slave women had little to say about how their bodies might be used.[11] Indeed, the secondary plot of the play turns on whether Henriette will be given consent by her father to marry one of the two suitors who are courting her. So the *marotte*, while not actively referred to in this play, hovers trenchantly in the background to figure many of its latent themes. Animated through its assimilation with the viewing public, the represented headform also distills the troubling de-animation and disempowering of women in nineteenth-century France.

Another play, a one-act-monologue vaudeville from 1855, entitled "Les Débuts de la Modiste," exploits the unsettling potential of these heads to engage even more directly with questions of the animation and de-animation of women. In this short play, Alexandrine, a young *modiste* employed at her aunt's atelier, is working alone one Sunday while all the other shop workers are out for a party in the countryside. Unjustly put to work on a Sunday while the others have some leisure time, she illustrates the sense of frustration that young girls with limited options must have experienced in their daily grind. Alexandrine protests: "I'm condemned to a day in the shop and twelve hours of surveillance . . . what an indignity!"[12] As we shall see, the headforms reinforce both the *modiste*'s drudgery and the de-animation that the young fashion worker discovers in the fashion industry. But they also activate a fantasy of animation that ultimately leads to the protagonist's success as an actress.

With the scene constructed as an *atelier de modes*, the stage directions indicate: "To the right and to the left, tables with headforms."[13] The young apprentice is further aggrieved in that she does not even want to be a *modiste* but dreams rather of becoming an actress (her uncle, by the way, is a *directeur de spectacle*). She suffers from stage fright, though, and can only practice her chosen vocation for the silent dummies; she says: "the sight of a person looking at me and listening to me freezes me to the point that I lose my senses. I'm never so brave as when I perform my roles in front of these good headforms right here. There are only these respectable, good women who don't intimidate me."[14] In the space of one

11. For an analysis of this play and the broader contours of race in French vaudeville in the nineteenth century, see Schreier.

12. "je suis condamnée à une journée de magasin et douze heures de surveillance . . . quelle indignité !" (1).

13. "A droite, et à gauche, des tables avec des têtes à chapeaux" (1).

14. "la vue d'une personne qui me regarde et m'écoute m'interdit au point que je perds tous mes moyens. Je ne suis jamais si hardie que lorsque je récite ici mes rôles devant les estimables têtes à chapeaux que voilà. Il n'y a que ces dignes et braves femmes qui ne m'intimident pas . . ." (2).

sentence she has replaced *têtes à chapeaux* with *dames*, and has brought her audience to life: "Let's go, Ladies, get dressed, put on your new hats . . . I invite you all to attend the début of Mlle Alexandrine. . . . Are you there . . . That's it! Form the gallery and please don't talk!"[15]

Fully recognizing why these *têtes* do not intimidate her, she nonetheless proceeds to anthropomorphize them: they become *braves femmes*, *mesdames*, *vous*, and *aimables spectatrices*. She coifs the anonymous and identical *têtes* in order to give each of them a distinct identity, and she talks to them as if they are reacting to the show, even modifying her performance to please one in particular. A *tête* in the rear, wearing a green hat, is making a face because of the improper nature of Alexandrine's dance. Her fantasy animation of the *marottes* works to demystify the idea of the theater public. And, in fact, Alexandrine gives such a fine performance that her spying (i.e., lecherous) uncle hires her, and her dream of acting comes true. In classic vaudeville fashion, visibly blurring the lines between stage and public and thus shattering the so-called "fourth wall," Alexandrine turns to the audience to sing her last air, having overcome her stage fright, and demands the requisite round of applause. The "network of gazes" that I referred to with respect to Numa's 1830 print (see fig. 2.3), one that included the presumed illicit male spectator, is reactivated here, solidifying the object status of women in fashion iconography and beyond. For, despite the conceit of animation that this short play evokes and exploits, the overriding message is that the little *modiste* is her creepy uncle's mannequin to pose at will on his stage and, perhaps, in his bed.

In this short monologue, the animation of lifeless headforms and their assimilation to the viewing public raise fundamental questions of agency. For if lifeless and interchangeable dummies are but one step removed from this public, if indeed they can stand in, even fancifully, for the living spectators of the play, then this comic vaudeville is saying something important about both the bourgeois consumer and the exploitation of workers. This is not necessarily what we expect from a vaudeville play, and yet, the relationship between fashion worker and fashion consumer is clearly being developed in these plays. Finally, the uncanny presence of headforms is significant in these representations of *modistes* in nineteenth-century popular culture, and it should be deciphered in relation to other similar forms used in the world of fashion to mimic women. Nineteenth-century popular culture clearly seized on the uncanny potential of the *marotte*, so ordinary to the fashion world but made strange in contexts outside of fashion, to represent, whether intentionally or not, the in-between status of women themselves. And the separation of head from body evoked at the outset of this essay leads inevitably to considerations of the commodification and objectification that fashion's work necessitated for its continued, cyclical survival.

---

15. "Allons, Mesdames, faites toilette, mettez vos chapeaux neufs . . . je vous invite toutes à venir assister aux débuts de Mlle Alexandrine. . . . Y êtes-vous ? . . . c'est ça ! Formez la galerie et ne bavardez pas surtout !" (2).

The Commodity Fetish of the Lady's Hat

If the *marotte* was an unwittingly uncanny object, promoting the commodification of women and simultaneously betraying the underlying violence of fashion's play for women as consumable and consuming objects, the product that the *marotte* and *modiste* both served—the lady's hat—took on lifelike proportions in nineteenth-century France. In his 1852 book *Le Tableau de Paris*, Edmond Texier, who was also the editor of the renowned weekly *l'Illustration*, invites his readers to enter the *modiste*'s atelier, where we find her in her habitat. Here, according to Texier, each girl knows her place within the hierarchy of workers as they labor together to produce the exquisite object that is the lady's hat. But the *première demoiselle*—the most talented *modiste* and, typically, the successor to the *maîtresse*—earns this rank through her gift for inventing fine new fashions. Texier devotes several paragraphs to the creation of this magical work of art: this hat is *not* a *chapeau de commande*, a hat commissioned by a client, but, rather, it is the result of the *modiste*'s creative vision and wields the power to initiate fashion trends. This hat, he says, is: "the improvised hat, the one that dictates fantasy, that can only coif a head never before seen by the artist, but rather, dreamed."[16]

After a whirlwind of frenetic measuring, turning, and gathering the gauzy fabric, the *modiste* cuts with confidence, while her attendants, the *demoiselles de magasin*, take up the various tasks she gives them—forming the cap, the frame, and the borders. Within fifteen minutes, the hat has taken shape. While the description references the labors of the fashion workers and suggests that at least seven of them are involved in the construction of such a hat, only the *première*, the author tells us, is capable of "giving it the breath of life."[17] What is Texier implying here? That the *modiste* has the power to *animate* the inanimate, and to make the fashion object par excellence, the lady's hat, absolutely essential to the successful *toilette* of the female consumer.

If Texier's fictionalized depiction seems to offer an objective window into the activities of the atelier and the material reality of the components of hat making, the author is also playing into a circulating mythology of the *modiste*, which turns on her loose morals. And this is a mythology that stems directly from her public presence on the street. There is no discussion of squalor or long hours, no mention of harsh mistresses, nothing about sexual predation, or the arduous labor of stitching tiny, fragile decorations onto a stiff fabric. Not only are the *modiste* and her work idealized, but her ability to animate a fashion object also romanticizes the hat itself. It becomes magical, a descriptor that would permeate discourse around hats for over a century.[18] The hat becomes a "phénomène vivant"—a living phenomenon—as the

---

16. "le chapeau improvisé, celui qui dicte la fantaisie, celui qui doit et ne peut coiffer qu'une tête que l'artiste n'a jamais vue, mais qu'elle a rêvée" (232).

17. "lui donner le souffle, la vie" (233).

18. It is important to note that this is precisely the same type of terminology that Marx uses to describe commodities.

Numa caricature illustrates (fig. 2.5). The very *fact* of the caricature in and of itself attests to the paramount importance of the hat to a lady's *toilette*, but this picture is doing more: it is calling attention to the disproportionate power of fashion commodities to usurp their human wearers.

The image depicts three bourgeois subjects—one man and two women—apparently enjoying a chance social encounter while out strolling in a parklike urban environment, as signaled by paving stones and distant trees. Numa's hat, worn by the smugly smiling lady at the center of the image, takes center stage and is clearly the "phénomène vivant" designated by the title of the picture. For the lady in the small *capote* draped in a blue shawl does not look at her smiling acquaintance but focuses all her straining attention on the towering hat. She leans forward with an upward gaze approaching adulation, her hands open as if supplicating this fantastic

Figure 2.5 "Phénomène vivant." Elke Rehder Collection.

object. The gentleman on the arm of the fantastically hatted lady seems to enjoy the hat's admiration as much as his companion does, as he looks on with prideful pleasure. The hat itself warrants the term *phénomène*, which suggests "extraordinary," "rare," rooted in the Greek "that which appears." It is indeed a feast for the eyes: apparently constructed of fine straw, its *calotte*, or the part of the hat that hugs the head, is exaggerated into a large tubular point and is decorated with two outsized blue ribbons, one at the tip and the other, jauntily set to the side, artfully placed to complement the hat's crowning glory. Three white feathers, one simply enormous, protrude from the blue bow, adding approximately three feet to the little lady's height.

What ought to have been a typical social meeting replete with small talk and mutual sizing up becomes instead an occasion for gawking with envy, in a scene prescient of Zola's opening shot of the department store's eerie windows with which we began. The "living" (*vivant*) aspect of this hat resides not only in the residue of life that is referenced by the elegantly swaying feathers, one of which is a *plume d'autruche*, the most coveted of hat ornaments. For hats were routinely festooned with "natural" embellishments—flowers, feathers—and made to look as though they were organic objects. But also, and more importantly, this hat overwhelms—we might even say, commandeers—the identity of the lady who wears it, such that her acquaintance no longer sees *her*, but only the "living" thing atop her head. Numa is of course ridiculing the excesses of contemporary fashion, and his punning title "phénomène vivant" applies equally satirically to the female subjects who fall under fashion's spell. *Phénomène vivant* also denotes a circus attraction, and it is but a short step from the gawking consumer to the ogling spectator. This image thus encapsulates fashion's spectacle and points to the strength of the commodity to overwhelm the very system that produces and consumes it (Smith 11). If the hat has become a living thing, then it follows that the woman from whom it derives its life force would suffer de-animation, or, at least, as the title suggests, extreme objectification in the form of a sideshow marvel. In this scenario, the man on her arm, although certainly ridiculously depicted with his dandified posture, corseted torso, and absurdly large lapels and collar, becomes literally her handler. Gender thus reinforces fashion's spectacle.

As has been well documented, in the nineteenth century, fashion was indeed highly gendered. Men adopted the bourgeois uniform of masculinity, and their wives were increasingly objectified as the ornamental markers of their husbands' wealth and position, an observation that was succinctly theorized by Thorstein Veblen at the end of the nineteenth century and has since been widely discussed by fashion historians and theorists.[19] This gendering is most visible in headgear, as any sampling of representative fashion plates depicting hats across the nineteenth century demonstrates. Hats both reflected and reinforced gender ideologies. The

19. Veblen, *Conspicuous Consumption*. On this subject, see also Perrot; Kuchta; Vinken; and Steele.

Figure 2.6 Men's fashion, 1856. University of Washington Libraries, Special Collections, UW 27105z.

male *haut-de-forme* was the incarnation of rational structure and simplicity—a column, at once stature enhancing and protective (fig. 2.6)—while the wide variety of women's hats reflected in magnified form how bourgeois women functioned as embellishment, or luxurious ornamentation, in relation to their male counterparts (see figs. 2.1 and 2.7). The astonishing diversity of women's headgear, from season to season, occasion to occasion, and for different moments of the day, each with its requisite activity—visiting, receiving, walking, and so forth—made ladies' hats and coifs crucial indicators of status, age, propriety, and identity as they marked out time and space and codified female behavior. Likewise, the superabundance of embellishments attached to ladies' hats—lace, bows, ribbons, flowers, and more—reflected the overflow of signification that bourgeois women as sole signifiers of their husbands' status were tasked with communicating.

As a hyperfeminine social symbol, the woman's hat offered a miniature, yet exaggerated, version of a dress. Like a dress, this luxury commodity, concealing its seams, pins, glue, and thread, was also removed from its conditions of production—it was what Marx termed a commodity fetish. Marx develops his discussion of the "fetishism of commodities" in terms of a "secret," and his analysis is in many ways an attempt at demystification (319). Alternately using the descriptors "mystical," "enigmatical," and "mysterious" to characterize the commodity in order to explain a product's transformation (one might even say, its *animation*) into a commodity, Marx writes:

> A commodity is therefore a mysterious thing, simply because in it the social character of men's labour appears to them as an objective character stamped upon the product of that labour; because the relation of the producers to the sum total of their own labour is presented to them as a social relation, existing not between themselves, but between the products of their labour. This is the reason why the products of labour become commodities, social things whose qualities are at the same time perceptible and imperceptible by the senses. (320–21)

As Marx explains it, the social relations among the people who create the products are transferred and "stamped" upon the products they have created; these products, then, as commodities, assume (fantastically) social relations among themselves. The essential human element that is rendered invisible by this transfer to the commodity is the labor expended in its production, but "traces of [that] exploited labour" remain, perhaps in that "living" quality the commodity seems to exude (Smith 11).

Defying through its excesses its use value and hiding the labor expended to create it, the commodity assumes a circulating social dimension. Considered as such, it is endowed with powers (social, economic) that ought to accrue to the workers who made it but that instead are attributed to an inanimate object—a hat. The famous *Chapeau de paille d'Italie*, Eugène Labiche's blockbuster vaudeville play from 1851, for example, takes as its central object the most valued hat of the nineteenth century—prized for the supple fineness of its straw, which permitted such delicacy of sewing that the hat seemed to be made of only one piece. It was the very seamlessness of the product that elevated its status and made it the requisite summer hat throughout the century.[20] This erasure of the signs of the hat's fabrication and indeed of work more generally is even more striking in the many advertisements and illustrations of ladies' hats over the course of the nineteenth century in the fashion press, where the object is portrayed in all its magical glory, separated from the elements and processes of its creation, free-floating and often independent even from the heads of the women who purchased it (fig 2.7).

This image, like thousands of others, evokes just such an erasure. For, here, fine lace, ribbons, feathers, and artificial flowers ornament each hat's *calotte*. All these embellishing items would have been crafted by secondary artisans—lace makers (*dentellières*), ribbon makers (*fabricants de rubans*), feather workers (*plumassiers*), and flower makers (*fleuristes*)—none of whom were regularly credited with or appropriately remunerated for the laborious, and sometimes dangerous, artisanal work they accomplished. Alison Matthews David documents the dangers faced by flower makers: "the scale and nature of professional flowermaking exposed workers who assembled craft kits and dusted foliage to potentially lethal quantities of arsenic" (92). The anonymity and indeed erasure of these workers were essential to the marketing of the luxury object whose only signature it would bear (if any) was that of the *maîtresse-modiste*. For it was her task, or that of her *première*, to combine these dainty items in artful ways, explicitly hiding the processes of fabrication to produce a fashion article that seems to have effortlessly sprouted lace and flowers, feathers and silk, as though a natural process. Thread and glue are invisible, concealed beneath layers of ruffles, bouquets of fake blooms, and exotic plumes; in later decades, whole stuffed birds would be arranged upon hats, mimicking flight and offering an exaggerated example of the "ambiguity of in/animateness" characteristic of both the uncanny and fashion (Withy 19). Each of these fashion articles hovers disconcertingly between natural and artificial, animate and inanimate.

The four hats, one bonnet, and a lady's tie of figure 2.7 are carefully distributed on the page of this fashion journal to float in a kind of circular frame around the empty yet swelling bodice and chemise at the center of the image, as if offering themselves as potential accompaniments for the dress that the implied, yet anonymous, client will wear. Like the bodice and puffed, shaped sleeves of the chemise, the hats suggest the curves and impressions of a live human form, and yet they are empty and headless, to echo Zola's image from the outset of this chapter. Heads and bodies are absent from illustrations such as these, and yet the articles themselves, suspended in air, are depicted in ways as to suggest movement, animation, life. The effect is twofold: first, the object itself is imbued with living qualities it does not in fact possess, thus enhancing consumer desire and allowing consumers to imagine filling the empty shells of clothing themselves; second, the consumer

20. Bolomier 70; Müller and Kamitsis 36. I have discussed elsewhere the importance of the notion of "seamlessness" to the construction of proper bourgeois femininity with respect to fashion more broadly. See Hiner, *Accessories to Modernity* and "The *Modiste*'s Palette."

FIGURE 2.7 Hats and lingerie in *Les Modes parisiennes* from Paris, France, 1863. University of Washington Libraries, Special Collections, UW 38850.

becomes infinitely replaceable, thus reversing the hierarchy between animate and inanimate. The consumer herself thus becomes secondary under the spell cast by these hats, and the women who produced them vanish behind the name of the *maîtresse-modiste*—in this case, Mme Bouvy Sainsaullieux—even if the myth of the *modiste* as flirty and fashionable remains ubiquitous (Clayson). The consumer has become substitutable, like a paper doll whose outfits can change with the fold of a flap, and the fashion worker disappears behind the myth of the *modiste*, expert creator of lifelike accessories.

The Uncanny Work of Fashion

By way of conclusion, let us return to Zola's headless mannequins in order to refocus our discussion around the troubling question of ambiguous animation:

> The red breasts of the mannequins swelled the fabric, their heavy thighs exaggerated dainty waists, absent heads were replaced with giant tags, stuck with a pin into the red felt of the collar; while the mirrors, on either side of the window, through a clever trick, reflected and multiplied them infinitely, populated the street with these beautiful women for sale, and wore prices in large numbers, in the place of heads. (*Ladies' Paradise* 6)[21]

Denise's brothers are dumbfounded before these "beautiful ladies in the shop window," the one "immobile again, his mouth open," and the other "disturbed and delighted" (6–7).[22] As they gawk before the spectacle, the excessive realism of the fashion display yields up its crude, but uncanny, essence to the reader as the eye wanders up through the luxurious folds of fabric, swelling over the inanimate voluptuousness of the lifelike, yet decapitated mannequins, to settle on giant price tags—a not so subtle clue that the fantasy world of fashion is indeed a business proposition.

Munro has argued that such displays of fashion mannequins demonstrate the "firm implantation of a consumer-orientated society in fin-de-siècle France, in which the mannequin was both the subject and agent of commodity fetishism" (174). In what can only be described as a surreal visual landscape, these headless, tagged bodies are repeated ad infinitum in the mirrors to either side of the expansive window, producing a disturbing replication of fashionable, but de-animated, women. Not mannequins, but "belles *dames* de vitrine," they slip into subjectivity,

21. "La gorge rouge des mannequins gonflait l'étoffe, les hanches fortes exagéraient la finesse de la taille, la tête absente était remplacée par une grande étiquette, piquée avec une épingle dans le molleton rouge du col ; tandis que les glaces, aux deux côtés de la vitrine, par un jeu calculé, les reflétaient et les multipliaient sans fin, peuplaient la rue de ces belles femmes à vendre, et portaient des prix en gros chiffres, à la place des têtes" (11).

22. "les belles dames de la vitrine" (11); "immobile, la bouche ouverte" (11); "troublé et ravi" (11).

reflect the women who admire them, and are to be emulated as models of fashionable femininity. Their potential for subjectivity, and their endless replication through the mise en abyme of the female form produced by the mirrors, creates a disquieting exchange of subject for object, dummy for woman.

Several decades later, in the early days of fashion modeling in the twentieth century, the same phenomena of de-animation and disturbing replication persist. As Caroline Evans notes in her history of fashion shows and models, "the mirrored salons that multiply the mannequins' image, the repetitious nature of their task, modeling the same garment ten times a day and their indifferent manner. . . . All these features combine to make the fashion model something a little less than human: mechanical or doll-like in her smooth performance" (19). Here, of course, the living mannequin has replaced the inanimate one, but the aura of oddity remains. Evans invokes the "uncanny doubling between the inanimate and the living mannequin," suggesting further that both also double the purchasing client and spectator—she who must imagine herself in the object position to be seduced into a purchase, whether by means of an image, a mirror, a mannequin, or a model. This "series of antinomies (alive-dead, animate-inanimate, object-subject, working girls-leisured client)," Evans concludes, "lead ineluctably to their predicate: original and copy" (20).

The *marotte* raises precisely these same questions of animation and de-animation that undergird any discussion of the uncanny, and the hat, the embodiment of consumer desire, is its fetishized counterpart. What is the uncanny work of fashion then if not the production of belief in and desire for the life-giving power of beautiful objects and the concomitant dehumanizing of the consumer and erasure of the unlovely toil that makes this illusion possible? This is precisely the mechanism of the commodity fetish. These heads and hats, so ordinary in fashion illustration and in popular prints and literature of the period, conceal the active minds and nimble fingers behind fashion's work. By defamiliarizing these objects, however, and recognizing this uncanniness, we can see beyond the subtle erasure of real women in fashion's early economy and begin to reclaim some of their history.

Acknowledgments

I wish to acknowledge the generosity of the American Library of Paris, where as a spring 2015 visiting scholar, an early draft of this essay was composed. I am also grateful to Eva Woods Pieró and Jeffrey Schneider for their careful reading of drafts of this essay. Finally, I offer my sincere thanks to Heidi Brevik-Zender for conceiving of this project and bringing it to completion.

Works Cited

Barthélemy et Lhérie. *L'Art de ne pas monter sa garde, vaudeville en un acte*. Marchant, 1837.

Berger, John. *Ways of Seeing*. Penguin, 1977.

Brown, Bill. *A Sense of Things: The Object Matter of American Literature*. U of Chicago P, 2003.

———. "Thing Theory." *Things*, edited by Bill Brown. U of Chicago P, 2004, pp. 1–16.

Bolomier, Eliane. *Le chapeau: grand art et savoir-faire*. Somogy, 1996.

Clayson, Hollis. *Painted Love: Prostitution in French Art of the Impressionist Era*. Yale UP, 1991.

Coffin, Judith. *The Politics of Women's Work: The Paris Garment Trades, 1750–1915*. Princeton UP, 1996.

Demornex, Jacqueline. *Le Siècle en chapeaux: Claude Saint-Cyr, histoire d'une modiste*. Editions du May, 1991.

Evans, Caroline. *The Mechanical Smile: Modernism and the First Fashion Shows in France and America 1900–1924*. Yale UP, 2013.

Higonnet, Anne. "Real Fashion: Clothes Unmake the Working Woman." *Spectacles of Realism: Gender, Body, Genre*, edited by Margaret Cohen and Christopher Prendergast. U of Minnesota P, 1995, pp. 137–62.

Hiner, Susan. *Accessories to Modernity: Fashion and the Feminine in Nineteenth-Century France*. U of Pennsylvania P, 2010.

———. "The *Modiste*'s Palette and the Artist's Hat." *Degas, Impressionism, and the Paris Millinery Trade*, Exhibition Catalogue edited and co-curated by Simon Kelly and Esther Bell. St. Louis Art Museum and Fine Arts Museum of San Francisco, 2017, pp. 67–80.

Freud, Sigmund. *The Uncanny*. Translated by David McClintock. Penguin, 2003.

Iskin, Ruth. *Modern Women and Parisian Consumer Culture in Impressionist Painting*. Cambridge UP, 2007.

Jentsch, Ernst. "On the Psychology of the Uncanny," translated by Roy Sellars. *Angelaki: A New Journal in Philosophy, Literature and the Social Sciences*, vol. 2, no. 1, 1996, pp. 7–16.

Jones, Jennifer. *Sexing La Mode: Gender, Fashion, and Commercial Culture in Old Regime France*. Berg, 2004.

Jouhaud, Auguste. *Les Débuts de la modiste*, monologue-vaudeville en un acte, théâtre Beaumarchais, 27 février, 1855.

Kuchta, David. "The Making of the Self-Made Man: Class, Clothing, and English Masculinity, 1688–1832." *The Sex of Things: Gender and Consumption in Historical Perspective*, edited by Victoria de Grazia and Ellen Furlough. U of California P, 1996, pp. 54–78.

Marcus, Sharon. "Reflections on Victorian Fashion Plates." *Differences*, vol. 14, no. 3, 2003, pp. 4–33.

Marx, Karl. "Commodities." *The Marx-Engels Reader*, edited by Robert C. Tucker, 2nd edition. W. W. Norton, 1978, pp. 302–28.

Matthews David, Alison. *Fashion Victims: The Dangers of Dress Past and Present*. Bloomsbury, 2015.

Müller, Florence, and Lydia Kamitsis. *Les chapeaux: une histoire de tête*. Syros-Alternatives, 1993.

Munro, Jane. *Silent Partners: Artist and Mannequin from Function to Fetish*. Yale UP, 2014.

Park, Julie. *The Self and It: Novel Objects in Eighteenth-Century England*. Stanford UP, 2010.

Peers, Juliette. *The Fashion Doll: From Bébé Jumeau to Barbie*. Berg, 2004.

Perrot, Philippe. "The Vestimentary Landscapes of the Nineteenth Century." *Fashioning the Bourgeoisie: A History of Clothing in the Nineteenth Century*, translated by Richard Bienvenu. Princeton UP, 1994 (1981), pp. 26–35.

Riotor, Léon. *Le Mannequin*. Bibliothèque Artistique et Littéraire, 1900.

Ross, Kristin. "Introduction: Shopping." Emile Zola, *The Ladies' Paradise: A Realist Novel*. U of California P, 1992, pp. v–xxiii.

Schreier, Lise. "Esclaves de la scène: Blackface et acteurs noirs dans le vaudeville français du dix-neuvième siècle." *French Cultural Studies*, vol. 27, no. 2, 2016, pp. 135–54.

Smith, Andrew. *The Ghost Story 1840–1920: A Cultural History*. Manchester UP, 2013.

Steele, Valerie. *Paris Fashion: A Cultural History*. Bloomsbury Academic, 1998.

Texier, Edmond. "Les Magasins." *Tableau de Paris*, t. 2. Paulin et Le Chevalier, 1852–53, pp. 230–33.

Veblen, Thorstein. *Conspicuous Consumption*. Penguin, 2006.

Vinken, Barbara. *Fashion Zeitgeist*. Berg, 2005.

Withy, Katherine. *Heidegger on Being Uncanny*. Harvard UP, 2015.

Zola, Émile. *Au bonheur des dames*. Edited by Robert Sctrick. Pocket, 1990.

———. *The Ladies' Paradise*. Translated by Brian Nelson. Oxford UP, 1995.

CHAPTER 3

GLOVES IN NINETEENTH-CENTURY FRANCE

Materiality and Metaphor

Anne Green

The changing circumstances of nineteenth-century France are strangely echoed in the changing fortunes of its gloves. From modest beginnings at the start of the century, glove production expanded rapidly to become one of France's most important industries as glovers strove to keep pace with ever-increasing consumer demand. Touching on almost every aspect of French culture, the glove phenomenon intersected not only with class, morality, and sexuality but with politics, economics, technology, and even agriculture and medicine. Contemporary writers soon recognized gloves' symbolic potential, and in nineteenth-century novels, poems, and plays, gloves undergo a fascinating evolution as they take on different literary functions. The main section of this chapter explores that evolution, but before examining how gloves were written about, and the meanings and metaphors that accrue to them, we should first consider them in all their materiality, and look at how they were made and how they were worn.

Making Gloves

At the beginning of the nineteenth century leather gloves were made entirely by hand, as they had been for centuries. Carefully prepared skins were cut with shears and the pieces hand-stitched with needle and thread (figs. 3.1(a) and 3.1(b)). But the French glove industry languished, undermined first by the trade embargoes of the Napoleonic wars, then by high export tariffs and a shortage of fine leather, which was being bought up by the British.[1] In an attempt to relieve their hardship, the glove workers of Grenoble organized France's first mutual society and petitioned

1. For example, in 1787 the Grenoble glove industry employed 6,254 people, but by 1807 the number had fallen to about 2,800. Britain's import ban lasted until 1826, with French gloves entering the country only as contraband. See *Bulletin de la société de statistique, des sciences naturelles et des arts industriels du département de l'Isère* (201–08).

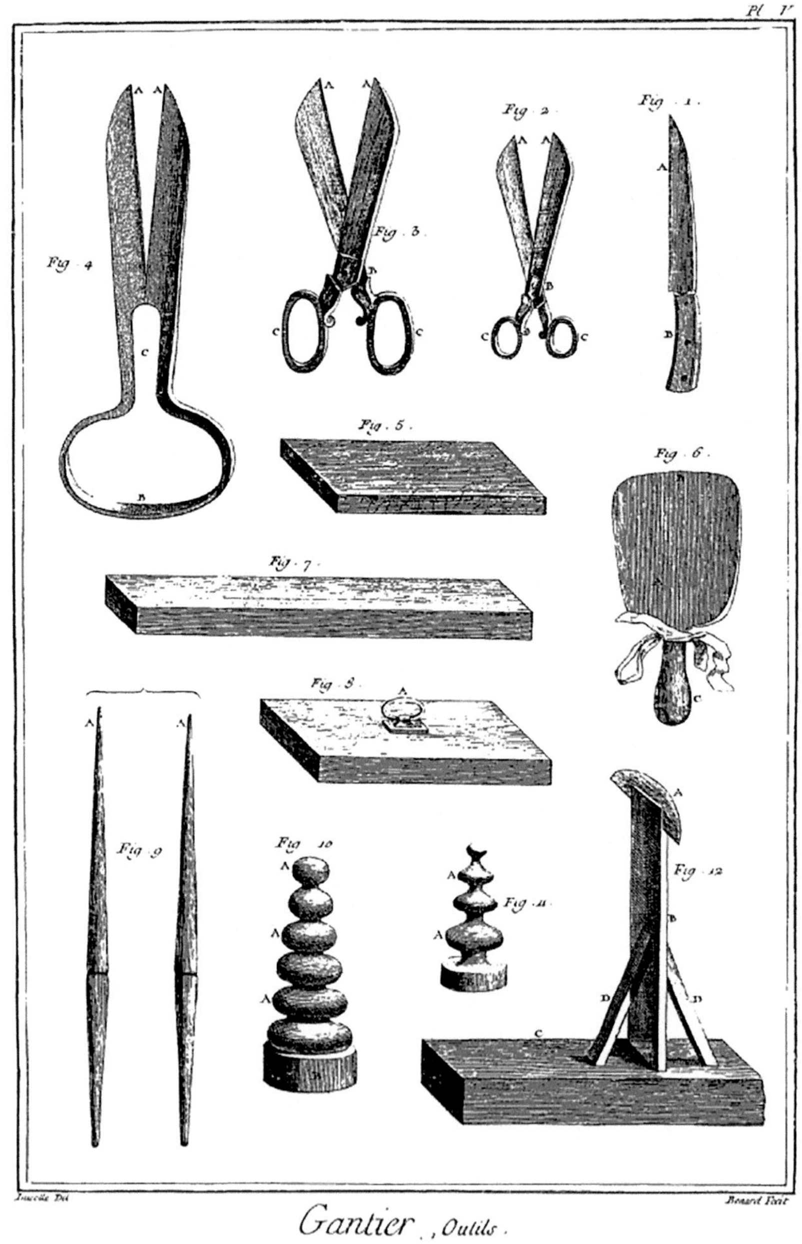

FIGURE 3.1(a) Plate 1 from "Ganterie" entry in Diderot and D'Alembert's *Encyclopédie* of 1751, showing glove-making tools. Bibliothèque nationale de France, Paris.

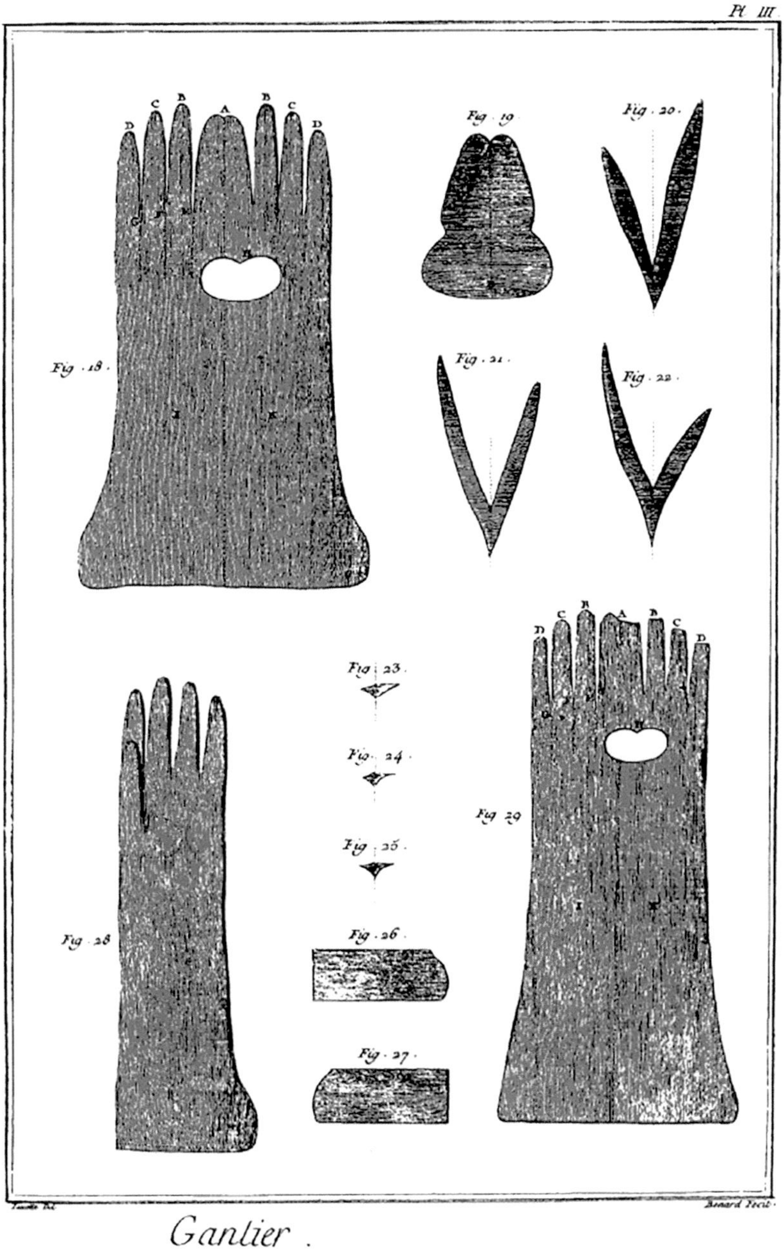

Figure 3.1(b) Plate 3 from "Ganterie" entry in Diderot and D'Alembert's *Encyclopédie* of 1751, showing glove pieces. Bibliothèque nationale de France, Paris.

the government for a ban on the export of glove leather, but without success (Rey 68, 105). Not even the introduction from England in 1816 of the *mécanique*—a toothed clamp that held the pieces of skin together to facilitate even stitching—could ensure a recovery. The industry's astonishing renaissance was largely due to the inventive son of a Grenoble glove maker. After spending over five years studying the shapes and sizes of patients' hands at the town's hospital, Xavier Jouvin devised a mathematical system of 320 glove sizes that guaranteed a perfect fit for any hand. Selecting gloves to fit an individual customer was no longer a time-consuming process of trial and error, and as a result, gloves could be sold more quickly and efficiently. Production was further enhanced a few years later when Jouvin introduced his *main de fer* (iron hand), a calibrated mechanical cutter that could stamp out precisely measured glove pieces from six layers of skin at a time (figs. 3.2 and 3.3).

He took out French patents on his inventions between 1834 and 1838, and as well-fitting Jouvin gloves became increasingly sought after at home and abroad, Grenoble's glove industry prospered. The expiration of these patents in 1849 caused a massive surge in France's production of leather gloves as other centers adopted the new technology: worth twenty million francs in 1847, national output had soared to forty-seven million francs by 1851, making it one of France's largest industries (Rey 110). While this huge expansion boosted the national economy, it also had an impact on animal husbandry, for on average it took the skins of eight kids to produce a dozen gloves. The *Bulletin de la société de statistique* for 1851 calculated that that year, Grenoble alone had needed 2,560,000 kid skins to produce its *gants chevreau*, while the town had used 75,000 eggs a week to treat the fine glove leather—about three times as many as were consumed by the inhabitants (Rey 203, 205). The qualities that made French leather gloves so sought after are summed up in an 1855 report from Paris's Universal Exhibition: "it is the distinctiveness of color, the regularity of cut, the suppleness of the leather and the seaming's fine finish that ensure the superiority of our manufacturers" (Alcan et al. 733).[2]

Production kept rising, as did demand. By 1867 France's leather glove industry employed sixty-five to seventy thousand workers and produced about two million dozen pairs—an output of roughly forty-eight million leather gloves a year (*Exposition* 330–31).[3] A shortage of skilled needlewomen led to what had formerly been an urban industry spreading into the surrounding countryside, as country girls were recruited to this relatively well-paid work during the winter months when they were not needed in the fields. Although the seasonal nature of their output inconvenienced glove manufacturers and helped to send lace-making and weaving industries into decline by taking these women away from their traditional crafts, their new source of income helped regenerate depressed rural areas, as is evident when

2. "c'est la netteté de la nuance, la régularité de la coupe, la souplesse de la peau et le fini de la couture qui établissent la supériorité de nos fabriquants." All English translations in this chapter are by Anne Green.

3. About three-quarters of these were exported, mainly to England, while most of England's own glove output was exported to America. See also Alcan et al. 54.

Figure 3.2 Grenoble statue of Xavier Jouvin holding a *main de fer*. Photograph by Matthieu Riegler. Wikimedia Commons.

FIGURE 3.3 A *main de fer* (iron hand). © Musée dauphinoise, Grenoble. Accession number 79.8.10.

Gérard de Nerval's Sylvie exchanges her lace bobbins for a glove maker's *mécanique* and dismays the narrator by adopting urban tastes and manners (Nerval 559).[4]

New inventions continued to appear as France became increasingly industrialized. In 1849, for example, a patent was granted for a machine that rapidly smoothed and folded gloves, allowing for neat stacking and packaging by the dozen. Since the close fit of the glove and the position and shape of the thumb were of particular concern, there were experiments with cutting machines that altered the position of pieces and seams to improve tightness without loss of flexibility.[5] The introduction of the dome fastener in 1855 also enabled a tighter fit; glove stretchers soon followed, as did machines for attaching buttons, for polishing, and for finishing (fig. 3.4). Attempts to produce a sewing machine suitable for leather gloves long proved problematic, and although the Danish clockmaker Hans Peter Henriksen exhibited

4. See also Jean-François Vallet d'Artois, *Manuel de fabriquant de gants, considéré dans ses rapports avec la mégisserie, la chamoiserie etc.*, 502–05. In his novel *Le Gouffre*, Elie Berthet writes of the benefits to women engaged in glove making in the countryside around Grenoble and observes that "the purely agricultural population was submerged, as it were, by this industrial population" ("la population purement agricole y était comme noyée au milieu de cette population industrielle") (57).

5. See, for example, *Le Génie industriel: Revue des inventions françaises et étrangères* for details of a modified glove pattern, patented in 1845, designed to allow the thumb more freedom of movement without straining the leather (253).

Figure 3.4 Nineteenth-century wooden glove stretchers. Photograph by Anne Green.

a machine in 1867, it was unsuitable for commercial use. The 1878 Exposition Universelle, however, displayed a variety of new glove-stitching machines, including one that operated throughout the exhibition for the public to admire. But despite a constant increase in productivity, the glove market was still far from saturated: the exhibition report commented that only by machine stitching could glove makers keep up with an ever-increasing demand, and indeed the majority of gloves sold that year were sewn by machine (*Études* 341).[6] As they became increasingly ubiquitous, gloves generated their own accessories, including glove stretchers, talcum powder shakers, button hooks, and ornate, lockable glove boxes. Miniature versions were even produced for dolls, to go with their own tiny leather gloves.

Wearing Gloves

How can one account for the phenomenal increase in demand for gloves in nineteenth-century France? As social anthropologists Mary Douglas and Baron Isherwood have observed, demand can never be explained by looking only at the physical or material properties of goods: "Man needs goods for communicating with others and for making sense of what is going on around him" (95). During a period of rapid social change, gloves came to fulfill that function admirably. Whereas Diderot and d'Alembert's *Encyclopédie* of 1751 had defined the glove

6. In *Le Gouffre*, Berthet contrasts the income and working conditions of a poor, sick, rural glove seamstress, who has to sew for fourteen hours a day to earn twenty sous, with those of Grenoble girls who sew by machine and can produce twelve gloves a day (111–13).

simply as a type of winter garment intended to protect the hands from the cold, in the following century that basic function was submerged by ever-increasing layers of meaning. For Georges Guenot-Lecointe, the author of a *Physiologie du gant* published in 1841, the remarkable changes he had seen in glove manufacturing even by that date were emblematic of France's evolution from barbarism to civilization. For him, the old days of badly stitched gloves before the introduction of the *mécanique* evoked the "first centuries of barbarism," whereas a well-made straw-colored glove was "the most advanced expression of modern civilization" (66, 84).[7] In the early years of the nineteenth century, however, gloves had relatively limited social significance. Then, as Guenot-Lecointe explains, "gloves played only a very minor role in our habits; they were rarely mentioned, and . . . no-one paid much attention to them" (72).[8] By the time he published his *Physiologie*, however, the glove had "invaded all social classes" (84).[9] Douglas and Isherwood note that people's "choice of goods continuously creates certain patterns of discrimination, overlaying or reinforcing others" (66), which is precisely what happened as more and more people adopted Guenot-Lecointe's conviction that "the glove alone indicates which rung we occupy on Jacob's ladder" and enlisted gloves in their attempts to best position themselves within a rapidly evolving social hierarchy (84).[10] No longer the province only of the upper class, by the 1840s glove wearing had been adopted as a social marker by an aspiring bourgeoisie, while to the lower classes gloves were an enviable emblem of luxury and leisure. Madame de Girardin describes little girls' delight at being given old gloves to play with, since "old gloves are something to be proud of; to working-class children gloves mean dignity; they represent luxury par excellence, they are a symptom of leisure!" (1: 150).[11] Although serving little practical purpose, wearing gloves had become increasingly indispensable. As Gustave Flaubert observed, people were more reluctant to leave the house without them than without a purse (*Corr.* 1: 355).

While some contemporary commentators fancied that gloves' new ubiquity signaled a new egalitarianism, most recognized that that was an illusion and that subtle variations indicated crucial social difference. Madame de Girardin tartly observed that despite what many people seemed to think, the mere fact of wearing white gloves and a black coat did not suddenly qualify a man to marry an heiress (2: 261). Simply wearing gloves was not enough. As Guenot-Lecointe pointed out: "it is not enough just to have gloves, you must also know how to wear them" (84).[12] Knowing

7. "premiers siècles de la barbarie"; "l'expression la plus avancée de la civilisation moderne."

8. "le gant n'avait joué qu'un rôle très-mesquin dans nos mœurs ; on en parlait à peine, et . . . on ne s'[en] occupait guère."

9. "envahi toutes les classes."

10. "le gant seul indique le rang que nous occupons sur l'échelle de Jacob."

11. "de vieux gants, c'est de l'orgueil ; les gants sont une dignité chez les enfants du peuple ; c'est le luxe par excellence, c'est un symptôme d'oisiveté !"

12. "il ne suffit pas d'avoir des gants, il faut encore les savoir mettre." He also meant this

which gloves to wear, and knowing when and how to wear them, was an essential indication of where one stood on the social ladder. As glove production grew, therefore, so too did the number of publications offering advice on an increasingly elaborate set of prescriptions and prohibitions surrounding glove wearing.

Interestingly, and despite the best efforts of contemporary fashion journals, gloves were largely immune to the whims of fashion. "Fashion has little influence on gloves," noted the art critic Charles Blanc in *L'Art dans la parure et dans le vêtement* (259).[13] Clearly, the *savoir-vivre* displayed in how a glove was worn was more significant than the material object itself. Taken to extremes, the putting on or removal of a glove became a display in itself. The piano virtuoso Franz Liszt, for example, would ceremoniously remove his white gloves on the concert platform to thunderous applause and toss them on the floor before playing; this was part of the performance, and his discarded gloves gained such iconic status that admirers fought over their fragments (Huneker 256–57, 298). The glove-wearing rituals of upper-class men described by the writer and illustrator Bertall were elaborate, though less flamboyant:

> The most elegant gentlemen change their gloves four or five times a day. Riding gloves in the morning, semi-formal gloves for going to lunch, formal kidskin or suede gloves for visits, dog-skin gloves for driving in the Bois, gloves for dining in town, gloves for going to a ball, to the theater, or to a club in the evening. (1: 58)[14]

Bertall did, however, admit that few could afford to fulfill all these so-called "obligations." But other commentators issued equally strict decrees: gloves were always to be worn in the street, on walks, in church, on journeys, at clubs, soirées, balls, and theaters. Coat and hat must be removed on arrival at the house of one's host, but gloves taken off only when the guest was seated at the dining table. A gentleman should never wear gloves when being presented to a sovereign or head of state, or when swearing an oath or signing a legal document. His valets and male servants waiting at table should wear white cotton gloves, but only when in livery or *habit noir*, and never when serving lunch. Gloves were not to be worn by chambermaids (Staffe 336, 337, 161). When in mourning, only knitted or fabric gloves were appropriate—never leather (Fère 153). In church, gloves must be removed when going to confession, taking communion, or taking holy water (G-M 29; Anon., *Usages* 98; Bradi 15–16); it was customary before a baptism for the godfather to send six pairs of gloves to the godmother (Anon., *Usages* 148); and during a marriage ceremony

---

literally, and he gave detailed instructions on how to insert one's hand into a long, tight glove (Guenot-Lecointe 84–85).

13. "La mode n'a pas grande prise sur les gants."

14. "Les hommes de haute élégance changent de gants quatre ou cinq fois par jour. Gant de cheval, le matin, gant de demi-toilette pour aller déjeuner, gant de toilette pour visite, chevreau ou peau de suède, gants de peau de chien pour conduire au Bois, gants pour aller dîner en ville, gants pour aller au bal, au théâtre, ou au club le soir."

the bride and groom's white gloves were to be removed only when the priest blessed the rings (Anon., *Le Livre de la famille* 99). Putty-colored gloves were specified for men forming part of the wedding cortege, whereas those attending only the wedding Mass should wear gloves of suede. Suede gloves were also prescribed for ladies wearing cretonne dresses—to pair glacé leather with cretonne was considered a solecism (Alq 107). Even the language surrounding these culturally loaded artifacts was caught up in social distinctions: the middle-class *porte des gants*, but the upper-class *se gante* (Guenot-Lecointe 109).

Choice of leather and color were crucial. "The color of gloves is an almost infallible indication of their owner's intimate habits," asserted Guenot-Lecointe (85),[15] while Eugène Chapus, writing under the pseudonym of the Vicomte de Marennes, exclaimed over the infinite variety of shades of glove leather available and asserted that it was possible to tell what a well-dressed man was about to do merely by observing his gloves (70). Certain basic rules pertained: darker gloves during the day, paler ones in the evening, when to be seen in dark gloves was considered "an enormity" (Bertall 1: 58)[16] (fig. 3.5). (The Vicomte de Marennes reported, nevertheless, that after the death of Charles X in 1836, opportunists took both black and yellow gloves to the theater or opera so that they could extend a hand in mourning to a Legitimist, but appear conventionally gloved for an Orleanist [70].) Women, however, were advised to avoid very pale gloves, which might distract from their fashionably pale complexions (Blanc 260–61). In a culture that set great store by the whiteness of a woman's skin, Madame Celnart warned dark-skinned women that the contrast with white gloves was "really intolerable" and suggested they wore long flesh-colored gloves of thick crêpe to hide what she referred to as "that horrid shade" (135–36).[17] For Guenot-Lecointe, it was yellow gloves—particularly favored by dandies and earning them their nickname of *gants jaunes*—that denoted the acme of modern civilization (86), and yellow gloves remained fashionable throughout the century: maize or straw colored for the morning, paler cream for evening.[18] Neutral colors such as pearl gray or putty were also acceptable for men and women, although Charles Blanc advised against

---

15. "La couleur des gants est un indice presque certain des moeurs intimes de leur propriétaire." Cf. "One can tell how distinguished a man is by the shade of his gloves" ("On reconnaît la distinction d'un homme à la nuance de ses gants") (Guenot-Lecointe 109).

16. "une énormité."

17. "vraiment intolérable"; "cette horrible teinte."

18. Visiting the Salon of 1837, Madame de Girardin waspishly observed that the fashionable glovers Privat and Boivin seemed to have been the inspiration behind many of the paintings on display. She particularly mocked a portrait of a young man leaning in melancholy pose against a tombstone on which his hat and yellow gloves had been carefully positioned: "Why put yellow gloves on a tomb ! Black gloves would have been preferable, they would have been more seemly" ("Pourquoi gants jaunes sur un tombeau ! Nous aurions préféré des gants noirs, c'était plus convenable") (1: 102–03).

tones such as steel gray, bronze, or slate—colors associated with hard materials that might, he warned, detract from the glove's essential quality of suppleness (178). On the other hand, brighter tones such as *sang de boeuf*, violet, poppy, or green—especially green—were a sign of vulgarity or *petit bourgeois* provincialism (Guenot-Lecointe 85–86; Bertall 1: 58).

Figure 3.5 Gloves at the theater: Pierre-Auguste Renoir (1841–1919), *La Loge* (*Theater Box*), 1874. Oil on canvas, 80 x 63.5 cm. The Samuel Courtauld Trust, The Courtauld Gallery, London.

A glove's fit was a further indicator of distinction. Although in 1833 Mme Celnart told her readers that "it is unsightly and common to have gloves that are too wide" (222),[19] later in the century a more frequent error was for women to squeeze their hands into gloves that were too tight, in an attempt to make them look smaller. Social commentators warned that this would have the opposite effect, for "a container is always bigger than its contents" (Blanc 259; Guenot-Lecointe 85).[20] It was obviously distasteful to have one's gloves split or tear in such circumstances, although split seams were forgivable and possibly even admirable if caused by applauding enthusiastically at the theater.[21]

Wearing faded or soiled gloves, however, was beyond the pale. There was no uglier sight than a soiled glove, Baroness Staffe asserted, reminding her readers that well-bred ladies spoke of "soiled gloves," never "dirty gloves,"[22] for the latter was a "naturalist" term that evoked far too unpleasant an image (*Secrets* 131). Honoré de Balzac's comment, in his *Traité de la vie élégante*, "A tear is a misfortune, a stain is a vice" (257),[23] was particularly true of gloves. Although nineteenth-century manuals of *savoir-vivre* offered extensive advice on how to clean gloves with substances ranging from toast crumbs to cyanide (Celnart 222–23; Juranville 175), in the best circles wearing gloves that had been cleaned rather than discarded was unthinkable. "A cleaned glove is like a reheated dinner; it is never any good," declared Guenot-Lecointe (111).[24] In fashionable society, gloves had the very briefest of lives: "the more often one changes them, the more highly one is regarded," he wrote, claiming that whereas in his grandparents' day a pair of gloves was as durable as a pair of breeches, now they lasted no longer than a delicate rose or a declaration of love (112–13).[25] This is no doubt why Flaubert once concluded his list of New Year's greetings to his teenage niece Caroline by wishing her "fifteen billion pairs of new

---

19. "il est disgracieux et commun d'avoir des gants trop larges."

20. "le contenant est toujours plus grand que le contenu."

21. See Champfleury's description of a performance of *Hamlet* in *Contes d'automne*: "Applause is then a sacred duty; the proprieties no longer need be respected, one tears one's gloves and shouts out loud; there has to be a violent eruption of emotion" ("Alors l'applaudissement est une dette sacrée ; il n'y a plus de convenances à garder, on déchire ses gants, on crie, il faut que l'émotion sorte violemment") (209). Cf. Théophile Gautier's poem "La Diva": "All voices cried out, all hands clapped, / White gloves burst from applauding so hard" ("Toutes les voix criaient, toutes les mains frappaient, / A force d'applaudir les gants blancs se rompaient") (155).

22. "des gants souillés"; "des gants sales."

23. "Une déchirure est un malheur, une tache est un vice."

24. "Un gant décrassé ressemble à un dîner échauffé ; il ne vaut jamais rien." The anonymous author of *Les Usages du monde* writes that the only thing more repulsive than a torn glove is one that emits a disgusting smell because it has been cleaned with benzene or ammonia (71).

25. "plus on en change, plus on est considéré."

butter-yellow gloves" (*Corr.* 3: 192).[26] The pressure to conform to such strictures is evident from the frequent references in nineteenth-century texts to "irreproachable gloves." The freshness of one's gloves was a sign of one's moral virtue, and gloves, like their wearers, must be beyond reproach.[27]

By the 1880s glove wearing as a mark of social distinction had come almost full circle. Baroness Staffe records that certain gentlemen, exasperated by the lower classes' adoption of gloves, chose to signal their superiority by flouting the rules and appearing in public barehanded. Staffe strongly disapproved:

> It is a form of protest, a kind of opposition ever since the glove became democratized . . . men who wanted to distinguish themselves tossed their gloves to the back of a drawer and flaunted their fine hands, telling all and sundry that it takes five centuries of leisure in one's bloodline to acquire a beautiful hand. What pretentious nonsense! (*Usages* 337)[28]

Commentators did agree, however, that gloves revealed everything about a person. While style might sometimes deceive, gloves never did, claimed Octave Uzanne in *Les Ornements de la femme* (234), while Madame de Girardin—who once declined an introduction to a woman on the grounds that she could tell by her gloves that the two of them would never get on—declared, "A woman's gloves betray her whole character" (3: 157).[29] Guenot-Lecointe even made the fanciful claim that if the whole of France were reduced to rubble, it would be possible to distinguish its eighty-six *départements* and the social classes of their former inhabitants by inspecting gloves retrieved from the debris (78). Clearly, gloves were now doing much more than protecting hands from the cold. The formula that appears repeatedly in such texts is "Show me your glove, and I shall tell you who you are" (Uzanne 226; Guenot-Lecointe 111).[30] Gloves, it seemed, could not lie.

---

26. "quinze milliards de paires de gants beurre frais."

27. "des gants irréprochables." Marennes, *Manuel*, asserts that a glove "sums up and expresses a host of moral inclinations" ("résume et exprime une foule de dispositions morales") (69).

28. "C'est une espèce de protestation, une sorte d'opposition depuis que le gant s'est démocratisé. . . . les hommes qui cherchent à se distinguer, rejetèrent leurs gants au fond des tiroirs et étalèrent leurs mains fines, répétant partout qu'il faut cinq siècles d'oisiveté dans une race pour acquérir une belle main. Sottise et prétention !" Cf. Bertall (58): "I know a great lord whose hands are of an admirable shape, color and elegance, and who always holds his gloves in his hand and never puts them on, claiming that only the deformed are obliged to wear them . . . I believe he is in the wrong" ("Je connais un grand seigneur dont les mains sont admirables de forme, de couleur et d'élégance, qui tient toujours ses gants à la main, et ne les met jamais, prétendant que les gens difformes sont seuls forcés d'en mettre . . . Je le crois dans son tort").

29. "Les gants d'une femme trahissent tout son caractère."

30. "Montrez-moi votre gant, je dirai qui vous êtes."

Writing about Gloves

If Guenot-Lecointe recognized that "the glove is a symbol" (78),[31] so too did writers of fiction, who realized that gloves offered a wealth of figurative possibilities. Yet in the first decades of the century—before Xavier Jouvin's intervention—gloves are virtually absent from French literature. Even Stendhal, so ready to depict characters concerned with the niceties of style and status, barely mentions them. The first to exploit their cultural significance was Balzac, and for him, as for the social commentators, gloves told the truth. As early as 1830, in *Étude de moeurs par les gants*, he has a countess claim to her friends that she will determine their character and actions simply by inspecting their gloves the morning after a ball. A colonel's crumpled but perfectly clean pair reveals that instead of dancing he spent the evening at the gaming tables, twisting and tearing his gloves in the anxiety of losing; another man's discolored gloves betray the fact that he danced too often with the same partner, the dye of whose gloves has transferred itself to his; and a third man's claim that an upset stomach kept him from the dancefloor is disproved when tell-tale liqueur stains and traces of food still smelling of vanilla and pistachio show him to have preferred dining to dancing (20: 437–41).

Because of their capacity to retain physical and mental traces of their wearers, gloves in fiction frequently offer clues or shed light on mysteries. As Charles Blanc put it, "How much there is in an object that has been worn by a man's hand and that retains the imprint of his trembling fingers and the nervous movements made while he was lost in thought" (179).[32] In the first half of the nineteenth century, however, fictional gloves function mainly as convenient markers of class or social aspiration, or as shortcut indicators of character. Thus, in Balzac's *Eugénie Grandet* the contrast between Monsieur Grandet's stiff, heavy gloves that last him a year and a half and the fine white leather of Charles's beautifully delicate pair neatly sums up the difference between the provincial miser and his foppish Parisian nephew (3: 1058).

Offering opportunities for wry comment on a society in flux, gloves were quickly welcomed by realist writers concerned to incorporate details from everyday life into their fiction. So we find ladies placing their evening gloves in their wine glasses to indicate no alcohol, as well as countless instances of characters picking up their gloves to signal that a visit is at an end, or of a glove splitting because too large (and by implication too ill-bred) a hand has been forced into it. Gloves are a frequent source of shame or embarrassment for those fictional wearers who are aware of society's demands but unable to meet them,[33] while those who transgress

31. "le gant est un symbole." Cf. Marennes (69): "Nowadays [gloves] play an important, symbolic role . . ." ("Aujourd'hui [les gants] jouent un grand rôle, rôle symbolique . . .").

32. "Que de choses dans un objet dont s'est revêtue la main de l'homme et où est restée l'empreinte de ses mouvements nerveux et du frémissement de ses doigts, sous l'empire de la pensée."

33. For example, in Flaubert's *L'Éducation sentimentale* Frédéric is always at pains to be "irreproachably gloved" ("irréprochablement ganté") when visiting Madame Arnoux, but

the rules without a sense of shame are clearly shown to belong on the lower rungs of the social ladder.[34] Moreover, the gap between individual behavior and society's decrees provides a rich source of comedy for playwrights, who flatter and entertain their middle-class audiences by depicting lower-class individuals whose aspiration to glove wearing merely emphasizes their social inferiority. Eugène Labiche's play *L'Avare en gants jaunes*, for example, features a young man who carries several pairs of gloves in public, changing into old or dirty ones when he thinks no one will notice. The disjunction between such parsimony and the message of wealth supposedly signaled by gloves was a particularly fruitful trope for writers eager to mock the pretensions of social upstarts. Wearing the right gloves was a central concern for suitors hoping to snare a wealthy bride, for instance, and in *Ces petits messieurs*, Louise Colet's narrator spells out the expense involved in trying to keep up appearances over a long period:

> the fashion was for straw-colored gloves. A dandy worthy of the name wore them even in broad daylight, which meant two pairs of gloves every day: one pair for afternoon visits, and another pair (at least) for evening. With Jouvin gloves the price they were, this was serious. (83)[35]

No one is surprised that Elie has run up a thirty thousand–franc bill at the famous glove maker's, but the narrator points out that although this seems an enormous sum, careful calculation shows it to be insufficient. For Elie to have frequented the Paris salons regularly over a twenty-year period, as he claimed, he would have needed between twelve and fourteen thousand pairs of gloves at four francs a pair; his sorties into high society must therefore have been far more limited. Elie is indeed less well off than he pretends. His solution is to court an aging heiress, using his usual method: "he bought lots more straw-colored gloves . . ." (83).[36]

But writers gradually came to realize that gloves opened up possibilities that went beyond everyday realism or class commentary. Revealing or concealing flesh, mediating contact, layering skin upon skin, capable of being turned inside out, and hovering uneasily between human hand and artifact, gloves were flexible in more senses than one. Flaubert was particularly alert to gloves' metaphorical potential. For him, gloves had negative connotations. Sensitive to how they constrained the hand's movements, he evoked them to express literary problems. Thus, for example, the image of

---

when he loses his inheritance and can no longer afford appropriate gloves, he fears he will never be able to see her again: "He could not turn up wearing shabby black gloves that had gone blue at the fingertips. . . . No, no! Never!" ("Il ne pouvait . . . se présenter avec de pauvres gants noirs bleuis du bout. . . . Non, non ! Jamais !") (59, 91).

34. See, for example, Louise Colet, *Les Coeurs brisés* (2: 359–60).

35. "la mode était aux gants paille. Un dandy, fût-il émérite, en portait même en plein jour, ce qui signifiait deux paires de gants quotidiennes : une paire pour les visites de l'après-midi, et une autre paire (au moins) pour le soir. Au prix que coûtaient les gants Jouvin, c'était grave."

36. "il redoubla de gants paille . . . "

an overtight glove bursting under the pressure of a large hand is used to communicate the way in which great ideas strain against the confines of language and make it buckle under their force (*Mémoires* 470).[37] Gloves, he argued, suppress or blunt creativity, whereas he wished for the form—literary as well as physical—to let the soul shine through (*Corr.* 2: 520).[38] In his mind, tight gloves were linked with the constraint and falsity he associated with bourgeois culture; complaining that contemporary literature was stifled and airless, he dismissed it as "barbarism in white gloves!" (*Corr.* 2: 538).[39] But above all, Flaubert was sensitive to the unsettling, uncanny quality of this thing that was both like and unlike a hand, a sense he articulated in one of his notebooks under the heading *Théorie du gant* (*Theory of the Glove*):

> It idealizes the hand by depriving it of its color, just as rice flour does for the face; it makes it inexpressive (think of the unpleasant effect that gloves have on stage), but typical; only the shape is preserved and accentuated. That artificial color, gray, white or yellow, blends in with the sleeve of the costume and [without] conveying the idea of something different (since the outline is preserved), it introduces novelty into the known, and so makes this covered member resemble the limb of a statue. And yet this anti-natural thing can move (in this it differs from a mask, though a mask does have movement through the eyes). There is nothing more disturbing than a gloved hand.[40] (*Carnets* 234)

Although gloves' truly unsettling qualities rarely come to the fore in literary texts until later in the century, during the Second Empire their metaphorical associations start to change. In an intriguing reversal of their previous connotations, literary gloves begin to be associated not with truth and revelation, but with concealment. The propriety with which they had been linked is increasingly seen as a deceptive veneer concealing something repugnant that implicates society itself; gloves start to function as emblems of hypocrisy. As Flaubert commented in 1856,

---

37. Flaubert uses a similar image in *Smarh*, where the central figure, tormented by the desire to write, cries: "my soul is swelling, it is stifling me, it is about to burst the body that covers it, like a swollen hand splitting a glove" ("mon âme se gonfle, elle m'étouffe, elle va crever le corps qui la recouvre comme une main gonflée qui déchire le gant") (610).

38. In the same letter Flaubert rages against opera singers who wear Jouvin gloves even when performing *Guillaume Tell*.

39. "barbarie en gants blancs !"

40. "C'est qu'il idéalise la main, en la privant de sa couleur, comme fait la poudre de riz pour le visage ; il la rend inexpressive (voir le villain effet des gants sur la scène), mais typique ; la forme seule est conservée et plus accusée. Cette couleur factice, grise, blanche ou jaune, s'harmonise avec la manche du vêtement, et, [sans] donner l'idée d'une nature autre (puisque le dessin est conservé), met de la nouveauté dans le connu, et rapproche ainsi ce membre couvert, d'un membre de statue. Et cependant, cette chose anti-naturelle a du movement (différent en cela du masque, mais le masque a du movement par les yeux). Rien n'est plus troublant qu'une main gantée."

Paris would allow a man to die of starvation, yet insist that he wear gloves (*Corr.* 2: 630).[41] In *La Curée*, Émile Zola recognizes their falsely decorous quality when he has Larsonneau observe that "the good thing about gloves [is that] you can touch anything without getting dirty" (269).[42] It is the hypocrisy of those who do wrong without soiling their hands that causes the Goncourts' Renée Mauperin to exclaim that she would prefer out-and-out villains, since "they do not wear gloves to commit foul deeds!" (*Renée Mauperin* 168–69).[43] This growing sense that the metaphorical glove may cover something other than fair white flesh gives rise to a common trope in the literature of the 1850s and '60s: a sinister and often politicized presence glimpsed between a glove's split seams, or something repellent piercing a glove from within. Victor Hugo's scathing poem "Aux femmes," for example, has the Emperor's soldiers donning gloves in an unsuccessful attempt to disguise their cruel claws (*Les Châtiments* 198),[44] while a poem by Émile Deschamps uses the image of a poisonous fingernail protruding from a glove to convey the Second Empire's failed attempts to conceal its corrupt nature ("Sur les *Fleurs du mal*" 403).[45]

As the century progresses, literary texts represent gloves less as emblems of irreproachable freshness than as objects of derision or disgust. In Joris-Karl Huysmans's *Les Soeurs Vatard*, for example, there is much ribald laughter over a pair of oiled leather gloves seen advertised in a shop window as "Venetian gloves for the night," while "worn, faded gloves" are listed as examples of human wretchedness alongside physical imperfections such as scars, pock-marked skin, sore eyes, and herpes blisters (106, 111).[46] Elsewhere in the same novel the implied upper-class elegance of a long, many-buttoned glove is undermined by the filthy condition of its sweat-stiffened fingers (136). The unromanticized physicality of the hand here asserts itself through the glove's refined veneer in a fine example of the type of naturalist *gant sale* that so horrified Baroness Staffe.

Less distasteful, however, was a woman's flirtatiously dropped glove—one of many instances of the glove's amorous associations[47]—and for novelists the gesture

---

41. Cf. the "glove" entry in Flaubert's *Dictionnaire des idées reçues*: "GLOVES. Give an air of respectability" ("GANTS. Donnent l'air comme il faut") (522).

42. "les gants ont du bon . . . on touche à tout sans se salir."

43. "ils ne font pas des infamies avec des gants !"

44. "in vain . . . did they put gloves over their claws to please you" ("en vain . . . / Pour vous plaire ils ont mis à leurs griffes des gants").

45. Several other writers, including Flaubert, Gautier, and Hippolyte Taine, use a pierced-glove image to indicate a disjunction between social class and social origins. For example, attributing a wealthy young man-about-town's bad behavior to his lower-class ancestry, Taine writes that "the coarse hand of his grandfather, the cattle merchant, still pokes through his yellow glove" ("la grosse main de son grand-père, le marchand de boeufs, perce encore sous son gant jaune") (147).

46. "gants vénitiens pour la nuit"; "des gants défraichis."

47. Others include gloves being used to conceal *billets-doux*, or, as in J. F. A. Bayard and T. M. F. Sauvage's play, *Le Gant et l'Éventail*, to send coded signals to a lover.

FIGURE 3.6 A dropped glove: Carolus-Duran, *La Dame au gant* (1869). Musée d'Orsay. © RMN-Grand Palais / Art Resource, NY / photograph by Hervé Lewandowski.

often served as a useful plot device for bringing two characters together (fig. 3.6). In *Le Chemin le plus court* Alphonse Karr gave the dropped glove trope a sardonic twist by narrating how a young man, Hughes, would fall in love with

> the first young woman . . . to drop a little white glove that Hughes could pick up, giving him both the chance and the courage to address a few words to her about the whiteness of a rather large hand which the little white glove enclosed with some difficulty. (8)[48]

The dropped glove, however, functioned as more than a literary ruse for instigating contact between a man and a woman, for in many texts the glove becomes a metonym for the woman herself as the distinction between flesh and glove starts to dissolve. One such example occurs in Edmond de Goncourt's *Chérie*, where an elaborate glove-dropping episode not only reveals the extent to which woman and glove are conflated in young Vatinelle's mind, but where the empty object simultaneously evokes the woman's presence and absence: "The glove was the thing he most desired from a woman, it was the mold and imprint of her hand, an object that preserved some of the life of her fingers" (165).[49] Balzac already understood such a conflation when, in *Le Père Goriot*, he had Madame de Beauséant give Rastignac a farewell gift of her empty glove box, with the words: "there is much of myself inside this, a whole Madame de Beauséant who no longer exists" (3: 265–66).[50] Absent gloves that the box no longer contains stand for the Madame de Beauséant who will no longer grace Parisian high society; like a coffin, the gloveless casket holds all that now remains of the woman facing eternal "burial" in the provinces.

Offering or acquiring a glove as a love token was one form of that identification between woman and glove, and a lady's glove, preserved and fetishized as a memento of an affair, features in many novels.[51] Evoking both her gloved and ungloved hand, by extension it evoked her clothed and unclothed body. In early drafts

48. "celle . . . qui la première laissa tomber un petit gant blanc que Hughes put ramasser, ce qui lui donna l'occasion, la hardiesse de lui adresser quelques mots sur la blancheur d'une main assez grosse que renfermait un peu difficilement le petit gant blanc." Cf. Prosper Mérimée, *Chronique du règne de Charles IX*, where, in a chapter entitled "Le Gant," a seductively dropped glove is retrieved by the wrong person.

49. "Le gant était la chose qu'il désirait le plus d'une femme, c'était le moule et l'empreinte de sa main, un objet gardant un peu de la vie de ses doigts." Exploiting this notion, the Belle Époque cabaret singer Yvette Guilbert came to be identified with the long black gloves she always wore on stage.

50. "il y a beaucoup de moi là-dedans, il y a toute une Mme de Beauséant qui n'est plus."

51. For example, in Georges Pradel's novel *Le Gant de suède* the protagonist's memories are triggered by finding the glove of the fiancée he had jilted years before, and he eventually tracks her down and proposes marriage again. (She rejects him.) Etienne-Prosper Dubois-Gachan's poem "La Paire de gants" in *Les Caprices d'un homme sérieux* offers a variant on the theme: in this case the male protagonist has preserved his own gloves as a memento of the young woman who gave them to him many years earlier.

of *Madame Bovary*, Rodolphe's tin of old love letters included a lady's glove, just as Flaubert himself had kept a glove belonging to his mistress, Louise Colet, alongside her letters, and had told her that its scent evoked the smell of her shoulder and the warmth of her bare arm (*Corr.* 1: 298–99).

As the century progressed, writers explored the glove's carnal associations further, from the sensual delicacy of "the little hand at work" (Coppée 15) as it buttons or unbuttons a glove,[52] to the more knowingly erotic "undressing" evoked by Maupassant in *Fort comme la mort* as he describes the act of peeling off a long glove to reveal the nudity beneath:

> She had long gloves that came up to the elbow. To remove one, she took hold of it by the top edge and slid it down rapidly, turning it inside out as if she were skinning a snake. The arm appeared, pale, plump and rounded, unclothed so quickly that it suggested the idea of complete, bold nudity. (14)[53]

In keeping with the old expression *perdre ses gants* (to lose one's gloves), which implied the loss of a girl's virginity, gloves' sexual connotations became even more graphic as writers realized that the innocent glove could be exploited to dramatize aspects of desire that could not be more explicitly described. Early manuscript drafts of *Madame Bovary* offer particularly striking examples. In one deleted episode, the lecherous lawyer, Guillaumin, toys with Emma's fingers and, breathing heavily, tries to force his hand inside her glove (*Madame Bovary* mss. "Brouillons," 6: fol. 136v). In another, Léon creeps downstairs in the night to retrieve a pale yellow glove dropped by Emma and take it back to bed with him; the glove still bears her scent and retains the form of her hand—the imprints of her fingernails, creases over the joints, and the curve of the leather where it stretched across the fleshy base of her thumb. Léon sniffs it, kisses it, inserts his fingers into it, and eventually falls asleep with his face resting on it ("Brouillons," 2: fol. 161).[54] In a marginal note to himself, Flaubert makes his intention perfectly clear: "make it understood that he masturbates with this glove" (*Madame Bovary* mss. "Plans et scenarios," fol. 19). Unsurprisingly, neither episode appeared in the final version. Yet even where the sexual innuendo is less explicit, gloves often feature in later literary texts in ways that are erotically transgressive. In *Le Bonheur dans le crime*, for example, Barbey d'Aurevilly—a writer whose predilection for using red ink was echoed in the idiosyncratic scarlet *nervures* of his own white gloves—imbues a glove with a disturbing

52. "la petite main qui travaille." Alphonse Karr includes the seductive gesture of removing a glove to take holy water in his list of the thirty-two infidelities a faithful wife can commit between home and church (*Clothilde* 354).

53. "Elle avait de longs gants, montant jusqu'au coude. Pour en ôter un, elle le prit tout en haut par le bord et vivement le fit glisser, en le retournant à la façon d'une peau de serpent qu'on arrache. Le bras apparut, pâle, gras, rond, dévêtu si vite qu'il fit surgir l'idée d'une nudité complète et hardie."

54. "faire comprendre qu'il se branle avec ce gant."

and violent sexuality. In an extraordinary scene set at the zoo where a woman and a panther stare into each other's eyes in a silent power struggle, he dramatizes both the tension and the affinity between woman and beast, between the civilized female and her dangerous sexual animality, by means of a violet glove that is suddenly reabsorbed into its original animal state:

> the unknown woman was like a human panther, confronting the real panther that she outshone. . . . So without saying a word, she undid the twelve buttons of the violet glove that molded her magnificent forearm and removed it; and passing her hand daringly between the bars of the cage, she slapped the panther's short muzzle with it. The panther made only one movement . . . but what a movement! . . . with a snap of teeth, as swift as lightning! . . . A cry went up from the group we were in. We thought her wrist had been bitten off: it was only the glove. The panther had swallowed it. . . .
>
> —You are mad!—said the man, seizing the beautiful wrist that had just eluded the sharpest of bites. . . . and he kissed that wrist, passionately.

The woman watches her naked wrist being kissed, and then the couple move away from the panther's cage, "with their faces turned toward one another, pressed together as if they wanted to penetrate one other, with him entering her and her entering him, to become one single body" (126–27).[55] The swallowing of the glove thus prefigures and enacts this erotic union.

Although in 1841 Guenot-Lecointe saw gloves as emblems of distinction and civilization, by the 1880s such prestige is rarely evident when gloves appear in literary texts. Reassessed, they take on deeply unsettling qualities, as Flaubert had already sensed, and as Pierre Loti's gloved hands seemed to the local women he encountered in Morocco. "His hands have two skins!" they exclaimed in astonishment,

---

55. "la femme, l'inconnue, était comme une panthère humaine, dressée devant la panthère animale qu'elle éclipsait. . . . Aussi, défaisant sans mot dire les douze boutons du gant violet qui moulait son magnifique avant-bras, elle ôta ce gant, et, passant audacieusement sa main entre les barreaux de la cage, elle en fouetta le museau court de la panthère, qui ne fit qu'un mouvement . . . mais quel mouvement ! . . . et d'un coup de dents, rapide comme l'éclair ! . . . Un cri partit du groupe où nous étions. Nous avions cru le poignet emporté : ce n'était que le gant. La panthère l'avait englouti. . . . — Folle !—dit l'homme, en saisissant ce beau poignet, qui venait d'échapper à la plus coupante des morsures. . . . et il le baisa, ce poignet, avec emportement."; "leurs visages tournés l'un vers l'autre, se serrant flanc contre flanc, comme s'ils avaient voulu se pénétrer, entrer, lui dans elle, elle dans lui, et ne faire qu'un seul corps à eux deux." This is not the only nineteenth-century text to associate passion with a swallowed glove. In Victor Hugo's *Les Misérables* a suitor declares his love by telling his sweetheart that he would eat her gloves if she cooked them as beignets (1: 201). In Eugène Labiche's play *Le Plus heureux des trois*, most of a girl's glove is swallowed by an ostrich as she feeds it a bun at the zoo; her companion's valor in retrieving three of the fingers makes her decide to marry him (*Théâtre complet* 6: 69–70).

their external perspective stripping gloves of all their acquired cultural significance and reducing them to a baffling extra dermal layer (*Au Maroc*, *OC* 5: 581).[56]

Although it has been argued that the consumption of goods is a ritual that seeks to make sense of the flux of events (Douglas and Isherwood 65), in the troubled aftermath of the Franco-Prussian War and the Commune the gloves that appear in large numbers in French fiction seem to exemplify chaos rather than making sense of it. Breaking free of their associations with the proprieties of a ritualized social order, they increasingly appear burst, torn, fragmented, lost, or abandoned. Frequently found detached from their partners and from hands, they convey physical, moral, and social disarray, like the dust-colored fingers that emerge from a tangle of clothes in a room filled with "irreparable disorder" in Huysmans's *En ménage*, for example (16), or the discarded gloves trailing on the floor of Nana's room that help Zola to convey her "female disorderliness" (*Nana* 367–68).[57] In his *Au bonheur des dames*, gloves are further divorced from function. Unwearable and epitomizing the grotesqueness of consumer excess, they are constructed into a monstrous shop display in the unlikely form of a Swiss chalet whose ground floor consists entirely of black gloves, with gloves of other colors edging the windows, outlining the balconies and forming the roof tiles. In that novel the store's glove counter is a focus for corruption and embezzlement, and customers shoplift gloves on a massive scale: one woman is caught with sixty pairs stuffed inside her clothing, while another is found to have stolen 248 pairs of pink gloves from stores across Paris, as gloves come to epitomize depravity and excess.[58]

Divorced from their earlier associations with distinction, morality, and truth—and, indeed, with hands—gloves have, as it were, been turned inside out. No longer suggestive of a healthy and vibrant society, by the late nineteenth century they convey the opposite. If they were once hailed as the perfect expression of French civilization, that civilization had come to be widely perceived as moribund, and literary gloves reflect that shift as they take on overtones of mortality. Those overtones were not limited to literature, however, for in the closing decades of the century it began to be recognized that despite technological advances, glove making had its own dark side. A medical treatise of 1883 not only details the permanent discolorations and deformities that glove-making processes inflicted on workers' hands, but it records research showing that leather-glove workers had one of the lowest life expectancies of all artisans. Pneumonia caused by a work environment full of leather dust killed over 70 percent; their average age at death was thirty-one (Rouvier 57).

It seems apt, therefore, to find Edmond de Goncourt in *La Faustin* likening a pair of very tight-fitting gloves to casts taken from the hands of a corpse (225). For

---

56. "il a des mains à deux peaux !"

57 "un irrémédiable désordre"; "désordre de bonne fille." In *Le Savoir-faire et le Savoir-vivre*, Juranville observes that a girl whose gloves often split or tear is very likely to become "a disorderly woman" ("une femme sans ordre") (41).

58. Cf. Edmond and Jules de Goncourt, *Germinie Lacerteux*, where the dishonest Jupillon works as a glove cutter.

Charles Blanc, too, gloves chart a slide from vitality to decay and death. In 1875 he recalled an incident soon after the 1848 revolution when he gained access to a room in the empty Tuileries Palace that had remained locked for seven years, untouched since the sudden death in a carriage accident of its occupant, the eldest son of Louis-Philippe. Blanc writes of the personal items that still lay strewn about the room, but it was the prince's gloves that left the strongest impression. While their diversity conveyed the young man's varied and active life, for Blanc their shriveled, desiccated skin denoted mortality. The gloves, like their young owner and the monarchy to which he was heir, were dead:

> What struck me most was to see gloves of all colors and types that had been tossed carelessly on a table. This young man's life, divided between pleasure, hunting, and war, was revealed by the appearance of these scattered gloves, some crumpled, some intact, some worn, others still in their box. Some were made of chamois leather for driving, or beaver for riding, or dog-skin, or fine white lambskin, or kid, and there, all these variations of dress had a remarkable and striking significance. . . . But the leather of these gloves had long since shrunk, the fine lambskin had stiffened, the kid had wrinkled, and these inert objects that so clearly spoke of the habits of the elegant young man who had worn them also told of his death. (180)[59]

Other writers saw gloves as symptomatic of morbidity on a far wider scale. On a journey to Algeria, for example, Ernest Feydeau had been dismayed to see a wedding trousseau that included gloves and parasols along with traditionally "oriental" pieces, and to find wealthy local women wearing cabbage-green leather gloves under their veils; complaining that "everything is falling apart all over the world," he interpreted gloves' infiltration of the Orient as evidence that Eastern civilization had been contaminated by the degenerate West (196–200).[60] Villiers de l'Isle Adam, too, linked gloves with a civilization in decline. In "La Machine à gloire," one of his *Contes cruels*, gloves not only convey the mechanical conformism of contemporary society, but predict its imminent collapse. Villiers pictures an enormous mechanism built into a theater auditorium, with a pair of beautifully sculpted wooden hands folded away under every seat, each hand clad in an immaculate yellow calfskin

59. "Ce qui me frappa le plus, ce fut de voir sur une table, jetés ça et là, des gants de toute couleur et de toute espèce. La vie de ce jeune homme, partagée entre le plaisir, la chasse et la guerre, se révélait dans la physionomie de ces gants épars, les uns froissés, les autres intacts, les uns essayés, les autres encore dans leur boîte. Il y en avait en chamois pour conduire, en castor pour monter à cheval, en peau de chien, en canepin blanc, en chevreau, et toutes ces variantes de la toilette avaient là une signification singulière et saisissante. . . . Mais, depuis longtemps, les peaux de ces gants s'étaient retirées, le canepin s'était raidi, le chevreau s'était parcheminé, et ces objets inertes, qui racontaient si clairement les habitudes du jeune élégant qui les avait portés, disaient aussi sa mort."

60. "tout s'en va par toute la terre."

glove. The inanimate gloved hands produce artificial applause that the audience follows like sheep, in a mindless reflex that will literally bring the house down if the machine's controls are turned to maximum volume (61–85).

As they spiral ever further from their original associations, fictional gloves take on macabre forms that hover disturbingly between artifact and hand, like the nightmarish street sign in the shape of a gigantic purple glove that looms over the Passage des Panoramas in Zola's *Nana*, described as resembling a bleeding, severed hand suspended from a yellow cuff (222); or the "glove" of blood that forms on Auguste's hand in *Le Ventre de Paris* after he plunges it into a bucket of blood from the pig he has just slaughtered (100); or—even more unsettling—the freshly amputated left arm that rests on a cushion of purple silk in Villiers de l'Isle Adam's *L'Eve future*, a pearl-gray glove still grasped in its slim fingers. That severed limb turns out to be made of artificial flesh covered with artificial skin, as smooth and supple as the finest glove leather (20–21). The idealized skin envelops the form to produce a disconcertingly faithful copy of the arm and hand of a beautiful young woman, in what is perhaps the ultimate illustration of what Flaubert had sensed in his *Théorie du gant* note: that in its juxtaposition of living and dead skin there was something unnervingly uncanny about "this anti-natural thing" that troubled the boundaries between hand and glove, between authenticity and falseness, and ultimately between life and death. As the century nears its end, those detached and bloody gloves convey a sense of disintegration and violence that seems in keeping with the unsettled aftermath of the traumatic Franco-Prussian War.

In their journey from artisanal to industrial mass production, nineteenth-century French gloves thus resonate with meanings that transcend their materiality. They map not only the nation's increasing prosperity and technological progress, but fundamental changes in manners, hierarchy, and social cohesion. By the final years of the nineteenth century, the aura of distinction and elegance that had once caused the French glove to be seen as "the most advanced expression of modern civilization" (Guenot-Lecointe 84) has been eclipsed, leaving in its place a dark, dystopian vision of a new modernity.[61]

Works Cited

Alcan et al. *Visite à l'exposition universelle de Paris en 1855*. Hachette, 1855.

Alq, Louise d'. *Le Maître et la maîtresse de maison*. Bureau des Causeries familières, 1887.

Anon. *Le Livre de la famille: les personnes et les choses, savoir-vivre et savoir-faire, morale, éducation, économie domestique, hygiène, soin aux enfants, etc.* Séguin frères, 1892.

Anon. *Les Usages du monde: Le savoir-vivre et la politesse chez soi, en visite, en soirée, au théâtre*. T. Lefèvre, 1880.

Balzac, Honoré de. *Étude de moeurs par les gants. Œuvres complètes*, vol. 20. Michel Lévy, 1870.

———. *Eugénie Grandet: La Comédie humaine*, vol. 3. Edited by P-G Castex. Gallimard, 1976–81.

61. "l'expression la plus avancée de la civilisation moderne."

———. *Le Père Goriot: La Comédie humaine*, vol. 3. Edited by P-G Castex. Gallimard, 1976–81.

———. *Traité de la vie élégante: La Comédie humaine*, vol. 12. Edited by P-G Castex. Gallimard, 1976–81.

Barbey d'Aurevilly, Jules Amédée. "Le Bonheur dans le crime." 1874. *Les Diaboliques*. Garnier Flammarion, 1967.

Bayard, J. F. A., and T. M. F. Sauvage. *Le Gant et l'éventail*. J. A. Lelong, 1846.

Bertall. *La Comédie de notre temps: études au crayon et à la plume. La civilité, les habitudes, les moeurs, les costumes, les manières et les manies de notre époque*. 3 vols. E. Plon, 1874–76.

Berthet, Elie. *Le Gouffre*. E. Dentu, 1872.

Blanc, Charles. *L'Art dans la parure et dans le vêtement*. Renouard, 1875.

Bradi, Mme la comtesse de. *Du savoir-vivre en France au dix-neuvième siècle, ou Instruction d'un père à ses enfants*. Levrault, 1841.

Bulletin de la société de statistique, des sciences naturelles et des arts industriels du département de l'Isère. Maisonville, 1851.

Celnart, Madame (Elisabeth-Félicie Bayle-Mouillard). *Manuel des dames, ou l'Art de l'élégance, sous le rapport de la toilette, des honneurs de la maison, des plaisirs, des occupations agréables*. Roret, 1833.

Champfleury (Jules-François-Félix Fleury-Husson). *Contes d'automne*. V. Lecou, 1854.

Colet, Louise. *Ces petits messieurs*. Dentu, 1869.

———. *Les Coeurs brisés*, 2 vols. Berquet & Pétion, 1843.

Coppée, François. *Promenades et intérieurs: Poésies complètes*. A. Lemerre, 1925.

Deschamps, Émile. "Sur les *Fleurs du mal*." *Les Fleurs du mal*, by Charles Baudelaire. Michel Levy frères, 1868.

Douglas, Mary, and Baron Isherwood. *The World of Goods: Towards an Anthropology of Consumption*. Penguin, 1980.

Dubois-Gachan, Etienne-Prosper. *Les Caprices d'un homme sérieux, esquisses poétiques*, 2nd ed. Didier, 1872.

Études sur l'exposition universelle de 1878: Annales et archives de l'industrie au XIXe siècle, vol. 4. E. Lacroix, 1878.

Exposition universelle de 1867: Rapports du jury international, vol. 4. Paul Dupont, 1868.

Fère, A. de la. *Savoir vivre, savoir parler, savoir écrire, à l'usage des gens du monde*, 7th ed. Nouvelle librairie scientifique et littéraire, 1889.

Feydeau, Ernest. *Alger*. Michel Lévy frères, 1862.

Flaubert, Gustave. *Carnets de travail*. Edited by P. M. de Biasi. Balland, 1988.

———. *Correspondance*, 5 vols. Edited by Jean Bruneau and Yvan Leclerc. Gallimard-Pléiade, 1973–2007.

———. *L'Éducation sentimentale*. Edited by P. M. Wetherill. Garnier, 1984.

———. *Le Dictionnaire des idées reçues: Bouvard et Pécuchet*. Edited by Claudine Gothot-Mersch. Gallimard, 1979.

———. *Les Mémoires d'un fou: Œuvres de jeunesse*. Edited by Claudine Gothot-Mersch and Guy Sagnes. Gallimard Pléiade, 2001.

———. *Madame Bovary* manuscripts. (L'Atelier Bovary) Centre Flaubert, Université de Rouen. www.Flaubert.univ-rouen.fr/bovary/index.php.

———. *Smarh: Œuvres de jeunesse*. Edited by Claudine Gothot-Mersch and Guy Sagnes. Gallimard Pléiade, 2001.

Gautier, Théophile. "La Diva." *La Comédie de la mort*. Desessart, 1838.

Girardin, Madame Emile de. *Lettres parisiennes*, 4 vols. Michel Lévy frères, 1857.

G-M., F. *Manuel de politesse à l'usage de la jeunesse: savoir-vivre, savoir-parler, savoir-écrire, savoir-travailler*. A. Mame et fils, 1908.

Goncourt, Edmond de. *Chérie*. 1884. Flammarion and Fasquelle, 1921.

———. *La Faustin*. Charpentier, 1882.

Goncourt, Edmond, and Jules de. *Germinie Lacerteux*. Charpentier, 1864.

———. *Renée Mauperin*. Charpentier, 1864.

Guenot-Lecointe, Georges. *Physiologie du gant*. Desloges, 1841.

Hugo, Victor. *Les Châtiments*. J. Hetzel, 1870.

———. *Les Misérables*, 3 vols. 1862. Nelson, 1933.

Huneker, James. *Franz Liszt*. C. Scribner's Sons, 1911.

Huysmans, Joris-Karl. *En ménage*. Charpentier, 1881.

———. *Les Soeurs Vatard*. Charpentier, 1879.

Juranville, Clarisse. *Le Savoir-faire et le savoir-vivre dans les diverses circonstances de la vie: guide pratique de la vie usuelle à l'usage des jeunes filles*. A. Boyer, 1879.

Karr, Alphonse. *Clothilde*. Bureaux du Siècle, 1865.

———. *Le Chemin le plus court*. Michel Lévy frères, 1860.

Labiche, Eugène. *L'Avare en gants jaunes: Théâtre complet*, vol. 6. Calmann-Lévy, 1898.

———. *Le Plus heureux des trois: Théâtre complet*, vol. 6. Calmann-Lévy, 1898.

Le Génie industriel: Revue des inventions françaises et étrangères, vol. 2. Armengaud, 1852.

Loti, Pierre. *Au Maroc. Œuvres complètes*, vol. 5. Calmann-Lévy, 1893–1911.

Maupassant, Guy de. *Fort comme la mort*. 1889. Albin Michel, 1965.

Marennes, Vicomte de (Eugène Chapus). *Manuel de l'homme et de la femme comme il faut*. Librairie nouvelle, 1855.

Mérimée, Prosper. *Chronique du règne de Charles IX*. Charpentier, 1869.

Nerval, Gérard de. Sylvie. *Œuvres complètes*, vol. 3, edited by J. Guillaume and C. Pichois. Gallimard Pléiade, 1993.

Pradel, Georges. *Le Gant de suède*. E. Rouveyre & G. Blond, 1883.

Rey, Edouard. *Xavier Jouvin*. F. Allier père et fils, 1868.

Rouvier, Louis. *Des altérations professionnelles des ouvriers gantiers et palissonneurs, envisagées au point de vue de l'identité*. A. Derenne, 1883.

Staffe, Baronne (Blanche-Augustine-Angèle Soyer). *Mes secrets*. G. Havard, 1896.

———. *Usages du monde: Règles du savoir-vivre dans la société moderne*. 1889. Victor Havard, 1891.

Taine, Hippolyte. *Notes sur Paris: vie et opinions de M. Frédéric Thomas Graindorge*. Hachette, 1867.

Uzanne, Octave. *Les Ornements de la femme. L'éventail—L'ombrelle—Le gant—Le manchon*. Librairies-imprimeries réunies, 1892.

Vallet d'Artois, Jean-François. *Manuel de fabriquant de gants, considéré dans ses rapports avec la mégisserie, la chamoiserie etc.* 2nd ed. Boret, 1835.

Villiers de l'Isle Adam, Auguste. "La Machine à gloire." *Contes cruels.* C. Lévy, 1883.

———. *L'Eve future.* Brunhoff, 1886.

Zola, Émile. *La Curée.* A. Lacroix, Verboeckhoven et cie, 1872.

———. *Le Ventre de Paris.* Charpentier, 1873.

———. *Nana.* Charpentier, 1880.

CHAPTER 4

GAUTIER'S MODERN SPIN ON FASHION

Cary Hollinshead-Strick

> Around 1830 there was a newspaper in Paris with the name *Le Sylphe*. Find a ballet about newspapers.
>
> —Walter Benjamin, *The Arcades Project*

Théophile Gautier did not write a ballet about newspapers, but he did write both libretti for ballets and an extraordinary quantity of weekly theater reviews for the press. His motives for the former were partly amorous: the dancer Carlotta Grisi was a muse of sorts for Gautier, while journalism was how he earned a living, but both activities relied on spinning bodies. Romantic ballet featured pirouettes, often executed by otherworldly figures dressed in white. In print shops, newspapers were produced faster and faster, as rotary presses drew paper from large spools over cylindrical drums of type.[1]

Rotary presses and the continuous bands of paper that allowed them to work without interruption had been developed during the nineteenth century from technology used to print identical patterns on cloth during the eighteenth century. By using rollers to print, presses could move away from the hand-press model, in which sheets of paper were squeezed against frames of type, to the rotary model, in which curved casts of those frames of print (*clichés*) made it possible to run paper over type that protruded from drums. In Paris, newspapers were printed on presses known as *mécaniques* in the 1830s and then on the more advanced *rotatives* Marinoni in the 1860s. Each advance in technology significantly reduced the time required to print newspapers and the number of workers needed to do so.[2]

The *mousseline* that whirled between ballerinas and their audiences and the paper speeding between spinning drums were both media of modern communication to

---

1. For an excellent pedagogical leaflet, see http://www.arts-et-metiers.net/sites/arts-et metiers.net/files/asset/document/carnet_marinoni.pdf.

2. See Feyel, "Coût de la presse."

FIGURE 4.1 Presse typographique rotative à plieuse système Marinoni, 1880–86. © Musée des arts et métiers-Cnam, Paris / photograph by Michèle Favareille.

FIGURE 4.2 "Valse favorite de Giselle : Dansée par Mme Carlotta Grisi et Mr. Petipa," 1841, lithograph. Bibliothèque nationale de France, Paris.

which Gautier was attentive (figs. 4.1 and 4.2). Cloth or paper bands in circular motion and relatively speedy textual production were central to Gautier's understanding of both fashion and the art of writing. Though he began his career as a Romantic "young Turk," over time Gautier's writings on clothing took on a modern reflexivity about their own role as media. Martine Lavaud even suggests that the brief crystalline forms of the poems of *Émaux et Camées* (1852) might be Gautier's "corseted" reaction against the quantity of prose that he had to produce for his *feuilleton* (*Civilisation* 1176). If so, his journalism forms the ample skirts of the figure that is his oeuvre. Gautier's writing on mid-nineteenth-century fashion connects classical ideals, oriental fantasy, and contemporary forms of motion. Hair, skin, and clothing that are sculpted and reflect, that are shaped and caress, become metaphors for the production of Gautier's text itself, both in his poetry and in his writing on dress more broadly. Touch and turn, rather than Baudelairean fixing and freezing, shape both Gautier's texts and the fashions that they represent.

Gautier was, after all, known for his fashions before he made a name for himself as a writer. At eighteen, he was perhaps the most visible member of the rowdy audience at the premiere of Hugo's *Hernani*, when a fight broke out between defenders of classical drama and those who favored Hugo's new romantic approach to theater. Gautier's long hair and made-to-order red silk vest successfully set him apart from the sea of black suits that surrounded him. He and his fashions became emblematic of youth and of the new school of literature (fig. 4.3). Knowing how to make a new impression was part of Gautier's talent as a man of fashion and as an author. When he wasn't splashing color into a theater audience, he dressed "like a Turk" in a turn to orientalism as a source of aesthetics that differed from those that surrounded him in Paris. Gautier's preface to *Mlle de Maupin*, usually remembered as a manifesto of art for art's sake, a treatise against all that is pragmatic in writing, especially journalism, is also, as Carole Furmanek points out, a refusal of biographism. *Le biographisme*, an approach most associated with conservative critic Charles Augustin Sainte-Beuve, linked qualities of writers' work to their backgrounds. Sainte-Beuve extended this logic to text production, too, claiming that "you're a journalist, even if you are a novelist, because your novels appear in newspapers, and you can tell; they retain the cuts, the expectations and the lapses of the *feuilleton*; they bear the brand and the crease."[3] Gautier, too, invested folds in paper and cloth with judgments about aesthetic value, but his conclusions were different from Sainte-Beuve's.

Folds were an apt figure for the press's contamination of literature in that the use of advertisement to finance press distribution had, indeed, led to increases in the size of newspapers over the course of the nineteenth century.[4] Papers grew to

3. "on est journaliste ; on l'est, fût-on romancier, car c'est en feuilletons que paraissent vos livres même, et l'on s'en aperçoit ; ils se ressentent des coupures, des attentes et des suspensions d'intérêt du feuilleton ; ils en portent la marque et le pli" (175–76).

4. To accommodate more advertising, nineteenth-century newspapers had been enlarged in 1828, 1837, 1845, and 1856–57, bringing them to 470 x 650 mm, a size that certainly required folding to be manageable. See Feyel, "L'économie de la presse," 148.

FIGURE 4.3 Théodore Chassériau, *Théophile Gautier*, 1840s, engraving by A. Bodin. Bibliothèque nationale de France, Paris.

accommodate ads, and larger papers had to be folded. Where Sainte-Beuve saw irremediable contamination, though, Gautier saw an opportunity for dynamic sculpture. In "De la mode," an essay he wrote in 1867, Gautier uses a portrait of a press baron (Ingres's 1832 portrait of Louis-François Bertin, which *Le Charivari* sent up as the very image of press prostitution)[5] to locate the value of a fold in the work of the artist who reproduced it, rather than the actions that had wrinkled the cloth represented. Folds in Bertin's *redingote* serve as Gautier's example of the aesthetic potential of contemporary dress. Though he himself dressed in opposition to the black suit that bourgeois men of the period wore, Gautier defends the suit on the grounds that Rembrandt would have been able to make beautiful paintings of it. Or, he proposes, "If you prefer line to color, see Ingres' portrait of Monsieur Bertin. Are the folds of the coat and the trousers not firm, noble, and pure like the folds of a cloak or a toga? Does the body not live under its prosaic garb like that of a statue under its drapery?"[6]

The noble folds of M. Bertin's clothing are stretched across a midsection made ample by a successful career in newspapers. If his garb is prosaic, that is because it was bought with profits made from prose. Ingres can elevate the material to a sculptural level, but the model, Bertin, was a press magnate whom the rest of the press did not hesitate to call prostituted for his multiple self-interested newspaper deals. Gautier had nothing against prostitutes, and made his own living by getting along with pressmen under a variety of regimes, but the focus on the folds here suggests that neither current press practices (advertisement and folding) nor current fashion (the black suit) were as anathema to Gautier as his Turkish dress and "anything but utilitarian journalism" positions might suggest.

Not only does Gautier refuse to condemn the ubiquitous black suit, in his essay on fashion, but he even defends the crinoline because, he says, "[f]rom this abundance of folds, which flare out like the skirt of a whirling dervish, the waist emerges elegant and slim; the torso is set off flatteringly, the entire figure pyramids in a gracious way. This mass of rich fabrics forms a kind of pedestal for the bust and the head, the only parts that matter, now that nudity is no longer allowed."[7] He continues to say that at the Javanese court and among the Greek gods, bodies were clothed from the waist down, so a skirt that hides women's legs participates in a variety of courtly traditions. Gautier's unusual use of *pyramide* as a verb, along with

---

5. *Charivari*, May 15, 1833, 3.

6. "Si vous préférez le dessin à la couleur, voyez le portrait de M. Bertin par M. Ingres. Les plis de la redingote et du pantalon ne sont-ils pas fermes, nobles et purs comme les plis d'une chlamyde ou d'une toge ? Le corps ne vit-il pas sous son vêtement prosaïque comme celui d'une statue sous son draperie ?" (*De la mode* 20).

7. "De cette abondance de plis, qui vont s'évasant comme la fustanelle d'un derviche tourneur, la taille sort élégante et mince ; le haut du corps se détache avantageusement, toute la personne pyramide d'une manière gracieuse. Cette masse de riches étoffes fait comme un piédestal au buste et à la tête, seules parties importantes, maintenant que la nudité n'est plus admise" (30).

his comparison between whirling dervishes and crinoline wearers, suggests that this pedestal is not a stationary one. Like Constantin Guys's sketches of Parisiennes, which Baudelaire so famously appreciated, Gautier's analysis emphasizes the movement of a crinolined skirt. As Ulrich Lehmann points out, Guys paid attention to moments when women stepped up or down, revealing the fetishized foot, and used them as opportunities to draw folds of cloth in motion (44). As the following image by Guys indicates, this sense of movement is also accentuated by the young woman's *bavolet*, or *suivez-moi jeune homme*—the bit of cloth, ribbon, or sometimes hair that floats behind her as she moves (fig. 4.4).

In his discussion of Walter Benjamin's dialectical understanding of fashion, Lehmann points out that, because of its slightly dislocated relationship to time, fashion serves, for Benjamin, as a kind of allegory of revolution. In Gautier's case, the material revolutions of cloth around bodies, paper around drums, a hairdo around the arc of a cranium, are movements indicative of both the gestures and technology of the present and the production of writing, itself, under the conditions of the mid-nineteenth century. Gautier's attention to such movement produces a more fluid form of modernism than most of Baudelaire's poetry does, but it still brings together disparate time periods to create an analysis of process. Gautier himself, in his preface to *Les Fleurs du mal*, sees Baudelaire's focus on the flutter of cloth as literary, and as modern. Indeed, for the purposes of his preface, Gautier sets up his own "sculptural" taste in opposition to Baudelaire (and Balzac's) "literary" approach (see my note 25).[8] In Gautier's own kinetic modernism, making *pyramide* a verb reveals an understanding of clothing and storytelling as actions.[9]

When Gautier tells stories of attractive young women, particularly if the women in question are neither entirely mortal nor French, he unrolls his tales by unspooling the clothing of his heroines. For example, a key element of *La Péri*, a ballet starring Carlotta Grisi, for which Gautier wrote the libretto, was the *danse de l'abeille*, in which the heroine, on the pretext of finding a bee that is stinging her, dances out of much of her costume. Likewise, in the *Roman de la momie* (1858), the removal of the bands that wrap the mummified body of Tahoser, a gorgeous sixteen-year-old pharaoh queen, reveals both her jewels and her form, in what Melanie Hawthorne has referred to as a striptease for an English lord, a German Egyptologist, and a Greek entrepreneur (719). The seductive removal of clothing motivates readerly desire to "see" more, while simultaneously transmitting details of Egyptian burial dress. Gautier's hybrid novella uses its Egyptian subject matter to enact the dual purpose of the press, be it the fashion press or ordinary newspapers: to instruct and to seduce. Claire Lyu, in her 2005 article "Unswathing the Mummy," uses a framework from Peter Brooks to read the unearthing and unwrapping of the body of Tahoser "as an

8. "Charles Baudelaire," liv.

9. Lehmann characterizes Gautier's later aesthetics as static and invested in the status quo (15). While Gautier's work does not underline temporal juxtapositions the same way that Baudelaire's does, it nonetheless jumps between historical periods in its characterization of the present.

Figure 4.4 Constantin Guys, "Jeune femme relevant sa jupe et marchant vers la gauche," n.d., gray ink, watercolor, and pencil. Musée du Louvre, Paris. © RMN-Grand Palais / photograph by Michel Urtado.

'epistemophilic' project," one which is structured by the frame narrative characters' desire to learn more about the circumstances of the beautiful Tahoser's death and mummification (314). Their desire to know more (love of knowledge, epistemophilia) is paired with their desire to look upon Tahoser's beautiful body.

The Egyptomania that had swept France from the late eighteenth century into the nineteenth century, especially with Jean-François Champollion's rock-star turn as the brilliant young decipherer of hieroglyphics in 1822, contributed to making parchment and papyrus frequently imagined companions to, or even extensions of, mummies' bands.[10] In the *Roman de la momie* Tahoser's story is supposedly found written in hieroglyphs on a papyrus that is interleaved with her winding-cloth.[11]

Gautier, writing after Balzac's exploration of plant-based papermaking in *Illusions perdues*, and as progress in that domain was slowly starting to change the composition of paper, imagines the source of Tahoser's story to be a document written on plant paper. If papyrus scrolls could survive until the present, surely words printed on great spools of paper made with increasing quantities of vegetable fiber had potential to last.

Tahoser's lovely form is rather miraculously preserved, we are assured, by the best and most expensive oils and substances. Gautier's insistence on the link between the quality of her embalming oils and their efficacy sounds similar to the *réclames* for new cosmetics that filled the back pages of most newspapers (and subsidized their production).[12] This well-preserved body is one source of desire, but the story buried with her is the one that will keep the nineteenth-century newspaper reader's epistemophilia going. For, like the German Egyptologist Rumphius, carefully rolling Tahoser's bands upon themselves, Gautier spun out his account in a serial publication between March 11 and May 6 of 1857. The descriptions of dress and architecture in the *Roman de la momie* were based on research Gautier did in the personal Egyptian collection of Ernest Feydeau, father of the playwright. His story participates in the sort of vulgarization that newspapers like *Le Moniteur universel*, the official newspaper of the government regime under the Second Empire, felt to be part of their purpose. The novella's genre is hybrid, like that of the commercial daily paper, with archaeology, fiction, and a Bible-related story mixed into one tale.

It is a tale of its time and its medium, then, and indeed Gautier got so frustrated with rapidly juggling the prints he consulted as he composed the *Roman de la momie* that he recruited his eleven-year-old daughter, Judith, to put Feydeau's images back in order when he was done with them. The arrangement worked well

10. Adam Geczy's *Fashion and Orientalism* gives a good overview of Egyptomania in fashion (chapter 2) and the turn to Turkish styles in which Gautier was an important figure (chapter 3).

11. It is also perhaps worth noting that French typographers had made metal type for hieroglyphs by the 1851 Exposition.

12. Gardair makes a similar link to the aesthetics of publicity in his preface to Gautier, *Roman de la momie*.

for father and daughter alike. Judith describes the balance between rigor and speed with which they worked:

> Despite the difficulty of the work and the detailed archaeological research involved in writing nearly every page, *Le Roman de la momie* appeared serially, as it was being written. My father naturally was not much ahead of time, and had to hurry so as not to let the printers get ahead of him. This research was done on in-folio prints, which quickly got mixed up and lost, and made him lose precious time.

To make this process more efficient, Judith was placed on the worktable and made responsible for finding and sorting Feydeau's prints.[13]

Although Gautier's editor worried that readers would find some of the archaeological details of the *Roman de la momie* difficult to follow because they were described using specialized vocabulary, one of the novel's early readers, Judith herself, seems not to have needed additional explanations. She tells how pleased her father was to discover that she had mummified and buried a doll that her mother had given her not long after the book's publication. Judith adapted the well-established practice of communicating fashions via dolls[14] to the archaeological vulgarization her father's novella sought to effect. She proved that she had understood the meanings of the mummy's "fashions" by reproducing them in miniature, while also choosing her father's vocation as a writer over her mother's encouragement of girlish ways. As interstitial narratives go, the way Judith dressed her doll was a declaration of intention to emulate her father.[15] When the mummified doll was unearthed from a planter on the Gautiers' balcony, Théophile pronounced: "If all the burial rites have been observed . . . I will take you under my protection, and you will not be scolded. . . . My doll emerged, carefully enveloped in strips of cloth, her face molded by a mask of gold paper."[16] Gautier was so pleased with his daughter's work that he kept the mummy-doll on his mantelpiece.

This mutual interest in a form of orientalism motivated by the picturesque, but invested in some sorts of accuracy, played out in a different direction seven years later, when Ding Dunling, a Chinese scholar stranded in France by the death of

---

13. "Malgré la difficulté du travail et les minutieuses recherches archaéologiques, qu'exigeait presque chaque page, *Le Roman de la momie* paraissait en feuilleton, à mesure qu'il était écrit. Mon père n'avait naturellement que fort peu d'avance et devait se hâter, pour ne pas se laisser dépasser par les imprimeurs. Ces recherches, à travers ses in-folios à planches mobiles, qui s'embrouillaiaient vite et se perdaient, lui faisaient dépender un temps précieux . . ." (*Collier jours* 185).

14. See Marcus, *Between Women*, 152.

15. Brevik-Zender, "Interstitial Narratives," 91.

16. "'Si tous les rites de l'ensevelissement sont observés . . . je te prends sous ma protection ; tu ne seras pas grondée' . . . Ma poupée apparaît, alors, soigneusement enveloppée de bandelettes, la figure étroitement moulée par un masque en papier d'or" (J. Gautier, *Collier des jours* 200).

his employer and possibly a political past he didn't want to revisit in China, came to live with the Gautiers as a tutor to Judith and her sister, Estelle. According to Pauline Yu's account, the Gautiers' friend, Charles Clermont-Ganneau, had encountered Ding Dunling wandering the streets in shabby clothing and had encouraged him to dress and do his hair in a Chinese style ("Chinese Poetry" 261). Curious to meet him, the Gautiers asked their friend to bring him for lunch.

In a metaphor that, by then, would have been familiar to father and daughter, Théophile Gautier proposed Chinese lessons to Judith with an injunction to "*unwind* [*dévider*] this yellow man and see what lies hidden in his mysterious brain" (emphasis mine) (Yu, "Your Alabaster" 469). In the *Roman de la momie*, unwrapping Tahoser's bands became a metaphor for producing a fiction supposedly translated from hieroglyphics. Here, Judith's recollection of how she began to learn to read Chinese characters is also cast as an unspooling. Having started her literary education by sorting reproductions of Egyptian monuments and hieroglyphs, Judith continued it by studying from a flawed but monumental dictionary of Chinese, under a tutor who was also a poet in his own right. Judith's resulting education in Chinese led her to create *Le Livre de Jade* (1867), translations of work by several classical Chinese poets, with a few by Ding Dunling included (Yu, "Your Alabaster" 466).

Judith and Théophile's collaborations on the *Roman de la momie*, and then on Judith's efforts to learn Chinese, led to evolutions in Théophile Gautier's perspective on both Egyptian mummies and Chinese art at the 1867 Exposition Universelle. His imagined unspoolings of a fictional mummy and of a language teacher's knowledge were rendered uncomfortably literal in some of the events and the representations of the Exposition.

As the author of the *Roman de la momie*, Théophile Gautier was one of a handful of guests invited to witness the unwrapping of a real mummy at the Exposition. His description of the experience skews toward the fantastic:

> Nothing could be stranger than this great doll of rags, with a cadaver as its armature, swaying under the hands that undressed it in a sort of parody of life . . . the pale lightning flashes lit up the yellowed old heads and the grimacing faces of six hundred skulls in the displays of the anthropological museum, and the low grumble of thunder accompanied the waltz of Nes-Khons, daughter of Horus and Rouas, *pirouetting* between the impatient hands of her unwrappers.[17] (emphasis mine)

17. "Rien n'était plus étrange que cette grande poupée de chiffons ayant pour armature un cadavre et démenant d'un air raide et gauche sous les mains qui la déshabillaient avec une sorte de parodie horrible de la vie . . . de blafardes lueurs d'éclairs illuminaient sur les rayons des armoires les vieux crânes jaunes et les rictus grimaçants de six cents têtes de mort du musée anthropologique, et la tonnerre avec des grondements sourds servait d'accompagnement à la valse de Nes-Khons, fille de Horus et de Rouas, *pirouettante* entre les mains impatients de ses démailloteurs" (*L'Orient* 2: 103).

Unwrapping a mummy is grotesque—the telling of it, too, extends on paper the secrets that were meant to be preserved untouched for longer. Against the supposedly archaeological scientific agenda of the Exposition, Gautier tells the experience as a strange ghost story, and yet this is also his fiction coming true. Gautier's mummy stories put the pressures of an industrializing print industry that was rumored, probably incorrectly, to peel rags from mummies in order to keep up with the demand for the raw materials from which paper was made, into a supernaturally inflected tale of expo-curiosity gone awry.[18]

The fascinated discomfort with which Gautier observed the unwinding of the mummy was accompanied by another impingement of reality on the orientalist fantasies he had harbored. In an infamous episode of the Opium Wars, British and French troops had burned the Summer Palace in Beijing in 1860, after looting its treasures. In response to a question about the event, Victor Hugo wrote,

> There was, in a corner of the world, a wonder of the world. This wonder was called the Summer Palace. Art has two principles, the idea, which produces European art, and the chimera, which produces oriental art. The Summer Palace was to chimerical art what the Parthenon is to ideal art. All that the imagination of a nearly supernatural people could invent was there. . . . The French empire pocketed half of this victory and today, with a sort of naive ownership, it displays the splendid bric-a-brac of the Summer Palace. I hope that a day will come when France, delivered and cleansed, will send this booty back to looted China. Until then, there is a theft, and two thieves.[19]

While Hugo wrote from exile, Gautier wrote newspaper columns about the Summer Palace artworks—now transformed into fashionable "bric-a-brac"—that had made it as far as France, tacitly acknowledging that the recent war had been brutal to the real place that was the source of so many fantasies for him.[20] In fact, in his coverage of the Exposition, Gautier uses the same word as Hugo—*chimère*—to characterize what has been lost, "China has its pavilion in the Exposition park. Since the taking

18. See Dane, "The Curse of the Mummy Paper," for an account of how stories of making paper from mummies' bands might have spread.

19. "Il y avait, dans un coin du monde, une merveille du monde ; cette merveille s'appelait le Palais d'été. L'art a deux principes, l'Idée, qui produit l'art européen, et la Chimère, qui produit l'art oriental. Le Palais d'été était à l'art chimérique ce que le Parthénon est à l'art idéal. Tout ce que peut enfanter l'imagination d'un peuple presque extra-humain était là. . . . L'empire français a empoché la moitié de cette victoire, et il étale aujourd'hui, avec une sorte de naïveté de propriétaire le splendide bric-à-brac du Palais d'été. J'espère qu'un jour viendra où la France, délivrée et nettoyée, renverra ce butin à la Chine spoliée. En attendant, il y a un vol et deux voleurs" (161).

20. Angela Pao explains how newspaper coverage itself contributed to public awareness of wars and therefore rearranged orientalist fantasies. Pao, *The Orient of the Boulevards*, 109 and 125.

of Peking the middle empire is no longer as chimerical a country as it was before; it is moving from dream to reality. You start not to believe anymore that the sky is of red or black lacquer with golden trees and silver-winged cranes, above a ground composed entirely of kaolin."[21] His nostalgic description of all the aesthetic images of China on which one can no longer base one's reveries about the country is followed by a description of the young Chinese women tending the tea counter: "They are dressed in long dark dresses attached at the neck, which look a great deal like the narrow dresses that women wear these days. Their hair is put up 'in the Chinese fashion.'" The quotation marks here indicate that Gautier expected such a hairdo to be recognizable by name for his French readers.[22]

In fact, Parisian hairdos are an area in which Gautier is confident that his era can compete, not only with current global fashions, but also with classical sculpture. In "De la mode" he maintains that when it comes to hairstyles,

> [t]he Parisian comb rivals the Greek chisel, and hair obeys more easily than marble from Paros or Pentelikon. . . . See with what taste these bows, these curls, these braids *roll upon themselves* like a horn of Ammon or the volute of an Ionian temple! An Athenian sculptor, a Renaissance painter, would he arrange them with more grace, ingenuity, and style? We do not think so. . . . The Venus de Milo, if she got her arms back and if a fashionable lady loaned her a top, could go to a party with her hair as it is—what an honor for our time![23] (emphasis mine)

Here the rolled-up-ness of hairdos is what associates them with classical ideals. As we have seen, modern beauty seems, for Gautier, to involve orientalist or trans-medium winding and unwinding of similarly coiled fabric, hair, or knowledge. Explanations of such beauty are printed on bands of paper passed over spinning drums.

---

21. "La Chine a son pavillon dans le parc de l'Exposition universelle. Depuis la prise de Pékin, l'empire du milieu n'est plus un pays aussi chimérique qu'autrefois ; il passe du rêve à la réalité. On commence à ne plus croire que le ciel y soit en laque rouge ou noire sur lequel se découpent des arbres d'or et volent des grues aux ailes argentées, au-dessus d'un sol composé uniquement de kaolin . . . " (*L'Orient* 1: 257). Note, even here, the attention to the material of which these fantasies are made. Kaolin is used for porcelain.

22. "Elles sont vêtues de longues robes de couleur sombre s'agrafant au col et qui ressemblent beaucoup aux étroites gaines que portent les femmes aujourd'hui. Leurs cheveux sont retroussés 'à la chinoise'" (*L'Orient* 1: 259).

23. "Le peigne parisien vaut le ciseau grec, et les cheveux obéissent plus docilement que le marbre de Paros ou du Pentélique. . . . Voyez avec quel goût se massent sur la nuque ces noeuds, ces boucles, ces tresses enroulées sur elles-mêmes comme une corne d'Ammon, ou comme une volute de chapiteau ionien ! Un sculpteur athénien, un peintre de la Renaissance, les disposeraient-ils avec plus de grâce, d'ingéniosité et de style ?—Nous ne le croyons pas . . . la Vénus de Milo, si elle retrouvait ses bras et si une femme du monde voulait lui prêter un corsage, pourrait aller en soirée coiffée comme elle est. Quel éloge pour la mode de notre temps !" (24–29).

The Exposition where Gautier saw women with their hair done up "à la chinoise" was both a place where fashions were constantly on display and a driving force for the production of related print matter. Guides to the Exposition, as well as illustrated or comic accounts of what was on display, were in demand. In one such guide, *L'Album de l'exposition* of 1867, Charles Maquet explains Parisian fashion to a fictitious Viennese visitor confused by the different ranks of women he is likely to encounter. Given five Parisiennes, ranging from a society lady to a chambermaid, he discovers that the common elements of clothing and adornment are: "A false chignon, a *suivez-moi jeune homme*, a pair of boots, a very expensive dress with many ornaments, a bit of blush on the cheeks, flour on the forehead, slang on the lips."[24] Any finer points of class differentiation supposedly paled before the common code of false chignons and *suivez-moi jeune hommes*. As we will see, *bavolets* and *suivez-moi jeune hommes* emphasized the movement of their wearers in ways that could be made to characterize fashionable Parisiennes and orientalized visitors alike.

Gautier, for his part, liked moving ribbons and waving shawls well enough, but he differentiates his taste in such accessories from Baudelaire and Balzac's by saying that he prefers to retain antique sculpture as a point of reference, rather than focusing on dynamic clothing to the exclusion of the classical:

> (Baudelaire's) original understanding of modern beauty inverses the question, for it sees antique beauty as primitive, coarse, and barbarous, a paradoxical opinion, no doubt, but one which can certainly be defended. Balzac much preferred an elegant Parisian, slim, fetching, her long cashmere shawl clinging to her through a gesture of the elbows, going stealthily to some date, her lace veil pushed up on her nose, tilting her head at an angle that shows, between the trailing ribbons of the hat and the last fold of the shawl, one of those ivory necks where two or three charming curls twist in the light, to the Venus de Milo. This certainly has its charm, though the Venus de Milo is more to my taste. That's because my early education and disposition have made me more sculptural than literary.[25]

24. "Un faux chignon, Un *suivez-moi jeune homme*, Une paire de bottes, Une robe tres chère, avec beaucoup d'ornements, Un peu de rouge sur les joues, De farine sur le front, d'argot sur les lèvres" (Maquet 20).

25. "Cette comprehension (Baudelaire's) si originale de la beauté moderne retourne la question, car elle regarde comme primitive, grossière et barbare la beauté antique, opinion paradoxale sans doute, mais qui peut très-bien se soutenir. Balzac préférait de beaucoup, à la Vénus de Milo, une Parisienne élégante, fine, coquette, moulée dans son long cachemire par un mouvement de coudes, allant d'un pied furtif à quelque rendez-vous, sa voilette de Chantilly rabattue sur le nez, penchant la tête de manière à montrer, entre le bavolet du chapeau et le dernier pli du châle, une de ces nuques au ton d'ivoire où se tordent gracieusement dans la lumière deux ou trois frisons de cheveux follets. Cela a bien son charme, quoique,

The *bavolet* that Gautier sees as an emblematic element of Baudelaire's modern beauty is a ribbon that trails from the back of a hat, like the one depicted in figure 4.4. An equivalent flourish, be it of ribbon or hair, is called a *suivez-moi jeune homme*.

Cham, a prolific, and often racist, caricaturist of expositions throughout the Second Empire, noted, in an image from 1867, that fashionable women wore their *suivez-moi jeune hommes* as Chinese men did their braids (fig. 4.5). Expositions were opportunities for the display of fashions, both Parisian and foreign, and Cham took full advantage of the range of such displays to suggest that men might be equally entranced by fibers that trailed behind hats or heads, as markers of gendered or racialized difference. Braided hair could also serve, not just as enticement, but as a trace of attraction experienced. In figure 4.6, a Chinese visitor gets caught by the turns he has made around a sculpture of a voluptuous nude.[26] In other caricatures of salons from the 1860s, Gautier, too, is portrayed as avidly interested in nude statues. In one, he is depicted carrying away a curvy sculpture under one arm and paintings he has skewered with his pen under the other. The suggestion that a shapely nude might interest a penetrating critic is barely veiled.[27]

Somewhat paradoxically, then, the very hairstyle that set Chinese visitors apart as picturesque at the Exposition was also used to establish parallels between them and fashionable Parisiennes. Trailing ribbons or braids left a fleeting trace of the turns one had taken around a nude, or sometimes just around another exhibit. Turning around statues of nudes was a modern experience Gautier had already defended in 1847, when Clésinger's sculpture *La femme piquée par un serpent*, caused a scandal at the Salon. The uproar, encouraged by Clésinger, who wanted to be the talk of the town, focused partly on the torqued position of the model, who appeared to be in the throes of passion, and partly on the unidealized representation of the body of the woman in question. The fact that the model was Apollonie Sabatier, a *salonnière*, artist, and courtesan whose friends referred to her as La Présidente, added to the whiff of scandal surrounding the sculpture. Gautier, who attended Sabatier's salon and wrote erotic letters to La Présidente, defended the sculpture, identifying

---

pour notre goût, nous aimions davantage la Vénus de Milo ; mais cela tient à ce que, par suite d'une première éducation et d'un sens particulier, nous sommes plus plastique que littéraire" ("Charles Baudelaire" liv).

26. Gautier's writing on Courbet suggests that he considered Cham crude: "*The Return from the Fair* seems to us to be done in the taste of Cham or Pigal rather than according to a serious idea of the picturesque. . . . We have been severe with Mr. Courbet, but he is strong enough, his qualities are significant enough to withstand criticism" ("*Le retour de la foire* nous semble plus concu dans le gout de Cham ou de Pigal, que dans une idée sérieuesement pittoresque. . . . Nous avons été sévères envers M. Courbet, mais il est assez fort ; il possède assez de qualités robustes pour supporter la critique") (*Courbet* 33).

27. Ségolène Le Men describes this image, whose caption is "You can be sure that each will find enough material for his column" ("Chacun, soyez-en sûr, trouvera à faire son petit feuilleton") ("Les débuts de Félicien Rops" note 7).

Figure 4.5 Cham. "A question at the Exposition: Between the two *Suivez-moi jeune homme*, the young man need not hesitate" ["Une question pendant la durée de l'exposition. Entre les deux *Suivez-moi, jeune homme*, le jeune homme n'a pas à hésiter"], 1867, lithograph. *La comédie de l'Exposition: 1er acte*, Arnauld de Vresse, éditeur, p. 3. Bibliothèque nationale de France, Paris.

both its realistic portrayal of a woman and the multiplicity of points of view from which it had to be appreciated as modern. The nude's twisted position meant that there was no one vantage point from which the viewer could see the entire figure of the *Femme piquée par un serpent.* As Wendy Joyce Nolan points out, this "confronted spectators with the mechanics of art production and reception in a way that redefined the relationship between artist, model, and viewer and injected that relationship with a new kind of self-consciousness" (182). This consciousness of the process by which flesh becomes stone could also have been encouraged by Clésinger's use of a cast of Sabatier's body in his preparation of the sculpture. Indeed, the technologically mediated reproduction of every detail of Sabatier's flesh is perhaps as important a source of self-consciousness about production and reception as movement around the sculpture is. After all, Clésinger's sculpture is also reminiscent of the Louvre's hermaphrodite, a classical sculpture whose pose famously rewards circumambulation with the surprise of ambiguous sex. A detailed representation of a well-known courtesan could be provocative, but referencing the classical ideal of the

Inconvénient pour un visiteur chinois d'avoir trop tourné autour d'une statue pour l'admirer.

FIGURE 4.6 Cham, "The disadvantage of having turned around a statue to admire it too many times" ["Inconvénient pour un visiteur chinois d'avoir trop tourné autour d'une statue pour l'admirer"], 1867, lithograph. *La comédie de l'Exposition: 1er acte*, Arnauld de Vresse, éditeur, p. 14. Bibliothèque nationale de France, Paris.

androgyne could also create contemporary erotic *frisson*.[28] Gautier's earlier play on a similar theme in *Mlle de Maupin* made him a logical advocate for Clésinger's *Femme piquée par un serpent*, with its simultaneously explicit and classically inflected form.

Gautier remained attached to classical sculpture, but he liked to disrupt generic expectations. The female nude was interesting when it was modern in surface and pose, whereas contemporary dress was interesting when its aesthetics were reminiscent of those of classical sculpture. Fleshly imperfection was fine on a marble sculpture by Clésinger, but Parisiennes getting dressed for an evening out ought to make themselves up so that the living colors of their skin wouldn't clash with the sheen of their silks and satins.

---

28. See Brix 24.

Like the album that listed flour as one of the five common ingredients of fashionable Parisian dress, Gautier's "De la mode" names rice powder makeup as the fashionable cosmetic that allows women to aspire to the status of statues. Gautier writes,

> With the fine feeling for harmony that characterizes them, women have understood that there is a kind of dissonance between evening dress and the natural face. Just as skilled painters harmonize draperies and flesh with light glazes, women whiten their skin, which would look crude next to watered silks, lace, satins, and they give it a unity of tone which is preferable to the clash of white, yellow, and pink, which even the purest of complexions offers. Using this fine dust, they give their epidermis a marble sheen, and remove from their complexion this reddish health that is crude in our civilization, for it assumes a prevalence of physical appetites over intellectual instincts. Perhaps a vague sense of modesty even inspires women to cover their neck, their shoulders, their breast and their arms with this veil of white powder which attenuates nudity by removing the hot, provocative colors of life from it. And so, form draws near to statuary, it purifies and spiritualizes itself.[29]

There is a rich critical bibliography devoted to Gautier's Pygmalion and anti-Pygmalion impulses, which, Nigel Harkness reminds us, he was not the only author of his period to explore (24). Women and statues apparently mirrored each other irresistibly. It is certainly a trope Gautier revisited during his travels. In his writings on Egypt, as Sarga Moussa points out, "Gautier emphasizes, for women wearing Theban costume, their 'statuesque figure,' and for squatting men a posture that reminds him of 'the judges of Amenthis lined up one behind the other on the papyri of funeral rites.'"[30] Elsewhere in the same article, Moussa discusses overlap between words Gautier uses to describe countryside and those he uses to speak

---

29. "Avec le rare sentiment d'harmonie qui les caractérise, les femmes ont compris qu'il y avait une sorte de dissonance entre la grande toilette et la figure *naturelle*. De même que les peintres habiles établissent l'accord des chairs et des draperies par des glacis légers, les femmes blanchissent leur peau, qui paraîtrait bise à côté des moires, des dentelles, des satins, et lui donnent une unité de ton préférable à ces martelages de blanc, de jaune et de rose qu'offrent les teints les plus purs. Au moyen de cette fine poussière, elles font prendre à leur épiderme un mica de marbre, et ôtent à leur teint cette santé rougeaude qui est une grossièreté dans notre civilisation, car elle suppose la prédominance des appétits physiques sur les instincts intellectuels. Peut-être même un vague frisson de pudeur engage-t-il les femmes à poser sur leur col, leurs épaules, leur sein et leurs bras ce léger voile de poussière blanche qui atténue la nudité en lui retirant les chaudes et provocantes couleurs de la vie. La forme se rapproche ainsi de la statuaire ; elle se spiritualise et se purifie" (34–36).

30. "Gautier souligne, pour les femmes portant des gargoulettes de Thèbes, leur 'galbe de statue,' et, pour les hommes accroupis, une posture qui lui rappelle 'ces juges de l'Amenthis rangés par file les uns derrière les autres sur les papyrus des rituels funéraires'" (19).

of paint, saying, "Gautier estheticizes the real and symmetrically he 'materializes' painting, referring to the making of the painting, to a process, rather than to a finished state."[31] This emphasis on the process—of painting moving folds or skirts, of powdering one's skin to coordinate better with one's ballgown, of (as we will see) having a red *gilet* made by a tailor—was modern. The orientalism that began as an element of upstart romantic bohemianism for Gautier morphed with time and experience into a modern focus on the media of cloth and of printed text.

"Clothing, in the modern era, has become a sort of skin that humans don't take off under any pretext, and which sticks to them like the pelt of an animal, to such an extent that the real form of bodies has been forgotten,"[32] says Gautier. The Second Empire public is no longer used to nudes. As we have seen, this conviction contributes to Gautier's apology for the crinoline and for folds nobly drawn. By reading Gautier's meditations on fashion with Cham's cruder, and more overtly racist, caricatures of exposition visitors, we can trace the emergence of concerns about the cultural status of nude sculpture. In such caricatures, the sculpted female nude, which Lynda Nead has shown had been understood as the ultimate manifestation of Art, is eyed with less elevated expectations, and more desire, by many visitors to the Exposition. The expansion of audience for nude sculpture that the Exposition represented complicated its role within the hierarchy of the arts. In Cham's caricatures, hair and clothing—the fashions characteristic of the Exposition—provide clues as to how spectators are reading the art that is before them.

Using cloth to trace reactions to the aesthetic, and to provide clues for how to read sculpture, is something Gautier, too, was apt to do. In her discussion of the *Roman de la momie* Anne Green has pointed out Rumphius's inky trousers as the precursor and extension of the story supposedly translated for readers (126). Gautier does another provocative version of text/textile segue on a live body in his poem "À une robe rose," which was understood to be addressed to Apollonie Sabatier, La Présidente, who is clothed in this version. The particularity of the dress in question is its closeness to the tones of Sabatier's skin. Gautier imagines his model, "Dropping the veil that weighs on you, / Reality that art has dreamed / Like the Borghese Princess / You would pose for Canova. // And these pink folds are the lips / Of my unappeased desires / Placing on the body from which you wean them, A tunic of kisses."[33]

The poem gives voice to unappeased desires, making the poem itself the tunic of kisses that it calls the pink dress. As with the hieroglyphic tendencies that Tortonese

31. "Gautier esthétise le réel, et, symétriquement, il 'matérialise' la peinture, en renvoyant à la *fabrication* du tableau, donc à un processus plutôt qu'à un état fini" (9).

32. "Le vêtement, à l'époque moderne, est devenu pour l'homme une sorte de peau dont il ne se sépare sous aucun prétexte et qui lui adhère comme le pelage à un animal, à ce point que la forme réelle du corps est de nos jours tout à fait tombée en oubli" (*De la mode* 11–12).

33. "Jetant le voile qui te pèse, / Réalité que l'art rêva, / Comme la princesse Borghèse / Tu poserais pour Canova. // Et ces plis roses sont les lèvres / De mes désirs inapaisés, / Mettant au corps dont tu les sèvres / Une tunique de baisers" (*Émaux et Camées* 94).

identifies in Gautier's naming of fashion,[34] here the cloth and the words do the same work, kiss the same almost-accessible body. The dress is pink, already a provocative choice, since Valerie Steele points out that only women under thirty wore pink.[35] Sabatier was twenty-eight at the time of the poem's first publication, thirty when it appeared in volume form, and hardly playing the role of the demure demoiselle that pink could imply. This is, instead, a dress that, like the mummies' bands, "undresses you so well." The idea of modesty is dismissed outright: "Or is the cloth dyed / With the roses of your modesty? / No, twenty times sculpted and painted, / Your form knows its splendor."[36]

Like the powdered skin that goes well with silks in "De la mode," Sabatier's skin here is contiguous, visually and haptically, with the silk that covers it: "From the epidermis on the silk, / Slip silvery shivers / and the fabric of your flesh reflects, / Its pink highlights. / Where did you get this strange dress? / Which seems to be made of your flesh? / Living weave which mixes / Its pale pink with your skin?"[37]

In his poem addressed to her dress, Gautier's treatment of Sabatier's skin as a *trame vivante* suggests a productive combination of the lines of weaving and the color of life. Though weaving metaphors are as old as literature, Gautier's pink silk reads like a discussion of what he would like his words to do.[38]

Meditating on his day job in his poem "Après le feuilleton," Gautier separates the plot-pulling strings of the melodramas he is obliged to review for his weekly column from the silky threads of his other creative work. Once his column is written, the former are banished in the interest of freeing the expressive capacities—and the pleasures—of caprice. Describing his Mondays, Gautier explains, "The strings of melodramas / are no longer allowed to slip / Between the silky threads of the cloth / That my caprice likes to weave."[39]

The silky threads of caprice can be worn and written. In *Histoire du romantisme*, which is generally read as Gautier's literary testament, the author says that he knows that he will be remembered by those who never read him for the red vest he

---

34. Tortonese, *La vie extérieure*, 63. The poem has been analyzed as a model for Baudelaire by Pommier, and Maria Rubins's treatment of it as ekphrasis addresses the slippage from description to analysis of poetic medium that occurs, but neither pay much attention to the dress itself. Anastasaki and Chambers do wonderful readings of the textile as text, but don't extend them to Gautier's other journalistic writing. I simply propose to enlarge the context of their readings to include other instances of threads unwrapped from bodies in Gautier's prose as well as his poetry.

35. Steele, *Paris Fashion* 157 (citing Julie de Marguerittes).

36. "te deshabille si bien"; "Ou bien l'étoffe est-elle teinte / Dans les roses de ta pudeur ? / Non ; vingt fois modelée et peinte, / Ta forme connaît sa splendeur" (93).

37. "de l'epiderme sur la soie / Glissent des frissons argentés, / Et l'étoffe à ta chair renvoie / Ses éclairs roses reflétés. / D'où te vient cette robe étrange / Qui semble faite de ta chair, / Trame vivante qui mélange / Avec ta peau son rose claire ?" (93).

38. Gautier, *Œuvres poétiques*, 494–95.

39. "Les ficelles des mélodrames / N'ont plus le droit de se glisser / Parmi les fils soyeux des trames / Que mon caprice aime à tisser" (*Émaux et Camées* 172).

wore to *Hernani*, and he likes that the anecdote reveals his disdain for convention (128). There's no shame in being remembered for a fashion statement. For those who *are* reading him, though, Gautier reserves the pleasures of a description of the cloth from which his vest was cut:

> We pulled from a trunk a magnificent piece of satin—cherry-colored or Chinese vermilion—that we spread triumphantly before the eyes of the terrified tailor, with an air of tranquil satisfaction that made him worry for our sanity. The light shone and slipped over the sheen of the cloth, which we mussed to make the reflections flash . . . running the scales of the warmest, richest, most ardent, and delicate shades of red.[40]

Presenting his legacy for readers who will go beyond the red vest, Gautier pays as much attention to the stuff of its fabric as he does to the public reception of the final garment. It is a fabric that reflects, after all, its agenda (to stand out), its audience (a sea of bourgeois suits), itself (a statement.)

The range of reflections enabled by the shiny satin is reminiscent, again, of Gautier's creative practice as he wrote the *Histoire du romantisme*, gathering up reflections on a career characterized by clothing worn and texts written. Gautier adapted his practice to new conditions as moving bands of cloth and paper transformed both fashion and print technology. He unwrapped mummies when a story had to be moved along, and he mussed the fabric of his own legend to invite reflection about the color he brought to his century. Perhaps the texture of composition he achieves in "A une robe rose" even prefigures the revolutionary bits of satin that would dress Degas's *Petite danseuse de 14 ans* not much later. But where Degas's dancer would be cast in bronze after his death, Gautier's aesthetics are cast in ink, with clothing playing just as self-conscious and materially-grounded a role.

Works Cited

Charivari, May 15, 1833. https://artwithmark.wordpress.com/2014/05/26/ingres-bertin-portrait-take-2/.

Charivari, July 18, 1839. Benjamin Roubaud and Valérie Guillaume, *Benjamin Roubaud et le Panthéon charivarique: Maison de Balzac, 31 mai–31 août 1988*. Maison de Balzac, 1988, p. 30.

Anastasaki, Elena. "Plus qu'une 'coquetterie posthume' Matérialité et individualité des objets dans *Émaux et camées*." *Gautier et les arts de la danse*, edited by Martine Lavaud. Société Théophile Gautier, 2009, pp. 329–42.

---

40. "Nous tirâmes d'un bahut un magnifique morceau de satin cerise ou vermillon de la Chine, que nous déployâmes triomphalement sous les yeux du tailleur épouvanté, avec un air de tranquillité et de satisfaction qui l'alarma pour notre raison. La lumière miroitait et glissait sur les cassures de l'étoffe que nous chiffonnions pour en faire jouer les reflets et les brillants . . . Les gammes les plus chaudes, les plus riches, les plus ardentes, les plus délicates du rouge étaient parcourus" (131–32).

Aravamudan, Srinivas. *Enlightenment Orientalism: Resisting the Rise of the Novel*. Chicago: U of Chicago P, 2012.

Benjamin, Walter. *The Arcades Project*. Belknap/Harvard UP, 1999.

Bernard, Claudie. *Le Passé recomposé: le roman historique français du dix-neuvième siècle*. Hachette supérieur, 1996.

Brevik-Zender, Heidi. "Interstitial Narratives: Rethinking Feminine Spaces of Modernity in Nineteenth-Century French Fashion Plates." *Nineteenth-Century Contexts*, vol. 36, no. 2, 2014, pp. 91–123.

Brix, Michel. "Esthétique néo-classique et romantisme." *Nineteenth-Century French Studies*, vol. 35, no.1, 2006, pp. 22–35.

Burke, Edmund, and David Prochaska. *Genealogies of Orientalism: History, Theory, Politics*. U of Nebraska P, 2008.

Chambers, Ross. "Gautier et le complexe de Pygmalion." *Revue d'histoire littéraire de la France*, vol. 72, no. 4, 1972, pp. 641–58. http://www.jstor.org/stable/40524421.

———. "Pour une poétique du vêtement." *Michigan Romance Studies*, vol. 1, 1980, pp. 18–46.

Dane, Joseph A. "The Curse of the Mummy Paper." *Printing History*, vol. 17, no. 2, 1995, pp. 18–25.

David-Weill, Natalie. *Rêve de Pierre: la quête de la femme chez Théophile Gautier*. Droz, 1989.

De la Motte, Dean. "Utopia Commodified: Utilitarianism, Aestheticism, and the *presse à bon marché*." *Making the News: Modernity and the Mass Press in Nineteenth-Century France*, edited by Dean de la Motte and Jeannene M. Przyblyski. U of Massachusetts P, 1999, pp. 141–59.

Dobie, Madeleine. *Foreign Bodies: Gender, Language, and Culture in French Orientalism*. Stanford UP, 2001.

Doy, Gen. *Drapery: Classicism and Barbarism in Visual Culture*. I. B. Tauris, 2002.

Feyel, Gilles. "Le Coût de la presse quotidienne parisienne (1800–1844)." *Le Temps des médias*, vol. 1, no. 6, 2006, pp. 9–21. www.cairn.info/revue-le-temps-des-medias-2006-1-page-9.htm.

———. "L'Économie de la presse au XIXe siècle." *La Civilisation du journal: histoire culturelle et littéraire de la presse française au XIXe siècle*, edited by Dominique Kalifa et al. Nouveau monde, 2011, pp. 141–80.

Furmanek, Carole. "Tentatives de relégation—'l'art pour l'art', 'la poésie pure', malentendus et constructions idéologiques douteuses." *Fabula / Les colloques, De l'absolu littéraire à la relégation : le poète hors les murs*. http://www.fabula.org/colloques/document2464.php.

Gautier, Judith. *Le Collier des jours: souvenirs de ma vie*. Preface by Denise Brahimi. C. Pirot, 1994.

Gautier, Judith, and Agnès de Noblet. *Le Second Rang du collier: souvenirs littéraires*. Harmattan, 1999.

Gautier, Théophile. "Charles Baudelaire." Preface to Charles Baudelaire, *Les Fleurs du mal*. Calmann-Lévy, 1868.

———. *Courbet, Le Watteau du laid*. Edited by Christine Sagnier. Séguier, 2000.

———. *De la mode*. Actes Sud, 1993.

———. *Émaux et Camées*. G. Crès, 1913.

———. *Histoire du romantisme: suivi de Quarante portraits romantiques*. Edited by Adrien Goetz and Itaï Kovács. Gallimard, 2011.

———. *Œuvres complètes, Section I, Tome 5*. Edited by Alain Montandon and Corinne Saminadayar-Perrin. H. Champion, 2003.

———. *Œuvres poétiques complètes de Théophile Gautier*. Bartillat, 2004.

———. *L'Orient*, t. 1. Charpentier, 1882.

———. *L'Orient*, t. 2. Charpentier, 1882.

———. *Le Roman de la momie*. Gallimard, 1986.

Geczy, Adam. *Fashion and Orientalism: Dress, Textiles and Culture from the 17th to the 21st Century*. Bloomsbury Academic, 2013.

Green, Anne. *Changing France: Literature and Material Culture in the Second Empire*. Anthem, 2011.

Grigsby, Darcy Grimaldo. *Colossal: Engineering the Suez Canal, Statue of Liberty, Eiffel Tower, and Panama Canal*. Periscope, 2012.

Harkness Nigel. "Ut sculptura poesis? Literary-Sculptural Intersections from Balzac to Proust." *Au seuil de la modernité: Proust, Literature and the Arts*, edited by Nigel Harkness and Marion Schmid. Peter Lang, 2011, pp. 211–35.

Hawthorne, Melanie C. "Dis-covering the Female: Gautier's *Roman de la momie*." *The French Review*, vol. 66, no. 5, 1993, pp. 718–29. http://www.jstor.org/stable/396295.

Hugo, Victor. *Œuvres complètes de Victor Hugo: Actes et paroles*. A. Michel, 1937–40.

Joyce, Wendy Nolan. "Sculpting the Modern Muse: Auguste Clésinger's 'Femme piquée par un serpent.'" *Nineteenth-Century French Studies*, vol. 35, no. 1, 2006, pp. 166–88. http://www.jstor.org/stable/23538385.

Kerlouégan, François. *Ce fatal excès du désir: poétique du corps romantique*. Champion, 2006.

Lavaud, Martine. *Le Cothurne étroit du journalisme: Théophile Gautier et la contrainte médiatique*. Société Théophile Gautier, 2007.

———. "Théophile Gautier." *La Civilisation du journal: histoire culturelle et littéraire de la presse française au XIXe siècle*, edited by Dominique Kalifa et al. Nouveau monde, 2011, pp. 1169–76.

Le Men, Ségolène. "Les Débuts de Félicien Rops: entre art et caricature." *L'Art de la caricature*, edited by Ségolène Le Men. Presses Universitaires de Paris Ouest, 2014, pp. 53–71.

Lehmann, Ulrich. *Tigersprung: Fashion in Modernity*. MIT P, 2000.

Lyu, Claire. "Unswathing the Mummy: Body, Knowledge, and Writing in Gautier's *Le Roman de la momie*." *Nineteenth-Century French Studies*, vol. 33, no. 3/4, 2005, pp. 308–19. http://www.jstor.org/stable/23537987.

Mainardi, Patricia. *Art and Politics of the Second Empire*. Yale UP, 1987.

Maquet, Charles. "A propos des costumes du jour." *L'album de l'exposition illustrée*, edited by G. Richard, 1867, pp. 19–20. http://gallica.bnf.fr/ark:/12148/bpt6k6279501j.

Marcus, Sharon. *Between Women: Friendship, Desire, and Marriage in Victorian England*. Princeton UP, 2008.

Moussa, Sarga. "La Double Vue: Sur le voyage en Égypte (1869) de Théophile Gautier." *Le Temps des médias*, vol. 1, no. 8, 2007, pp. 34–45. http://www.cairn.info/article.php?ID_ARTICLE=TDM_008_0034.

Nead, Lynda. *The Female Nude: Art, Obscenity, and Sexuality.* Routledge, 1992.

Pao, Angela Chia-yi. *The Orient of the Boulevards: Exoticism, Empire, and Nineteenth-Century French Theater.* U of Pennsylvania P, 1998.

Pommier, Jean. *Dans les chemins de Baudelaire.* José Corti, 1945.

Rancière, Jacques, and Patrice Vauday. "En allant à l'expo: l'ouvrier, sa femme et les machines." *Les Révoltes logiques*, no. 1, 1975, pp. 5–22.

Rubins, Maria. *Crossroad of Arts, Crossroad of Cultures: Ecphrasis in Russian and French Poetry.* Palgrave, 2000.

Sainte-Beuve, Charles-Augustin. *Nouveaux lundis*, tome 9. Michel Lévy frères, 1863–70.

Steele, Valerie. *Paris Fashion: A Cultural History.* Oxford UP, 1988.

Tortonese, Paolo. "Les Hiéroglyphes, ou l'écriture de pierre." *L'Orient de Théophile Gautier.* 1. 1. Société Théophile Gautier, 1990.

———. *La vie extérieure: essai sur l'œuvre narrative de Théophile Gautier.* Lettres modernes, 1992.

Von Minden, Stephan. "Une expérience d'exotisme vécu : 'le Chinois de Théophile Gautier.'" *L'Orient de Théophile Gautier.* 1. 1. Société Théophile Gautier, 1990.

Yu, Pauline. "Judith Gautier and the Invention of Chinese Poetry." *Reading Medieval Chinese Poetry: Text, Context, and Culture*, edited by Paul W. Kroll. Brill, 2014, pp. 251–88.

———. "'Your Alabaster in This Porcelain': Judith Gautier's *Le Livre de jade.*" *PMLA*, vol. 122, no. 2, 2007, pp. 464–82. http://www.jstor.org/stable/25501716.

CHAPTER 5

FASHION'S TRACE

The Material Eternal in Sand's *Indiana*, Flaubert's *Madame Bovary*, and Maupassant's *Bel-Ami*

Heidi Brevik-Zender

> [Madeleine] had slipped on her wrap, a loose white flannel wrap that Duroy recognized at once. He found the sight of it unpleasant. Why? His wife possessed a good dozen of these morning coats, as he well knew. She could hardly destroy her whole wardrobe and buy a completely new one. All the same, he would have preferred her bedroom-wear, her nightwear, the clothes she wore when making love, to be different from those she had worn with her other husband. He felt that something of Forestier must have rubbed off on the warm, fleecy material.
>
> —Guy de Maupassant, *Bel-Ami*[1]

Gazing at his attractive bride Madeleine on the morning after their wedding, Georges Duroy, the antihero protagonist of Guy de Maupassant's *Bel-Ami*, struggles to comprehend why this vision of postnuptial intimacy is not enticing, as one might expect, but rather, the text indicates, "unpleasant." As Duroy fixates on Madeleine's white flannel robe, a garment that she has saved from her previous marriage to deceased husband Charles Forestier, the answer, Duroy realizes, lies in this article of clothing, the soft, warm folds of which seem to hold the imprint, Maupassant writes,

1. Translation Parmée (241). "[Madeleine] avait passé son peignoir, un grand peignoir de flanelle blanche, que Duroy reconnut aussitôt. Cette vue lui fut désagréable. Pourquoi ? Sa femme possédait, il le savait bien, une douzaine entière de ces vêtements de matinée. Elle ne pouvait pourtant point détruire son trousseau pour en acheter un neuf ? N'importe, il eût voulu que son linge de chambre, son linge de nuit, son linge d'amour ne fût plus le même qu'avec l'autre. Il lui semblât que l'étoffe moelleuse et tiède devait avoir gardé quelque chose du contact de Forestier" (Maupassant, *Romans* 355). Unless otherwise indicated, all translations are my own.

of "something of Forestier . . . rubbed off." If the disquieting "something" that the dead man has left behind is meant to be understood in layered symbolic terms—representing the access to Madeleine's body, affections, and writerly talents once afforded to Husband Number 1 whom Duroy now jealously resents, for instance—I would instead like to call attention to something of a far more material nature, that is, the object through which what lingers of Charles is mediated, and, specifically, to the garment's ability to harbor and communicate residuals of the departed first spouse. For it is not Madeleine herself but rather her clothing, Maupassant stresses, that seems to have retained what I will be calling "the trace" of the man otherwise dead and gone. It is through his contact with material fashion that something of Charles, from beyond the tomb, is powerfully preserved.

The trace of Charles that lingers on Madeleine's flannel attire is a useful introduction to this essay, wherein the goal is to assess, with new critical eyes, the well-known, but only partly explored, formulation of fashion as a literary metaphor for nineteenth-century French modernity. This formulation is one that we owe largely to another Charles, that is, Charles Baudelaire, who articulated a dialectical tension between, on the one hand, transition, mobility, and change, and, on the other hand, that which is eternal. Positing these as the conjoined conditions of both fashion and the modern, Baudelaire famously lauded efforts to "extract from fashion whatever element it may contain of poetry within history, to distill the eternal from the transitory" (*Painter* 12).[2] As frequently as this dictum is cited in relation to fashion[3] and literary works alike, it would seem that a stronger correlation has been established between the "ephemeral" side of the dialectical coin and the concerns of nineteenth-century novelists. Scholars[4] have adeptly examined the concept of change as a recurring trope in texts that explored major transformations characterizing this era—rising mass industry, increased consumption, human displacement, movement and transition at ever-increasing speeds—and correlated these to fashion's transitory nature. The basic connection put forth by Baudelaire of fashion to ephemerality in the context of novelistic writing is thereby well established. But what of his notion of *l'éternel*? How might the novelistic production of Baudelaire's century have rendered the eternalness of modernity?

---

2. "dégager de la mode ce qu'elle peut contenir de poétique dans l'historique, de tirer l'éternel du transitoire" (*Œuvres Complètes* 1163).

3. Roland Barthes reminds us in *Système de la mode* that the fashion system itself promotes the myth that change—a constantly updated wardrobe, for instance—is necessary. The myth of clothing's expendability and compulsory renewal must be perpetuated, he notes; otherwise, consumers would not be spurred on to purchase new garments with each passing season, thereby resulting in the overall collapse of the industry that constellates around fashion and dress.

4. For recent book-length studies, see for instance *Real Time: Accelerating Narrative from Balzac to Zola* by David F. Bell, *Le Grand Transit Moderne: Mobility, Modernity, and French Naturalist Fiction* by Larry Duffy, and *Changing France: Literature and Material Culture in the Second Empire* by Anne Green.

This essay considers the nexus of fashion's eternalness and novel writing through an examination of works by Guy de Maupassant, George Sand, and Gustave Flaubert, three novelists writing at different moments in the century who used fashion both to enact and to represent French modernity. It posits that the eternalness in novels can be fruitfully understood through the concept of "the trace," as theorized by Walter Benjamin, a familiar name in critical fashion studies, as well as by Jacques Derrida, a far less familiar name in this area of inquiry.[5] The discussion will focus on the materiality of fashion, a seeming antithesis to the eternal due to the impermanence and degradable nature of clothes as objects. Paradoxically, though, through close readings of dress in three canonical texts of the 1800s, we will see that, for some of the period's most influential novelists, it is authorial permanency that is made available in the materiality of fashion, and, moreover, this eternalness is conditioned by the ephemerality inherent to apparently transitory marks as exemplified by fashion traces. What will be explored is how traces on garments perform the very storytelling drive—the "narrative impetus"[6] in Fredric Jameson's words—characteristic of modern fiction from this era. If the thematic concerns of novelists of this period were widely varied, the sartorial trace present across their works communicates a more universal expression of authorial marking on their narratives, the lingering presence of the nineteenth-century writer deliberately inserted into texts to endure, not unlike a trace of the departed held fast in the folds of a flannel robe.

The Trace of Things

> You don't want to wear concepts . . . you want to wear a fabulous dress.
>
> —John Galliano[7]

In his study of how fashion became linked to philosophies of modernity in the nineteenth and twentieth centuries, Ulrich Lehmann appropriately begins with Baudelaire, adeptly summarizing the poet's preoccupation with the principle of modernity as an aspiration "to discover eternal beauty within the most fugitive expressions" (8). Beauty, that great poetic concern of Baudelaire's, often associates in his writings with antiquity, the sublime, and with death, all of these concepts constituting forms of "the eternal" that he saw in fashion, and inscribed, for instance, in the

5. One notable exception is Nancy J. Troy's discussion of Derrida's reading of the signature in relation to the fashion label or *griffe* (26–27). See also Alison Gill's "Jacques Derrida: Fashion Under Erasure," which usefully engages several of Derrida's recurring concepts, including the trace, within the context of contemporary fashion design. Gill concentrates on the fashion trace in relation to labor and construction—as seen in seams of garments, for instance—and history, as seen in "the signature motifs of past designers that are neither fully absent nor present" (259).

6. This is the titular subject of chapter 1 of Jameson's *The Antinomies of Realism*.

7. The haute-couture fashion designer John Galliano's remark is from an interview with Hamish Bowles published in the March 2015 issue of *Vogue* (533).

dark, heroic "undertakers" suit that men of the nineteenth century had adopted, as well as in the black mourning dress worn by the majestic, statuesque passerby in his poem "A une passante."[8] There is also the idea in Baudelaire, one to which Barthes would later attend in his consideration of the fashion cycle in ladies' magazines, of unending recurrences: fashion must forever be renewed in order to be fashionable, or, in Barbara Vinken's words, it operates as "the eternal return of the new" (66). This is the paradox that Baudelaire's painter of modern life, Constantin Guys, conveyed in his watercolors of stylish Parisians, which, counterintuitively, deployed ephemerality in painting technique, medium, and subject matter—rapid brushstrokes, watercolor, and fashionable clothing—to capture what the poet viewed as historically transcendent, eternal aesthetic ideals.

In his writings on Guys and fashion in *Le Peintre de la vie moderne*, Baudelaire's quest is to theorize modernity in symbolic terms, his engagement taking primarily the ocular point of view of the urban observer-flaneur. Novelists of the period, who typically took highly descriptive and documentary approaches to recording modern life,[9] expanded to the haptic, tactile, physicality of clothing in their desire to represent society comprehensively and "authentically" through, among other things, sensorial engagement with objects. To examine what we might call the material-object turn implicit in the realist literary project of the period thereby invites engagement with scholarship focusing on material garments as themselves primary objects of study. Recent research in this vein that has productive implications for literary criticism can be found in studies probing the dialogical relationships between bodies and attire. Witness, for instance, Paola Colaiacomo's account of how rigid bodywear gave way over time to relatively freer, looser styles:

> For centuries, dress had been perceived as one and the same as the body it covered. Renaissance and Baroque court dresses exacted an idol-like immobility from their wearers: when a niece of Francis I of France was married, at the age of twelve, she had to be carried to church in the arms of an assistant, so great was the weight of the gold and silver cloth of her bridal gown. By contrast, modern, or liberated, dress opens a *dialogue* with the body underneath. A *dialogue* always implies a distance, in some cases even a *difference*. This genealogy can be traced back to the French revolution and the end of the ancien régime. The Roman and Greek fashions characterizing the Empire style of the beginning of the nineteenth century were at once an experiment in vintage and an immediately popular "new look." Then, during the second half of the century, the debate about the artistic dignity of modern dress already signaled a world where body and dress play separate roles. (26)

8. See Barbara Vinken's "Eternity—A Frill on a Dress" (60–63) for Baudelaire's use of fashion to express the eternal in this poem.

9. For a fascinating discussion on reading description in Baudelaire's poetry allegorically to parse its modernity, see "Now You See It, Now You Don't" by Kevin Newmark.

Figure 5.1 A woman lifting her stylish crinoline skirt. Constantin Guys (French, 1802–92), "Woman with a Parasol," 1860–65. Digital image courtesy of the Getty's Open Content Program.

Colaiacomo's description of this historical move away from costume that fused with the human form, and toward a taste in the post-Revolutionary era for garments from which the body was liberated, first invokes the powerful materiality of clothing through the example of a gown whose weighty physicality turns the twelve-year-old bride into a kind of gilded statue. What is of particular interest here is the way in which this materiality then becomes linked to language. For, tellingly, as she goes on to discuss how clothing became increasingly separated from the body in modernity, Colaiacomo's analysis transitions to the vocabulary of literary deconstruction, her use of terms such as "dialogue" and "difference" calling to mind how modern dress, like language, might harbor the concept of *la trace* as explored by Jacques Derrida. Derrida's thoughts turned on numerous occasions to the notion of the trace, one early discussion appearing in *Of Grammatology* wherein he writes: "The trace is not only the disappearance of origin . . . it means that the origin did not even disappear, that it was never constituted except reciprocally by a nonorigin . . . although it *does not exist*, although it is never a *being-present* outside of all plenitude, its possibility is by rights anterior to all that one calls sign" (*Grammatology* 61–62). Or, as Gayatri Chakravorty Spivak interprets it in the original preface to her translation of Derrida's study, the trace can be comprehended in part as "the mark of the absence of a presence, an always already absent present" (xvii).

We can see how Spivak's description of Derrida's trace, as the mark of the absence of a presence, correlates with what is left on Madeleine's white flannel robe in *Bel-Ami*. The garment bears the lingering presence of Charles, his absence and his existence simultaneously inscribed by the trace that endures, ineffable, perhaps, but clearly still present enough to set Duroy on edge. The fashion item hosting the trace in turn acts as a "thing" as theorized by Bill Brown, who, differentiating between "things" and "objects," notes that "we begin to confront the thingness of objects when they stop working for us . . . when their flow within the circuits of production, distribution, consumption and exhibition, has been arrested, however momentarily" (4). In the modernist fiction that Brown studies, "the story of objects asserting themselves as things . . . is the story of a changed relation to the human subject and thus the story of how the thing really names less an object than a particular subject-object relation" (4). Analogously, in Maupassant's text, Madeleine's robe temporarily ceases to operate as a garment, becoming instead a "thing" that asserts itself not to name the object—the white flannel robe—but rather to point conspicuously to the trace of Forestier that now defines his posthumous, materially mediated relationship to Duroy. In defiance of the finite human life span, the trace stubbornly retains something of Forestier nestled in the nightgown (and the narrative), even as it points unnervingly to his, and Duroy's own, mortality, the always already nonpresence that relates them to one another as humans.

Here, both the general "thingness" of the robe and its particularity as a garment are drawn on by Maupassant, who highlights clothing's special aptitude to hold the human narrative—or *histoire*, to cite from Zola's long title for his own nineteenth-century realist epic, the *Rougon-Macquart*—as well as fashion's ability to catalyze the telling of these very "stories." The story of *Bel-Ami*, as we know, is that of Duroy's singular launch into and ultimate domination over modern society. Yet the novel also adheres in ways to the relatively formulaic nineteenth-century *bildungsroman* format and features the prototypical figure of the *arriviste*, two common novelistic configurations of the period that supported a standardizing effect on how literary stories developed in this period. These narrative frameworks in *Bel-Ami* are already in place well before Duroy arrives on the scene. We recall, for instance, Maupassant's succinct rendition of Forestier's trajectory in the opening chapter as the latter recounts it to Duroy—1) return from military service in Africa, 2) newspaper job, 3) marriage—which reads like a plot summary that Duroy is also on track to follow. Thus, when he spies Forestier on the boulevard and actively pursues him rather than allowing the chance encounter to end, it is as though the ambitious Duroy is instinctively seeking entrance into the story for himself. He is thereby poised and ready when the story's original protagonist, Forestier, prematurely dies, and the plot requires a main-character replacement. Naomi Schor, analyzing *Madame Bovary*, advances the useful notion of "substitution chains [which] organize the narrative" (504), noting that, in Flaubert's text, "Emma's death is not synchronic with the exhaustion of the narrative because, after her death, she is replaced by other characters" (504). A comparable structure of "substitution chains," one could say, informs Maupassant's novel, wherein similar patterns of replacement contribute to the sense of the narrative's indefinite continuation. Tellingly, in both novels it is fashion that communicates this narrative deferment, indicating that the story endures beyond the finite existence of any one protagonist; Schor reminds us that, in *Madame Bovary*, not only does the maid Félicité take her mistress's place by donning the dead protagonist's clothes, but Charles himself follows Emma's sartorial lead, adopting shiny boots, white cravats, and waxing his moustache in simulation of his fad-following departed wife (504). More to the point for our purposes, in *Bel-Ami* it is Forestier's quasi-animated trace on the white flannel robe that mediates his connection to Duroy, the character through whom the story will carry on.

Thus, the time-defying, self-perpetuating impetus of realist fiction in the nineteenth century seems to find in fashion a natural ally. This is the case, I suggest, because clothing is an exceptional carrier of traces. Garments, worn typically by all humans in the social world, archive our daily lives through the traces that we, and others, leave in and on them: holes worn into fabrics, spots and stains, perfumes of the body or from adjacent sources are records of our histories. Emily Spivack's *Worn Stories* literary arts project, which chronicles memories that people recount about themselves when describing articles of their own clothing, is founded on this basic premise and connects it to the construction of narrative. Explaining her reasons for choosing dress as a trigger for these narrated accounts, Spivack explains that it is because "clothes can be a rich and universal storytelling device" (7). Building on Brown's object-based analysis of literature in her provocatively titled *Stuff Theory*, Maurizia Boscagli highlights the role that clothing, particularly in contact with the organic human, can play in modernist narratives, arguing that in literature "the 'deep' materiality of the object . . . comes into being and functions in synergy with the body" (13). Sartorial items distinguish themselves from other "things" in part by way of proximity to the human epidermis, creating rich sensorial possibilities for authors to explore. "Clothes," Boscagli aptly remarks, "are charged with intimacy and thus occupy a potentially synesthetic position in regard to the subject" (88). We can discern this synesthetic "synergy with the body" and clothing's capacity to act out narrative in the aforementioned *Bel-Ami* example, wherein the optical image ("the sight") of Forestier's trace on Madeleine's robe transitions to the haptic ("the warm, fleecy material"). One effect of this is to highlight the material-body dialogue so that the "something of Forestier" seems both a physical and a narrative irritant, embedded into the folds of Madeleine's garment, aggravating Duroy (and, perhaps, the reader) until the first man's essence is eventually expunged and Duroy can replace him in the plot.

Tracing the Author's Tracks: George Sand's *Indiana*

> "Take your cloak and your boa," he said, stopping her.
> "Yes, of course, these traces of my presence might compromise you," she replied.[10]
>
> —George Sand, *Indiana*

If Stendhal once praised George Sand's talents for describing garments, even holding her up as a model for his own novelistic renderings of fashionable attire,[11] the frequent references to clothing in her texts also, predictably, provided fodder for chauvinistic contemporaries seeking to condemn the writings of this female author as flighty and inferior to the works of men.[12] As has been well studied, attire both in Sand's life—her famous cross-dressing—and as she deployed it in her literary works can be understood as crucial strategies in gender politics and narrative innovation

10. Translation Raphael (167). "—Prenez donc votre manteau et votre boa, lui dit-il en l'arrêtant.—Il est vrai, répondit-elle, ces traces de ma présence pourraient vous compromettre" (Sand, *Indiana* 222).

11. In notes that he took while struggling to write *Lucien Leuwen*, Stendhal instructs himself: "See George Sand for outfits . . . fashion, clothing, how to wear them, the strength of George Sand" ("Voir George Sand pour les toilettes . . . la mode, les vêtements, la façon de les porter, le fort de George Sand"). The compliment turns backhanded, however, in the next sentence: "Her philosophy (her ambition) her weakness" ("Sa philosophie (sa prétention) son faible") (cited in Hoog 83).

12. For instance, Flaubert's narrator in the 1848 version of *L'Éducation sentimentale* who ridicules the "seamstresses who read George Sand" ("couturières qui lisent George Sand"), simultaneously mocking the novelist for the regular inclusion of fashion in her works and scorning female garment workers—inferior readers, according to the narrator—who should not be confused with "intelligent people" ("gens d'esprit") (cited in Booker 231).

Figure 5.2 *Indienne* fabric. Skirt, 1840–60, French, cotton. Brooklyn Museum Costume Collection at The Metropolitan Museum of Art, Gift of the Brooklyn Museum, 2009; Gift of Arturo and Paul Peralta-Ramos, 1955.

alike,[13] strategies having lasting consequences to narrative fiction given Sand's influence on realist authors of the mid- and late-1800s. Fashion in her 1832 debut novel *Indiana* registers the trace of the eternal that we have seen Maupassant reprising on his own terms later in the century. But what is more, in a text that Patrick M. Bray has called "Sand's most realist novel" (127), dress in *Indiana* is a way for Sand to comment on the process of narrative building itself. In particular, as we will see, the fashion trace, which acts as the mark of Indiana's claim over a garment, parallels the mark of authorship on a story.

13. See work by Nigel Harkness and Jacinta Wright linking Barthes's notion of the text as *tissu* to intertextuality and fashion in Sand (3–4).

That fashion will be a theme in *Indiana* is foregrounded from the outset by the titular character's name, which, in addition to denoting her exotic birth origins in the islands of the Indian Ocean (*les Indes*), also calls up the textile referred to as *indienne*, a printed cotton calico deriving from overseas and one that by Sand's day had been widely embraced in French clothing styles worn by members of her fashionable circle. In his study of cloth, which appears in Arjun Appadurai's important volume *The Social Life of Things*, historian William M. Reddy has observed a rising market for French-produced *indiennes* as early as the eighteenth century, which implies that the textile's popularity was already so established as to stimulate the manufacture of domestic imitations (268).[14] Reddy describes *indienne* cloth as having Bengali origins, to which one must add the complication that in the eighteenth and nineteenth centuries the term *Indes* could refer to islands in the Indian Ocean, including l'île Bourbon (present-day Réunion), from which Indiana hails. When Sand refers to Indiana as "la belle Indienne" (81), she may well have been drawing a comparison to the fashionable fabric. This reading of a textile metaphor in the characters' names is supported by the fact that her "sister" counterpart, the creole maid Noun, is connected, in contrast, to "madras" (74, 106), a silk-cotton blend so named for the Indian city Madras, but also a term referring to a woman's hairstyle consisting of wrapped, colorful headscarves made of this fabric. Among other things Sand assigns this style the task of class differentiation, for the madras coiffure in the novel designates Noun's status as a servant.[15]

One of the most prominent sartorial episodes in *Indiana* takes place at the dramatic conclusion to the novel's first section, wherein Noun dons her mistress's clothes as part of her seduction of their mutual love interest, Raymon de Ramière. Fashion takes center stage as, under the cover of night and dressed warmly in Indiana's "fur-lined cloak with the hood up over her head" (61),[16] Noun meets the young man in the garden and escorts him to Indiana's bedroom where she sheds the fur-lined cloak, revealing Indiana's white ballgown beneath it. Raymon, gazing intoxicatedly at multiple reflections of the chambermaid in a double-paneled angled mirror, falls subject to the quasi-fantasy that Noun is actually Indiana, his error occurring despite the fact that the maid models the look poorly, lacking the title character's posh sartorial refinement, her modesty, and her dainty girlish frame:

> Indiana would have uncovered herself less . . . her modest bosom would have been glimpsed only under a bodice of three layers of gauze. She might have decorated her hair with natural camellias, but they would not have been arranged on her head in such provocative disorder. She might have encased her feet in satin slippers, but her chaste dress would

14. See the chapter "Cashmere Fever" in Hiner's *Accessories to Modernity* for a nuanced treatment of fashion's role in the nineteenth century's "domestication of the exotic."

15. I am grateful to Pratima Prasad for her insights about the complex nineteenth-century meanings evoked by the terms *Inde*, *les Indes*, and *indienne*.

16. "pelisse dont le capuchon était relevé sur sa tête" (100).

> not have revealed like this the secrets of her pretty legs. Taller and of bigger build than her mistress, Noun was dressed up rather than dressed in her fine attire. (62)[17]

This dissimilarity between the two female wearers notwithstanding, Raymon greedily kisses, inhales, and caresses the borrowed outfit's scarf, ribbons, and fabric, searching for the essence of Indiana. The unsuspecting Noun, meanwhile, does not realize that, in Raymon's mind, she has been supplanted by the invisible traces left on the outfit by its true owner:

> If [Noun] had not been drunk as he, she would have realized that at the height of his ecstasy Raymon was thinking of another. She would have seen him kiss the scarf and ribbons that Indiana had worn, breathe in the perfumes that reminded him of her, and crush in his eager hands the material that had covered her breast; but Noun took all these transports for herself, when *all that Raymon saw of her was Indiana's dress.* (64; emphasis added)[18]

That attire in this extraordinary scene has been scrutinized from numerous critical points of view, including its portrayal of racial ambiguity, hybridity, and Sand's overlapping critiques of marriage and slavery,[19] cannot come as a surprise, given that Sand deliberately makes Indiana's gown a protracted and multivalent metaphor. For our purposes, the importance of the dress, as well as Sand's signature and subversive ambiguity about how to parse its layered meanings, are particularly well encapsulated in the remark "all that Raymon saw of her was Indiana's dress," a comment made by the narrator to call attention to the garment, but one that stops short of limiting the text to any single interpretation of the now excessively charged sartorial "thing."

Reading the borrowed garment through Derrida, for instance, we can posit that Sand suggests that Indiana's trace on the dress implies erasure, most notably that of Noun. "The trace," Derrida explains, "is not a presence but is rather the

---

17. "Indiana eût été plus cachée . . . son sein modeste ne se fût trahi que sous la triple gaze de son corsage ; elle eût peut-être orné ses cheveux de camélias naturels, mais ce n'est pas dans ce désordre excitant qu'ils se fussent joués sur sa tête ; elle eût pu emprisonner ses pieds dans des souliers de satin, mais sa chaste robe n'eût pas ainsi trahi les mystères de sa jambe mignonne. Plus grande et plus forte que sa maîtresse, Noun était habillée et non pas vêtue avec ses parures" (101–02).

18. "Si [Noun] n'eût pas été ivre comme lui, elle eût compris qu'au plus fort de son délire Raymon songeait à une autre. Elle l'eût vu baiser l'écharpe et les rubans qu'avait portés Indiana, respirer les essences qui la lui rappelaient, froisser dans ses mains ardentes l'étoffe qui avait protégé son sein ; mais Noun prenait tous ces transports pour elle-même, lorsque *Raymon ne voyait d'elle que la robe d'Indiana*" (104; emphasis added).

19. See compelling articles by Véronique Machelidon and Pratima Prasad as listed in the works cited.

simulacrum of a presence that dislocates, displaces, and refers beyond itself. The trace has, properly speaking, no place, for effacement belongs to the very structure of the trace" (*Speech* 156). Indiana's trace on the attire that Noun wears "refers beyond itself" to that which is not present: the physically absent Indiana, of course, but, more poignantly, Noun, who, in slipping into the dress not with the intention of replacing but simply of resembling her elegant social superior, unwittingly reveals the impossibility of her own presence, since the racial and class realities inscribed into the garment indicate that Noun is not, and can never be, Indiana. Sand's self-consciously provocative phrase, "all that Raymon saw of her was Indiana's dress," thus proposes that the only dehumanizing form of representation now accorded to Noun is as the material object that denies her any existence: Indiana's dress. Indeed, when Noun tragically drowns herself still wearing the protagonist's white garment, and her floating body is rendered by Sand through Indiana's eyes as nothing more than "a woman's clothes, clothes she knew only too well" (76),[20] the maid's erasure as indicated by the mistress's trace on the twice referenced "clothes," or, narratively, fashion "things," is confirmed.

Going further, as much as Sand appears to invite endless interpretations of this clothing-item-turned-symbolic-field, such as the one we have just performed through a reading attentive to the trace, I would offer that one of fashion's most important functions in this episode relates to Sand's signaling her own status as the novel's storyteller, that is, as a narrative builder seeking authorial recognition. This is indicated through the narrator's intrusion some chapters later when not the white ballgown but rather the borrowed *cloak* reappears, this time worn by its true owner, Indiana. Wishing to shock a confession from Raymon that he slept with Noun on the fateful night examined earlier, Indiana confronts him costumed to evoke the phantom of the creole maid, wearing Noun's typical *île-Bourbonais* headscarf and shrouded in the pelisse as Raymon had last seen the unfortunate servant:

> Indiana had her back turned to him. She was wrapped in a fur-lined cloak; by a strange chance, it was the same one that Noun had chosen at the time of their last rendezvous to go to meet him in the grounds. *I don't know if you remember* that Raymon had had then, for a moment, the improbable idea that the woman wrapped up and concealed in the cloak was Madame Delmare. (139; emphasis added)[21]

The passage is rife with traces, perhaps less in the sense that we have thus far noted but rather in the sense of "tracks," which is another nuance implicit in the

20. "les vêtements d'une femme, des vêtements qu'elle connaissait trop bien" (119).

21. "Indiana lui tournait le dos, elle était enveloppée d'une pelisse doublée de fourrure. Par un étrange hasard, c'était la même que Noun avait prise à l'heure du dernier rendez-vous pour aller à sa rencontre dans le parc. *Je ne sais si vous vous souvenez* que Raymon eut alors pendant un instant l'idée invraisemblable que cette femme enveloppée et cachée était madame Delmare" (190; emphasis added).

Figure 5.3 Pelisse, ca. 1815, French, silk. The Metropolitan Museum of Art, Purchase, Irene Lewisohn Bequest, 1988.

word. Spivak acknowledges this additional meaning in Derrida's term, stating "I stick to 'trace' in my translation [of *De la grammatologie*], because it 'looks the same' as Derrida's word; the reader must remind himself of at least the track, even the spoor, contained within the French word" (xvii). The "spoor" connotation of the French word *trace*, equivalent to the German term *Spur* that Benjamin similarly deploys in his own writings on the trace, refers commonly to the tracks of animals, imprints that register their presence and that indicate their trail. What Sand does here, I argue, is that she uses the fashion "thing"—Indiana's pelisse—to designate the narrative track that has been carefully laid by none other than her. As if drawing on the animal origins of the fur that lines the coat, Sand invokes the spoor imprint of the author, showing her narrative trail's direction in similar manner to the prints of a furry mammal.[22] Thus, when the narrator describes Indiana's choice to don this particular cloak as a "strange chance," the comment might at first strike one as insignificant or even superfluous, since the fact that the cloak is thrown on without forethought does not appear to be relevant to how it later functions in the plot. However, it can be argued that the importance of this short phrase is that it draws on attire to bear witness to the very constructedness of narrative fiction, and, more importantly, to the novelist's essential role in it.

To better understand, let us examine the path of Sand's sartorial track laying by returning to the morning after Raymon's night of passion with Noun, wherein one narrative trail is proposed. Filled with regret at the thought that he has sullied his true intended's bed and dress with the bodily traces of his lust for her chambermaid, Raymon emits an extended melodramatic lament over Indiana's now supposedly compromised purity. Commencing with a classically Romantic exclamation of "Oh Indiana!," Raymon then cries out to the absent woman:

> Reject me . . . I sullied your gown with my accursed breath and your modest dress with my infamous kisses on another's breast . . . and the mad ardor which inflames the limbs of that sensual Creole, will it not come, like Deianeira's tunic, and cling to yours and gnaw at them? (65–66)[23]

Here, traces on fashion (in the sense of residual marks) stand in for two anxieties: 1) that Raymon has polluted Indiana's pure white dress, a stand-in for her honor and chastity, with the fluid remnants of his manhood, and 2) that Noun's feverish ardor (linked to her alleged creole lasciviousness) has similarly transferred to the dress and will now attach itself corrosively to Indiana. To intimate the grave danger of the latter, Raymon cites the ancient myth of Deianeira, wife of Hercules, who mistakenly killed her mighty husband by smearing poisoned blood on his tunic, which then burned the hero so terribly that he perished.

In fact, though, Raymon's ecstatic lament purportedly over Indiana's lost honor is really a self-serving declaration of normative patriarchal social codes: it allows for him to augment the imagined power of his virility, to deflect onto Noun the responsibility for possible harm to the title character, and to fantasize about the virginal

---

22. I thank Sonya Stephens for suggesting a connection between the pelisse's fur lining and the animal spoor metaphor.

23. "Repousse-moi . . . moi qui ai souillée ta robe de mon haleine maudite et ta ceinture pudique de mes infâmes baisers sur le sein d'une autre . . . et l'ardeur insensée qui consume les flancs de cette créole lascive ne viendra-t-elle pas, comme la robe de Déjanire, s'attacher aux tiens pour les ronger ?" (105–06).

Indiana as a sensual creole. Sand's rejection of Raymon's story is made apparent by the narrator, who immediately mocks the speech as a kind of false prayer and then has Noun cheerfully lock the frustrated young man inside Indiana's boudoir against his will. So much for the manly vitality of Raymon's trace, which Sand derides along with the bogus narrative track that he is trying to establish. As for Noun's creole wiles seeping into Indiana's gown, now likened to Deianeira's poisoned tunic, this sartorial suggestion, too, turns out to be a false trail. For, not only will Indiana never again wear the white ballgown adopted by the drowned chambermaid, but when she later envelopes herself in the pelisse, after providing its initial visual reminder of the deceased maid, the cloak seems to hold little trace of the servant who once borrowed it,[24] that job conferred far more forcefully to the lock of hair that Indiana brings with her, having earlier clipped it from the head of Noun's cadaver.[25] Thus, we might ask, in the passage cited earlier depicting Indiana dressed to look like Noun, what is the *narrative function* of the pelisse that the protagonist, by a "strange chance," puts on?

I would offer that the pelisse operates as a disruptive "thing," one intentionally declared a surprising coincidence in service of tracking the author's hand in constructing the story as it develops. Sand does this by using the cloak as the impetus for summarizing the earlier "last rendezvous," that is, the travesty-seduction scene in Indiana's bedroom. The latter is a passage that foregrounds narrative techniques and modes such as theatricality and affect that were among the hallmarks of Romantic melodrama in Sand's time. Simultaneously, it exhibits the same kind of material-detail-oriented realism that was then becoming a preoccupation in novelistic writing, an approach exemplified by Balzac, whose narrative style would later be famously explored by Erich Auerbach in his reading of the object-laden opening chapter of *Le Père Goriot* (a novel the installments of which began appearing two years *after Indiana*, we incidentally note). Sand, backtracking the reader to her earlier, masterfully penned, passage in *Indiana*, inscribes the novel within the Romantic fiction traditions of her day and at the same time draws attention to her adoption of the period's rising narrative techniques, constituting a powerful statement by a first-time novelist. Moreover, Sand underscores the writerliness of this maneuver by prominently inserting the narrator at the start of the phrase "I don't know if you remember," the first-person "I" reminding readers of the narrator and, by extension, of the author's essential part in blazing a text's narrative trail. It is the eternal trace of the *writer* in the text that the narrator privileges by way of fashion, when she or

24. In *Disguise in George Sand's Novels* Françoise Ghillebaert gives a contrasting reading of this scene, suggesting that "the clothes, saturated with the maid's sensuality, now arouse Indiana," and that through the headscarf Noun's passion "begins to infiltrate Indiana's senses and results in bringing out her latent sensuality" (82). For me, Indiana's weak acquiescence to, rather than seduction of, Raymon implies the opposite, that fashion in this instance has *not* passed the sensual trace from servant to mistress.

25. For a detailed analysis of this lock of hair see chapter 5 in Carol Rifelj's *Coiffures: Hair in Nineteenth-Century French Literature and Culture.*

he[26] recounts, and then references a second time, the key sartorial moment describing Indiana's indelible trace on the white gown.

Traces on Emma: Flaubert's *Madame Bovary*

Although *The Arcades Project* includes a handful of direct references to George Sand, with Benjamin relating her to a rather eclectic range of topics, from lesbianism in Baudelaire's writings to cross-dressing in the city to nineteenth-century socialism, perhaps the most striking echo of Sand in Benjamin is inadvertent, appearing in his Exposé of 1935, a text now understood as an intended framework for *The Arcades Project* as a whole. In this Exposé Benjamin criticizes fashion, arguing that it is imbued with "false consciousness" deriving from its deceptive promise to provide newness. His remark that "this semblance of the new is reflected, like one mirror in another, in the semblance of the ever recurrent" (11) uncannily recalls the sartorial mirror episode from Sand's *Indiana*, recasting the endless reflections of Noun wearing Indiana's fashionable dress not as the sensual fantasy that they represent for Raymon but rather as a horrifying image of that which never changes, or the "hell-time" of modernity, as Benjamin pessimistically put it. As this example implies, Benjamin's interests in fashion involved the ways in which it could be instrumental to his thinking about nonlinear history, which had become one of his major theoretical preoccupations. But at the same time, as Boscagli has explored, Benjamin's writings are grounded in materiality, in objects and the phenomenological experience—visual, haptic, aural, and, ultimately, synesthetic—of the physical manifestations of modernism that he chose to focus on, from children's toys, to *bibelots*, to silent films, to architectural structures, and so on. Regarding the fashion object specifically, Benjamin's sartorial remark that "the eternal is in any case far more the ruffle on a dress than some idea" (69),[27] indeed seems to privilege materiality—the aforementioned ruffle—as an overlooked but essential counterpart to the conceptuality of ideas.

Benjamin's critical interest in the material aspects of fashion is helpful to us particularly when considered alongside his thoughts on the trace, with the caveat that his writings on the latter give it multiple, even contradictory, meanings. In Convolute I, "The Interior, The Trace," for instance, he concentrates on the evidentiary quality of traces left on furniture in nineteenth-century interiors, noting, "Plush—the material in which traces are left especially easily" (*Arcades* 222). To add to Miriam Bratu Hansen's suggestion that the trace is here "rejected as the fetishizing

26. This is not to reductively suggest that author and narrator are one in the same; simply that the narrator (whoever he or she is) constantly calls attention throughout *Indiana* to authorship. For the intriguing proposition that the novel might be told from Ralph's point of view see "Who Is the Narrator in *Indiana*?" by Peter Dayan. Underscoring the writer in her fiction might be seen as a counterpoint to Sand's use of novelistic techniques when rendering her real life in letters and memoirs, as Anne McCall's work on epistolary autobiography has persuasively established.

27. For an expanded gloss of this quote by Benjamin, see Vinken.

signature of the bourgeois interior" (340), to my mind it seems equally related to a Foucauldian, surveilling type of bureaucracy, for, in what he then refers to as his "theory of the trace" (*Arcades* 227), Benjamin also cites the recording of government registers and the rise of organized administration as key examples. Opposite to these fairly negative connotations, in his essay "The Storyteller" Benjamin writes that "traces of the storyteller cling to the story the way the handprints of the potter cling to the clay vessel" (*Illuminations* 92), nostalgically celebrating the trace as the raconteur's unique mark on literature, a type of craftsmanship that seemed woefully under threat in the age of technological reproduction.

As we will see, these assorted functions of Benjamin's trace—as evidence, tools of surveillance, and marks of literary craftsmanship—inform depictions of clothing from that most fashion-forward novel of the mid-nineteenth century: Gustave Flaubert's *Madame Bovary* (1856). In terms of investigative evidence, for instance, traces on fashions in Flaubert's masterpiece repeatedly bear witness to the central "crime" of the text, to wit, the protagonist's infidelity. This is because, with some frequency, the garments and accessories that Emma wears during extramarital encounters typically end up besmirched: she arrives to a tryst with her frock covered in morning dew, prompting Rodolphe's exclamation, "Ah! your dress is wet" (134);[28] the habitual liaisons that then follow render her boots "all coated with mud—the mud of the rendezvous" (152);[29] during a tête-à-tête with her lover Emma has a nosebleed that will stain her handkerchief "with pale drops" (161).[30] Should Flaubert have been called to write detective mysteries in the style of some of his nineteenth-century contemporaries, such traces surely would have made for compelling forensic evidence to be gathered through investigative observation and used as proof of the title character's illicit adultery.

However, I argue that, for Flaubert, these traces on Emma's garments do not function principally as evidence of criminal acts in service of condemning her. Instead, such spots, clots, and drops on clothing seem more to be markers of the human experience, one that in Emma's case is relatively banal as opposed to remarkable but, nonetheless, is narratively recorded. Understood in this way, fashion traces in *Madame Bovary* highlight not the story but the storyteller, a writer achieving that unique mark of authorship that Benjamin praised, a writer for whom not plot but narrative craftsmanship is arguably the primary impetus for the telling of Emma's story. Let us consider, for example, Flaubert's account of the Bovarys' return from the Marquis d'Andervilliers's ball wherein we find Emma reverently stowing away her party clothes and we learn that traces of wax from the Marquis's polished wood floor have yellowed the soles of her shoes:

> She devoutly put away in her drawers her beautiful dress, down to the satin shoes whose soles were yellowed with the slippery wax of the

28. "Ah ! Ta robe est mouillée !" (441).
29. "tout empâtées de crotte—la crotte des rendez-vous" (463).
30. "de gouttelettes pâles" (475).

> dancing floor. *Her heart resembled them*: in its contact with wealth, *something had rubbed off on it that could not be removed* . . . some of the details [of the ball] faded but *the wistful feeling* remained with her. (49; emphasis added)[31]

The traces of wax on Emma's footwear, we are told, have a permanent quality, the yellow polish a metaphor, Flaubert specifies, for the "wistful feeling" that "could not be removed," which figuratively stands in for the unending "search for love's passion" (499), in Naomi Schor's words, that Emma's story ultimately recounts. The author's comparison of the stained slippers to his protagonist's heart in the phrase "her heart resembled them" is also a poignant comment on Emma's emotive center, upon which eternal longing has now been inscribed. The yellowish trace on Emma's footwear thereby highlights one of the main concerns of the novel as a whole, which is not Emma's fate per se but, rather, how to narrate affective tensions when desire is constantly thwarted by the impossibility of lasting human intimacy. Building on the fashion-inflected episode of Emma's waxy soles, this preoccupation will run as a sartorial leitmotif throughout the text, reintroduced in descriptions involving dress that communicate in material terms both the prospect and the unfeasibility of human contact.

For instance, during her dizzying waltz with the Vicomte, the activation of passion that Emma desperately seeks is carried out not through fleshly contact but rather by the grazing together of garments, as, Flaubert writes, "the train of Emma's dress caught against his trousers" (46).[32] Similarly, Emma's first amorous encounter with Rodolphe in the woods occurs initially through their clothes, the episode encapsulated in the phrase "the cloth of her dress clung to the velvet of his coat" (130)[33] that leads to the sexual act. Tellingly, however, if fashion in these instances communicates emotional charges—experienced like static electric shocks produced through clinging, rubbing fabrics—such clothing encounters, in the end, do not seem to hold a trace that might pass from one character to another, as in the case of Sand's *Indiana*. Instead, traces on garments, such as the mud and dew previously mentioned, come rather from the earthly environment surrounding the title character, inviting a reading of the relationship, mediated by fashion, between Emma and the natural world.

This connection is introduced as early in the text as the protagonists' wedding, a scene rendered by Flaubert in extensive sartorial detail that crystalizes metonymically in his portrayal of the snaking marriage processional from *mairie* to church

31. "Elle serra pieusement dans la commode sa belle toilette et jusqu'à ses souliers de satin, dont la semelle s'était jaunie à la cire glissante du parquet. *Son coeur était comme eux*: au frottement de la richesse, *il s'était placé dessus quelque chose qui ne s'effacerait pas* . . . quelques détails s'en allèrent, mais *le regret lui resta*" (342; emphasis added).

32. "la robe d'Emma, par le bas, s'éraflait au pantalon" (339).

33. "le drap de sa robe s'accrochait au velours de l'habit" (438).

Figure 5.4 Evening slippers, 1845–65, probably French, silk. Brooklyn Museum Costume Collection at The Metropolitan Museum of Art, Gift of the Brooklyn Museum, 2009; Gift of the estate of Sarah B. Russell, 1956.

to reception as a "colored scarf,"[34] that is, the wedding itself as an item of dress. Fashion as a metaphor for matrimony is reinforced, when, during the course of the Bovarys' scarf-like marital parade, prickly weeds affix themselves to the trailing hem of Emma's wedding gown: "Emma's dress, too long, trailed a little on the ground; from time to time she stopped to pull it up, and then delicately, with her gloved hands, she picked off the coarse grass and the thistles" (25).[35] In addition to prefiguring the traces of country fields that will stick to Emma's garments during future trips to visit her lover Rodolphe, thereby anticipating the protagonist's acts of adultery, ironically, on the day consecrating her marriage, the thistles in this early chapter communicate Emma's link to the novel's living ecosystem, the blades of grass and weeds clinging to her skirt like the mud and dewdrops that later attach to her boots and her dress. Thus, it would seem fitting that, at a corresponding narrative bookend to Emma's nuptials, that is to say, at the time of her death, the protagonist appears to return to the environment that had all along been attaching itself to her clothing. It is as if earthly, water, and plant life had been exerting tiny trace pulls on her by way of her garments throughout the novel until, finally, in the end, as Charles gazes upon her funeral-ready corpse, we read:

> The watered satin of her gown shimmered white as moonlight. Emma was disappearing, lost beneath it; and it seemed to him that, spreading beyond her own self, she blended confusedly with everything around

34. "écharpe de couleur" (316).

35. "La robe d'Emma, trop longue, traînait un peu par le bas ; de temps à autre, elle s'arrêtait pour la tirer, et alors délicatement, de ses doigts gantés, elle enlevait les herbes rudes avec les petits dards des chardons" (316).

her—the silence, the night, the passing wind, the damp odors rising from the ground. (263; translation slightly modified)[36]

As the shiny white gown envelopes her body, Emma seems, from Charles's point of view ("it seemed to him"), to merge synesthetically through the shimmers of her satin dress with the ethereal elements of nature: moonlight, wind, scents of the earth, the silent air of night. Through fashion, it appears, Emma is being released to the atmosphere to live on eternally as a part of the larger natural environment. This lyrical passage can be contrasted with the blunt and depressing sartorial phrase that earlier had reduced "her whole existence"[37] to "her dresses, the linen, the dressing-room" (234)[38] and had compared these items to a lifeless cadaver. Rather than reading garments through the morbid undertones evoked by the earlier autopsy metaphor, the later passage as seen by Charles underscores that clothing, among Emma's dearest possessions, might signal a continuation of her human life, the organic traces that lingered on her attire throughout the recounting of her story bearing witness to the fact that Emma was there, that she had lived, and, perhaps, in some new atmospheric form, might live on.

At the same time, we note that the serenity of Charles's vision is compromised by the narrator, who problematizes the image's airy peacefulness with the inclusion of the troubling terms "disappearing" and "lost," as though to suggest that Emma's funerary outfit harbors a destructive force that is in some way dissolving or, perhaps more accurately, vaporizing, its wearer. Moreover, the passage includes the adverb "confusedly," a term having unsettling undertones that disrupt the otherwise tranquil thought of Emma's gentle passing into the night wind. These disturbing details are the omniscient narrator's interjections, traces of the storyteller that remind readers not only that the literary universe—the allegedly "natural" or "realistic" world depicted—is still fundamentally a construction, but also that all is due to the writer, who invents and represents this fictional world. What I wish to highlight is that, for Flaubert and other nineteenth-century novelists, traces on clothing are repeatedly deployed as such reminders of the author's fingerprint on the narrative, or, to recall Benjamin's formulation cited earlier, the "traces of the storyteller cling[ing] to the story the way the handprints of the potter cling to the clay vessel."

In fact, the wax traces on Emma's dancing shoes that launched our discussion of *Madame Bovary* might be seen to exemplify the very production of narrative with which Flaubert was painstakingly engaged during this period: his well-studied *style indirect libre*, or indirect free discourse, a hybrid structure of first-person perspective and third-person omniscience through which, depending on the critic, affect

36. "Des moires frissonnaient sur la robe de satin, blanche comme un clair de lune. Emma disparaissait dessous ; et il lui semblait que, s'épandant au dehors d'elle-même, elle se perdait confusément dans l'entourage des choses, dans le silence, dans la nuit, dans le vent qui passait, dans les senteurs humides qui montaient" (596).

37. "son existence" (560).

38. "ses robes, le linge, le cabinet de toilette" (560).

is expressed and/or annihilated.[39] Of interest to us is how Flaubert turns to fashion "things" inflected with traces to communicate the novel's merging narrative points of view, that is, the way in which the encounters portrayed through the materiality of clothing items such as those studied in this chapter—floor polish rubbed onto *souliers*, thistles embedded in skirts, mud caked on boot soles—also perform the textual friction that Flaubert was toiling diligently in these years to master through the active development of what would become his signature narrative style.

One passage culled from many possible examples suffices to illustrate how fashion and Flaubert's *style indirect libre* are especially self-complementary. During the initial stages of the Bovarys' marriage we read that, each evening, Charles comes home to the pleasant discovery of "a well-dressed woman, charming and so freshly scented that it was impossible to say where the perfume came from; it might have been her skin that communicated its fragrance to her blouse" (52).[40] Here is the author's classic *style indirect libre*, in which the third-person narrator's objective presentation of Emma ("a well-dressed woman") morphs into Charles's phenomenological absorption of her through smell and his subjective uncertainty about the origins of the scent on her shirt ("it was impossible to say where the perfume came from"). To my mind, the Benjaminian trace of the storyteller lives in Flaubert's final phrase—"it might have been her skin that communicated its fragrance to her blouse"—for if these words on the one hand represent Charles's first-person viewpoint (as the one sniffing and whose nose is mystified), the proposal that Emma's skin might have transferred its trace scent to her blouse is also the narrator's own interjected suggestion. In addition to highlighting the author's trace this interjection makes the case for the evocative storytelling power of the marks that humans leave on the things that touch them intimately, as much on their narratives, for instance, as on their blouses.

If *Madame Bovary* is also about writing style itself, as Schor (511) and others aptly contend, this in turn invites the question of the novel's depiction of authorship. Schor convincingly points out that Emma takes up the role of author in Flaubert's novel (501), but she also mentions another possibility, which is Emma's father, Rouault (509). Rouault is a "poor" writer in the sense that he does not master spelling, but an important one for us given the way in which his textual efforts align him with the kind of trace-laden authorship that we have been examining here. In one of the annual letters that he writes to his daughter, for instance, the trace of authorship mediated by clothing is made quite literal:

---

39. As Jonathan D. Culler writes, for instance, for some, Flaubert's *style indirect libre* "reduces and deadens by omitting the effective and spontaneous engagement of characters in speech" (490). Gilbert D. Chaitin has helpfully outlined the ways in which numerous influential literary critics, including Auerbach, Lukács, Sartre, and Genette, among others, have rigorously studied this style characteristic not just of Flaubert but of many nineteenth-century novelists.

40. "une femme en toilette fine, charmante et sentant frais, à ne savoir même d'où venait cette odeur, ou si ce n'était pas sa peau qui parfumait sa chemise" (346).

FIGURE 5.5 Styles worn by "well-dressed" women of Emma's day. Dress, ca. 1858, French, silk. The Metropolitan Museum of Art, Gift of Frederic Edward Gibert, 1962.

> She held the coarse paper in her fingers for some minutes. A continuous stream of spelling mistakes ran through the letter . . . the writing had been dried with ashes from the hearth, for *a little grey powder slipped from the letter on her dress*, and she almost thought she saw her father bending over the hearth to take up the tongs. (140; emphasis added)[41]

Here, again, the fashion thing is marked by a foreign matter ("a little grey powder"), but this time the substance does double duty: it is both the trace memory of her father—the image of Rouault leaning over the fire—slipping into Emma's mind like powder onto her dress, and a literal fixer of the writer's written word, which is the function of the ash-producing cinders that dry Rouault's ink permanently to the page. Although Flaubert and Rouault are not "authors" of the same kind, and we are

41. "Elle resta quelques minutes à tenir entre ses doigts ce gros papier. Les fautes d'orthographe s'y enlaçaient les unes aux autres . . . on avait séché l'écriture avec les cendres du foyer, car *un peu de poussière grise glissa de la lettre sur sa robe*, et elle crut presque apercevoir son père se courbant vers l'âtre pour saisir les pincettes" (448–49; emphasis added).

Figure 5.6 Agricultural workers in blue smocks. Léon Lhermitte: *La Paye des moissonneurs*, 1882 (RF 333), Musée d'Orsay. © RMN-Grand Palais / Art Resource, NY / photograph by Hervé Lewandowski.

to be wary of a naive reading of Emma's quasi-literate father as an allegory for the person who penned *Madame Bovary*, we can posit, nonetheless, a basic connection of the two men through writing, one that is foregrounded by Flaubert in the detail of the ashy trace that Rouault's letter leaves on Emma's garment.[42]

In particular, we are focusing on Rouault-the-writer as opposed to other characters who take up the pen in Flaubert's novel, because Emma's father is the one subjected most conspicuously to an important reverse sartorial trace: an instance in which a garment is not marked but is itself the agent doing the marking. In the novel's penultimate chapter, following Emma's funeral and as Rouault prepares to depart Yonville (along with the narrative), we read: "Old Rouault put on his blue smock. It was new, and as he had repeatedly wiped his eyes on the sleeves during his journey, the dye had stained his face, and traces of tears lined the layer of dust

42. Perhaps, in his own way, Flaubert here anticipates Derrida's later writings on the eternalness of cinders, which take up Nietzsche's concept of the "eternal recurrence of the same," itself interpreting the universe as ash that perpetually (re)cycles living and nonliving matter. In *Cinders* (*Feu la cendre*) Derrida implies that the cinder might be another formulation for his notion of the trace (*Cinders* 43).

that covered it" (267).[43] We recall that this passage is part of an extraordinary chapter that begins with the retroactive story of Rouault's frantic journey to Yonville, a passage in which *style indirect libre* vividly communicates the father's hallucinatory panic and denial over Emma's death and in which narrative style, that is, the way that the story is told, seems at least as important as the plot's advancement. It is, in other words, a chapter in which writing itself takes center stage. Thus, as the dye from his new shirt stains Rouault's skin, and his tear tracks are recorded in a thin layer of "*poussière*"—the same word used to describe what fell out of his letter and now covers his face—we find at the end of this chapter a complete convergence of three of the novel's recurring concerns: the writing process, sartorial materiality, and the fashion trace. It is, we might conclude, no coincidence that this is also a passage communicating a link between the production of narrative and the eternal, for there are lines left by tears on the ink-like blue of clothing dye smudging Rouault's face, and it is these lines, we understand, that constitute the script that "writes" the unending story of a father's infinite grief.

This chapter has posited that the "eternal" that Baudelaire famously imagined as the dialectical counterpart to the "ephemeral" in modernity is present in nineteenth-century realist fiction through that which expresses both the transitoriness of the human body and authorial permanence in the narrative: the fashion trace. For one final example let us end where we began, that is, with Maupassant's *Bel-Ami* antihero, Georges Duroy. Readers will recall that early on the novel features a suit, specifically, the eveningwear that Duroy is told to rent so that he may attend the Forestiers' soirée. The garment serves its intended purpose by allowing the now-dapper protagonist his first crucial access into upper-class society. However, as hired clothing worn by countless other people, his formalwear is implicitly covered in the traces of others. These ghostly marks of former wearers seem at first invisible in the text, unmentioned, for instance, by Maupassant's narrator and unremarked by Duroy. Nonetheless, the reader intuits that these traces are there, sartorial remainders of stories already written onto the garments that harbor an endless string of narratives in which Duroy's story is but the next. As this and the examples previously studied by Sand and Flaubert indicate, the self-perpetuating "eternalness" in fiction of the 1800s found an effective metaphor in fashion. Traces from a garment's former owner, traces from others encountered, traces from the natural world, traces from oneself—these are the material manifestations of Baudelaire's ephemeral-eternal, ones embedded through a variety of techniques into the worn stories written by some of the most influential authors of nineteenth-century French literary realism.

43. "Le père Rouault repassa sa blouse bleue. Elle était neuve, et, comme il s'était, pendant la route, souvent essuyé les yeux avec les manches, elle avait déteint sur sa figure ; et la trace des pleurs y faisait des lignes dans la couche de poussière qui la salissait" (601).

Works Cited

Barthes, Roland. *Système de la mode*. Seuil, 1967.

Baudelaire, Charles. *Œuvres complètes*. Gallimard-Pléiade, 1961.

———. *The Painter of Modern Life and Other Essays*. Translated by Jonathan Mayne. Phaidon, 2008.

Bell, David F. *Real Time: Accelerating Narrative from Balzac to Zola*. U of Illinois P, 2004.

Benjamin, Walter. *The Arcades Project*. Translated by Howard Eiland and Kevin McLaughlin. Harvard UP, 1999.

———. *Illuminations*. Translated by Harry Zohn, edited by Hannah Arendt. Schocken Books, 2007.

Booker, John T. "*Indiana* and *Madame Bovary*: Intertextual Echoes." *Nineteenth-Century French Studies*, vol. 31, no. 3/4, 2003, pp. 226–36.

Boscagli, Maurizia. *Stuff Theory: Everyday Objects, Radical Materialism*. Bloomsbury, 2014.

Bowles, Hamish. "Bringing Back the Magic." *Vogue*, Mar. 2015, pp. 528–35.

Bray, Patrick M. *The Novel Map: Space and Subjectivity in Nineteenth-Century French Fiction*. Northwestern UP, 2013.

Brown, Bill. "Thing Theory." *Critical Inquiry*, vol. 28, no.1, 2001, pp. 1–22.

Chaitin, Gilbert D. "Listening Power: Flaubert, Zola, and the Politics of *Style Indirect Libre*." *The French Review*, vol. 72, no. 6, 1999, pp. 1023–27.

Colaiacomo, Paola. "Fashion's Model Bodies: A Genealogy." *Accessorizing the Body: Habits of Being I*, edited by Cristina Giorcelli and Paula Rabinowitz. U of Minnesota P, 2011, pp. 23–32.

Culler, Jonathan D. "From *Flaubert: The Uses of Uncertainty*." *Madame Bovary*. Translated by Eleanor Marx Aveling, revised by Paul de Man, edited by Margaret Cohen. W.W. Norton, 2004, pp. 479–91.

Dayan, Peter. "Who Is the Narrator in *Indiana*?" *French Studies*, vol. 52, no. 2, 1998, pp. 152–61.

Derrida, Jacques. *Cinders*. Translated by Ned Lukacher. U of Nebraska P, 1987.

———. *Of Grammatology*. Translated by Gayatri Chakravorty Spivak. Johns Hopkins UP, 1976.

———. Speech and Phenomena *and Other Essays on Husserl's Theory of Signs*. Translated by David B. Allison. Northwestern UP, 1973.

Duffy, Larry. *Le Grand Transit Moderne: Mobility, Modernity, and French Naturalist Fiction*. Rodopi, 2005.

Flaubert, Gustave. *Madame Bovary. Œuvres Complètes*, tome 1. Gallimard, 1951.

———. *Madame Bovary*. Translated by Eleanor Marx Aveling, revised by Paul de Man, edited by Margaret Cohen. W.W. Norton, 2004.

Ghillebaert, Françoise. *Disguise in George Sand's Novels*. Peter Lang, 2009.

Gill, Alison. "Jacques Derrida: Fashion Under Erasure." *Thinking Through Fashion: A Guide to Key Theorists*, edited by Agnes Rocamora and Anneke Smelik. I. B. Tauris, 2016, pp. 251–68.

Green, Anne. *Changing France: Literature and Material Culture in the Second Empire*. Anthem, 2011.

Hansen, Mariam Bratu. "Benjamin's Aura." *Critical Inquiry*, vol. 34, 2008, pp. 336–75.

Harkness, Nigel, and Jacinta Wright. "Introduction." *George Sand: Intertextualité et polyphonie I. Palimpsests, échanges, réécritures*, edited by Nigel Harkness and Jacinta Wright. Peter Lang, 2011, pp. 1–19.

Hiner, Susan. *Accessories to Modernity: Fashion and the Feminine in Nineteenth-Century France*. U of Pennsylvania P, 2010.

Hoog, Marie-Jacques. "George Sand: *Être/Paraître* ('To Be/To Appear')." *George Sand Papers: Conference Proceedings, 1978*. AMS UP, 1978, pp. 83–92.

Jameson, Fredric. *The Antinomies of Realism*. Verso, 2013.

Lehmann, Ulrich. *Tigersprung: Fashion in Modernity*. MIT P, 2000.

Machelidon, Véronique. "George Sand's Praise of Creoleness: Race, Slavery and (In)Visibility in *Indiana*." *George Sand Studies*, vol. 28, 2009, pp. 27–45.

Maupassant, Guy de. *Bel-Ami*. Translated by Douglas Parmée. Penguin, 1975.

———. *Romans*. Gallimard-Pléiade, 1987.

McCall, Anne E. "Of Textual Demise and Literary Renewal: George Sand and the Problematics of Epistolary Autobiography." *a/b: Auto/Biography Studies*, vol. 9, no. 2, 1994, pp. 212–30.

Newmark, Kevin. "Now You See It, Now You Don't: Baudelaire's *Modernité*." *Nineteenth-Century French Studies*, vol. 44, nos. 1 & 2, 2015–16, pp. 1–24.

Prasad, Pratima. "(De)masking the 'Other' Woman in George Sand's *Indiana*." *Romance Languages Annual*, vol. 8, 1997, pp. 104–09.

Reddy, William M. "The Structure of a Cultural Crisis: Thinking About Cloth in France Before and After the Revolution." *The Social Life of Things: Commodities in Cultural Perspective*, edited by Arjun Appadurai, Cambridge UP, 2013, pp. 261–84.

Rifelj, Carol. *Coiffures: Hair in Nineteenth-Century French Literature and Culture*. U of Delaware P, 2010.

Sand, Georges. *Indiana*. Folio Classique, 1984.

———. *Indiana*. Translated by Sylvia Raphael. Oxford UP, 2008.

Schor, Naomi. "Restricted Thematics: *Madame Bovary*." *Madame Bovary*. Translated by Eleanor Marx Aveling, revised by Paul de Man, edited by Margaret Cohen. W.W. Norton, 2004, pp. 499–511.

Spivack, Emily. *Worn Stories*. Princeton Architectural, 2014.

Troy, Nancy J. *Couture Culture: A Study in Modern Art and Fashion*. MIT P, 2003.

Vinken, Barbara. "Eternity—A Frill on the Dress." *Fashion Theory*, vol. 1, no.1, 1997, pp. 59–68.

CHAPTER 6

BEYOND THE SHADOW OF THE VEIL

Claude Monet's *The Beach at Trouville*

Marni Reva Kessler

For Linda Nochlin

In *The Beach at Trouville* of 1870 (fig. 6.1), Claude Monet represents a close-up view of two seated women who shield themselves from the sun, wind, and blowing sand with hats and parasols. Across the unusually empty stretch of beach behind them, we see a few barely suggested chairs, beyond which the squat form of a bathing tent meets the more distant horizon. What must be sailboats or fishing boats dot the water's edge, and, further out, a horizontal streak of leaden gray references what could be a passing ship. Closer in at the right, a flag billows atop a thin pole and a woman is recognizable as such because her weightless white dress is buffeted by the gusty wind. Ribbons of fleecy clouds mingle and whirl above like a material presence, nearly obfuscating the blue sky and filling almost half of the composition. Not one of the elements in Monet's small canvas is incidental. He establishes this context so that we fully understand that this painting is meant to depict a partially sunny and extremely windy day at a beach resort, in this case the very fashionable Trouville, formerly a small fishing village along the coast of Normandy.[1]

Like so many others who came for the socializing, casinos, and beautiful beach, Monet and his new wife Camille stayed in Trouville during July and August of 1870 following their June 28th nuptials in Paris.[2] While there, he painted at least nine known canvases outdoors, three of which feature Camille as a quintessentially elegant vacationer and four of which present more distant panoramic views of the chic strollers and idlers who populated the terrace and balconies of the recently

1. For more information on the history of Trouville and its status in 1870, see: Baudre; A. Joanne; P. B. Joanne; Nochlin 158–72; Herbert; Lemonedes et al.; and Hamilton 49–61.

2. The couple officially wed in a small ceremony on June 28, 1870 at the City Hall in the eighth arrondissement in Paris (Wildenstein, *Claude Monet* 46).

FIGURE 6.1 Claude Monet, *The Beach at Trouville*, 1870, oil on canvas, 14.96 x 18.3 in. © The National Gallery, London.

opened posh Hôtel des Roches Noires and the beach and boardwalk looking toward the hotel, in front of which the colorful flags of various countries regularly flew. Not one of the artist's canvases betrays the dark reality that loomed for the merrymakers in Trouville during the summer of 1870: the imminent outbreak of the Franco-Prussian War in late July of 1870—and its attendant fears of conscription for younger men like Monet[3]—which led to the dramatic downfall of Napoleon III's Second Empire and made way for the devastating Prussian siege of Paris that lasted from mid-September until late January of 1871. Nor do Monet's paintings from this summer reveal his own dangerously precarious financial situation, one that was so

3. Wildenstein points out that Monet had initially hoped that his marriage and earlier military service in North Africa would exempt him from conscription. By September, when it became obvious that the government was more interested in recruiting those who had already served in the army, Monet chose to flee to London, where Camille and Jean met him in October. The family returned to France in late 1871, after a brief stay in the Netherlands (Wildenstein, *Monet ou le triomphe* 46 and 51–52).

serious, in fact, that he was unable to pay his family's hotel bill.[4] Instead, all is buoyant and sunlit and the stylish people who inhabit his canvases sit quietly, swim, read, sew, promenade, chat, and play.

For *The Beach at Trouville*, Monet trains his lens on the foreground of the composition. The figure on the left is Camille,[5] and the woman slightly further back and cut off at the right edge is likely the wife of his friend and mentor, the painter Eugène Boudin, whom Monet first met when he was a teenager in 1858.[6] The Boudins, too, stayed at Trouville for part of the summer of 1870, and we know that the older couple spent a great deal of time with the newlyweds. So, it stands to reason that Camille's pictorial companion could well be Marie-Anne Boudin. Regardless of her identity, though, this figure is clearly not Monet's focus. Her facial features are, at best, synoptic. Elliptical brown strokes stand for her downcast eyes, a wisp of brown indicates her nose, and two mauve-ish lines represent the bare minimum of a mouth and the recessed space above her chin. Asymmetrical smears of rosy pigment lie unblended across her tanned cheeks. She is dressed in a black dress with a small white collar, a schematic black hat, and a black parasol that she props on her right shoulder. She exists as a veritable monochromatic blot in a scene that is otherwise filled with the light and airy hues of the cool beige sand and the frothy churn of a cloudy sky. The vibrant blue scribble of the bow at her neck, powdery

4. The Monets did not stay at the Hôtel des Roches Noires, which Linda Nochlin describes as having had "a specific aura of *arrivisme*," and instead took up residence at the much less expensive, though nearby, Hôtel Tivoli (158). For details on the cost of both hotels, see Herbert 138n26.

5. Although she has not been definitively identified as such, I am confident that this figure represents Camille Monet. In two of the eight other paintings Monet executed at the beach at Trouville between July and August of 1870, a similarly dressed woman is firmly recognized as Camille. Furthermore, finances were tight for the young couple at this time, and so Monet would not have been able to hire a model. Linda Nochlin also interprets the woman as Camille (167), as does Robert L. Herbert (26). Richard R. Brettell makes the good point that "although the figures [in Monet's paintings from the summer of 1870 in Trouville] surely include Camille and her friends, the aim of Monet's transcription was clearly not portraiture" (119).

6. The wall text for the painting at the National Gallery London informs us that "the woman on the right may be the wife of Eugène Boudin." To support her reading of this figure as Mme Boudin, Vivien Hamilton cites a letter from Boudin to Monet dated July 14, 1897, in which the former waxes nostalgic about their time together in Trouville during August of 1870. He writes that he had "'kept . . . a drawing which shows you on the beach. There are three women in white in it, still young. Two of them have died, my poor Marie-Anne and your wife. . . . Little Jean is playing in the sand and his father is sitting on the ground with a sketch in his hand . . . it is a souvenir of that period which I have always treasured'" (Hamilton 46). Linda Nochlin speculates that this figure may be an older friend or the Monets' son's nurse, which is compelling since, given Monet's esteem for Boudin, it would seem that he would have chosen to represent his mentor's wife in a less summarized manner (165). Robert L. Herbert calls her "a woman who assumes the role of a plain older companion, a familiar figure in passages on tourism in nineteenth-century novels" (26).

lilac white of her pointed collar, silvered sheen of the handle of her parasol, and the feathery gray of the needlepoint or sewing upon which she works[7] provide the only real optical relief for the unexpected starkness of the right side of the canvas.

There is something incongruous about this figure in her unrelentingly dark ensemble.[8] Even the places where Monet scumbles the black paint to reveal primed canvas—particularly across the top of her noticeably unornamented hat, parasol lining, and areas of the dress—barely lighten the overall visual effect of Mme Boudin, whose pitchy form only amplifies the luminosity of the bright star of the image, Camille Monet. These women are nearly inverses of one another, two points on a carefully calibrated black, gray, and white spectrum. An unoccupied chair sits at a slant between them, an object that serves both to separate and to bridge the two women. What Linda Nochlin has read as a child's drying slippers, which would likely have belonged to the Monets' son Jean, born out of wedlock three years earlier, hang on the ear of the chair (165). Light limns its upper and middle cross rails in impastoed sweeps of off-white and beige, and a dark gray swipe marks the center rung like a fragment of an idea that leads our eye to the slashes of a similar hue that define the underside of Camille's right arm and the three creases that score her skirt beneath it. On the chair's crudely articulated seat, a maroon object reads as a workbag for Mme Boudin's needlework. But what is most striking formally about the empty chair is the way that its taupe paint and the jagged rectangular views of sand between its cross rails—each edged by the soft gray of the primed canvas—mellows the black of Mme Boudin's garment into the lighter tones of Camille's.

Wearing a pale gray muslin dress trimmed in deeper gray and white ruffles and a black sash that ties at the back, Camille Monet is the epitome of sensible 1870 beachside chic. Her brunette hair is gathered loosely at the nape of her neck in a modish *chignon*, a black choker peeks from beneath her collar, and a small colorfully flowered *chapeau de paille* is perched obliquely on her head, its front dip grazing the bridge of her nose and eyebrow. Like so many of the summer hats advertised in the plates of popular fashion journals such as *Journal des demoiselles* during the summer of 1870 (fig. 6.2), Camille's petit chapeau is more decorative than serviceable. Her parasol, which she holds at an angle, does the real work of shading her from the sun. Its cheerful periwinkle underside distantly echoes not

---

7. Some have construed that the object that Mme Boudin holds is a newspaper, but its shape and color, along with the position of her one visible, though unfinished hand, lead me to conclude that she is working on some kind of sewing or stitchery. For an alternative reading to mine, see Brown 23–24.

8. This figure is sometimes interpreted as being in mourning, however it would not have been too uncommon for a woman to don a black dress for the beach. Monet's friend Boudin, who tended to take more distant views of his subjects, often represented women wearing black at the beach alongside others in gray or white. See, for example, his *The Beach at Trouville* from 1863 (National Gallery of Art, Washington, DC) and *Approaching Storm* of 1864 (The Art Institute of Chicago).

FIGURE 6.2 *Journal des demoiselles*, summer 1870, hand-colored lithograph, 10½ x 6¾ in. Costume Institute Fashion Plate Collection, Gift of Lee Simonson. Digital Collections of the Thomas J. Watson Library, Metropolitan Museum of Art.

just the unclouded parts of the cerulean sky and the soft gray of the water, but also the deeper hue of her cuff and bodice ruffles. This lavender blue also tightens the frame around Camille's head and even more closely refers to the small cobalt blossoms—one more defined than the other—tucked in among yellow and orange-red flowers, ribbons of black lace and smoother silk, and lengths of green vine, the embellishments that adorn the body and circumference of her plaited straw hat.

This parasol serves many functions pictorially, not the least of which is the way that it casts much of Camille as she sits in profile, in shadow. Stray flickers of light scatter across the front of her lap and the edge of her left cuff in thick smears of white paint. But the rest of her, we infer, because her dress comprises thinner, more matte ashy tones, appears to be protected from the direct rays of the harsh summer sun. And so, we are left with a conundrum: why is the upper two-thirds of the terrain of Camille's face smudged and darkened in such stark contrast to the lighter tanned flesh of her chin, neck, and right ear when Monet otherwise gives us no indication that anything but a uniformly shaded light could be hitting that region. In fact, the only part of Camille to receive uninterrupted sun is the stretch of her skirt where broad strokes of bleached white splash out and overlap one another. So, Monet distinctly parses shadow from light upon Camille's lap, where he juxtaposes viscous white pigment with the otherwise flat and duller gray of her dress. But the visual evidence does not explain the brazen discrepancy between the upper and lower portions of her face. Not surprisingly, scholars have not been able to agree upon a single explanation for this perplexing patch of darkness. Some have argued that Camille wears a veil, while others claim that the area represents shadow.[9] This striking variability in tone is indeed confounding, though its stunning visual effect—and the possible reasons for it—is partly what makes this image so especially intriguing to me. Nevertheless, distinguishing whether Monet depicts a shadow *or* a veil across his wife's eyes and nose is actually not, to my mind, the pressing issue, since, as I will demonstrate, *both* are implied and are, thus, in effect, there, marking the surface of Camille's face.

The Shadow of the Veil

According to art and cultural critic Charles Blanc in his *L'Art dans la parure et dans le vêtement*, the shadow created by a parasol upon a face was meant to be, like the tangible object itself, captivating, an essential ingredient, in fact, of a fashionable woman's toilette. He understands that it is not the parasol alone that generates its allure, but rather that it is its fusion with the shade that it casts upon the visage that makes it so alluring. Blanc writes:

---

9. The wall text that accompanies the painting at the National Gallery, London, reads: "The white dashes of paint indicating the dress of the left-hand figure are prominent. They contrast with the shadowed face, probably concealed by a veil . . ."

> Another instrument of their [women's] coquetry is the parasol. Do you think that women imagined it to protect their complexions from the work of the sun? . . . Yes, no doubt, but how many resources give women the need to cast a shadow upon their face, and how many women would be annoyed with the sun if it gave them no reason to protect themselves against its rays! In the work of art, which we call a woman's toilette, the parasol plays the role of *clair-obscur* [light-shadow]. It produces this charming effect that Rubens masterfully imitated in the portrait which is famously known as *Chapeau de paille*, and which consists of effacing the shadows of the face, to marry them with the light and melt the whole in luminous halftones. (*L'Art dans la parure* 268–70)[10]

Blanc further points out that for a parasol to create a pleasing shadow, its lining should be the same color as the woman's dress. However, even if a violet or mauve underside matches a woman's garments, he notes, it could nevertheless negatively alter the appearance of the complexion. As Blanc writes: "Let us recall the law of complementary colors. By casting a violet shade over the face, [the parasol] causes the skin to become colorless and dull, because the more or less yellow tones of the skin, devoured by the violet, are reduced to a neutral tone, to a sad gray, while a parasol lined, for example, in rose de Chine or carnation, would spread on the face a tone of animation and youth" (*L'Art dans la parure* 270).[11]

The lavender underside of Camille's parasol unmistakably does not literally match her light gray dress, though they are certainly related hues. But it would be too facile to assume that Monet was trying to represent the type of unbecoming shadow that Blanc describes when the artist laid that puzzling trapezoid of brownish gray pigment upon his canvas, upon the upper part of his new wife's face. The grammar of the painting alone undercuts such an interpretation. For the position of the women in relation to the sun—which, based on the position of their parasols, we can surmise is behind Mme Boudin and overhead on Camille's left—would not likely yield such a shadow. Since the latter's torso is uniformly shaded, a fact that

---

10. "Un autre instrument de leur coquetterie, c'est l'*ombrelle*. Vous croyez qu'elles l'ont imaginée pour préserver leur teint contre les ardeurs du soleil ? . . . Oui, sans doute, mais que de ressources leur fournit ce besoin de jeter une pénombre sur leur visage, et combien elles en voudraient au soleil s'il ne leur donnait aucun prétexte de se défendre contre ses rayons! Dans cette œuvre d'art qui s'appelle la toilette d'une femme, l'ombrelle joue le rôle du clair-obscur. Elle produit cet effet charmant que Rubens a imité en maître dans le portrait qui est célèbre sous le nom de *Chapeau de paille*, et qui consiste à effacer les ombres de la figure, à les marier avec le clair et à fondre ainsi le tout dans une demi-teinte lumineuse." All translations, unless otherwise noted, are mine.

11. "Rappelons-nous la loi des couleurs complémentaires. En mettant comme une gaze de violet sur le visage, on se fait une peau incolore et terne, parce que les tons plus ou moins jaunes de la chair, dévorés par le violet, se réduisent à une teinte neutre, à un gris triste, tandis qu'une ombrelle doublée, par exemple, en soie rose de Chine ou rouge-in-carnat, répandrait sur la figure une teinte d'animation et de jeunesse."

Monet makes blatant by so flamboyantly delineating the sun's action upon her skirt in sculptural licks of white paint, the sun should have cast the whole—and not just part—of her face into shadow. Things simply do not add up. But this is exactly my point: the artist's formal choices resist the possibility of a too literal analysis not just of the full painting, but also of this inscrutable passage. And so, it is most useful, I think, to imagine that Monet meant to represent both a shadow and the veil Camille might have worn on those breezy summer days when she sat for his painting.

To be sure, veils were fashionable accessories that would have been donned by respectable women both in the city and also at the seaside at the time. As I argued in *Sheer Presence: The Veil in Manet's Paris*, this garment became popular in the capital city particularly during the Second Empire and early Third Republic for a wide variety of reasons, chief among them, as protection from the dust generated by the renovations of the city under the Baron Haussmann, to distinguish class, create an ideal of feminine youthfulness, and to introduce an indirect reference to the Muslim veil worn in the French colonies to everyday Parisian life.[12] And at the seashore, more densely woven veils could be especially practical, as they would guard not only the sun but also all but the finest grains of sand from the face. A signifying accessory, in life as in visual representation, the veil was multilayered, its concrete uses not distinguishable from its myriad meanings and infinite effects. In other words, the materiality of the veil is inseparable from its work and the ever-shifting and ineffable shadows it casts. So, whether represented physically and/or metaphorically invoked, a veil falls across the upper part of Camille's face in *The Beach at Trouville*, and this understanding, to me, is essential to unpacking this spectacular yet quiet image of two women enjoying the filtered sunlight and soft breeze of a cloudy day at the beach.

Camille on the Beach in Trouville (fig. 6.3),[13] painted also during that post-wedding, summer holiday of 1870, may help us to begin to fathom the flurry of brushwork that muddles the play of fabric, shadow, and light upon Camille's visage into ambiguity in *The Beach at Trouville.* In this related image, Monet also represents his wife's body in profile, her head now turned toward the viewer. She jauntily holds the same off-white and periwinkle parasol behind her, wears a similar style of light summer dress,[14] and dons a small black straw hat, to which is attached a lavender veil. Camille's facial features are even more imprecise here than in the other painting, blurred now by the filmy netting that spreads across them. The veil gathers where diagonal strokes of lilac and silvery white stretch across the front band of her hat, her cheeks, and along the side of her head. Combined with Camille's hazy physiognomy, these folds serve as a kind of visual shorthand to index the veil that covers three-quarters of her face. The saturated periwinkle of the lining of the

12. For a detailed analysis of these and other aspects of the nineteenth-century Parisian veil, see Kessler.

13. Susan D. Greenberg provides an in-depth discussion of this painting in Greenberg.

14. Robert L. Herbert posits that Camille's dress in *Camille on the Beach in Trouville* is identical to the one worn by the woman on the left in *The Beach at Trouville* (28).

Figure 6.3 Claude Monet, *Camille on the Beach in Trouville*, 1870, oil on canvas, 15 x 8¼ in. Yale University Art Gallery Collection of Mr. and Mrs. John Hay Whitney. Photograph credit: Yale University Art Gallery.

parasol and the pale blue of the sky and the water where it meets the shoreline echo this tissue of fabric, the significance of which for Monet is further confirmed by the anemic patch of beige pigment and primed canvas that stands in for the more colorful blossoms that would have decorated the top of his wife's chapeau had he wanted to include them.

The tide swirls into shore at an acute angle behind Camille, the flags that indicated where to swim recede in the distance, a sailboat drifts beyond them, and five swimmers, each evoked by only a few well-placed dabs of brown and flesh-toned pigment, bob in the far middle ground. At the right, a child, possibly young Jean Monet, plays at the water's edge, overseen by a woman whose voluminous green veil trails in the wind behind her. All in this image is movement and whir, apart from Camille in the foreground who sits calmly, the still center around whom the breeze stirs. Indeed, the elements churn about her, but her veil protects her eyes and nose from the blowing wind and sand. I would even assert that this small area of translucent lilac pigment is made all the more integral to the syntax of the image by the clever visual and verbal play Monet must have known he was establishing between the pink sail—*la voile*—of the boat on the horizon and the soft purple veil—*le voile*—upon Camille's face. And in the context of my argument, the veil in this image becomes a kind of rejoinder to what I am contending is both a material and an implied one in *The Beach at Trouville.*

Comparing more closely Monet's technique for depicting Camille's face in these two images is also instructive. To indicate the creases in the veil that is so noticeable in *Camille on the Beach in Trouville*, he uses densely packed, relatively linear oblique strokes. The brushwork that constitutes the upper part of his wife's features in *The Beach at Trouville* (fig. 6.4) is also linear, though the direction of the marks is more varied, some dynamic diagonals reaching from her cheek toward her ear and upward from her cheek to her eye, whereas others veer toward verticality. It is, thus, useful to see that what at first blush appears to be a significant disparity between the two faces—one decidedly veiled and the other maybe so—is, in fact, not so especially oppositional, and that the formal affinities between them are actually quite remarkable. Indeed, Monet's explicit depiction of a veil in one should inflect our understanding of the other even if the artist did not necessarily mean for us to see or interpret these images in relation to one another. But, both the visual evidence and the circumstances of the paintings' creations are compellingly linked, and so considering them together provides a framework for analysis of each, and, for the purposes of my argument, a sharper lens with which to scrutinize the mystery generated by the clear distinction the artist makes between the upper two-thirds and lower third of Camille's face in *The Beach at Trouville.*

Monet does not simply vary color, but he also alters his brushwork to distinguish the two sections of his wife's visage. The more linear gray tones of her temple, cheek, and nose differ markedly from the creamy arabesques of fleshy pink pigment that establish the curve of her jawline and the shape of her neck. He wants us to interpret these areas as dissimilar, and his method for doing so obfuscates the very possibility of being able to articulate a definitive explanation for what does or does not lie across Camille's face, whether we see the portrayal of fabric or a shadow upon skin. But the very fact that we have this question means that we perceive both and by offering us both, Monet expands our experience of the painting. As we work to tease out and comprehend this protean form, we engage with the image intensely and begin to notice other small, yet telling, details. What are the smears of light brown that overlap Camille's hairline supposed to suggest? Do we detect the faintest whiff of a gossamer material where stray gray lines flicker along the edge of her profile, particularly around her nose? And what of the unblended skitters of blue pigment that lie just where her cheek meets her nose, where a nostril would be, under her eye, and out toward her temple? Camille's upper lip, we notice, is virtually obliterated by strokes of dark gray, the fleshy beige that rounds her chin also bisects her rosy lower lip, and her eye is barely evoked by three strokes of brown paint that form a triangle. The too-thick horizontal blot above it implies a fragment of an eyebrow. Everything seems to be in its proper place, but shapes are summarized and blurred, and it is as if we see Camille's facial features through fine mesh and the shadow it would cast. In our visual experience of it at least, her face is veiled.

Figure 6.4 A detail from Claude Monet, *The Beach at Trouville*, 1870, oil on canvas, 14.96 x 18.3 in. © The National Gallery, London.

Monet painted his wife veiled before that summer in Trouville, in *The Luncheon* (fig. 6.5), which dates from the winter of 1868–69 and was executed while the family lived temporarily in Étretat.[15] Best described as a fantasy of bourgeois domestic life

15. For a perceptive interpretation of *The Luncheon* in relation to what she sees as Monet's repudiation of figure painting in favor of the more "impersonal" subject of landscape based on internal conflicts between the realities of his personal domestic life—with its "passions and errors and weaknesses" (629)—and the fictional one he felt obliged to represent in the painting, see Anne M. Wagner's article.

FIGURE 6.5 Claude Monet, *The Luncheon*, 1868–69, oil on canvas, 91 x 59½ in. Städel Museum, Frankfurt am Main. © Städel Museum—U. Edelmann / ARTOTHEK.

replete with bountiful food and a maid, neither of which were realities for the very poor, as-yet unmarried couple, *The Luncheon* casts Camille as a mysterious visitor in outdoor clothing, still wearing gloves and a spotted black veil.[16] She may also have posed as herself, a mother who tends to an infant, the model for whom we must assume is the Monets' then-year-and-a-half-year-old son Jean.[17] Noticeably absent,

16. I base my understanding of these figures' identities on Wildenstein's (176).

17. Spate proposes that Camille may have been the model for both the visitor and the mother (60). In a letter to Frédéric Bazille dated December 1868, Monet conveys his plans for two paintings, one of which he describes as: "un intérieur avec bébé et deux femmes" (quoted in Wagner 629). That he notes that the picture he envisioned would have two women in it

though everywhere present—from his empty chair and fully realized place at the table in the foreground to the visible brushwork—is the paterfamilias, Monet himself.[18] This complex and rich painting certainly warrants careful scrutiny; however, for the advancement of my argument, I will focus on Camille's veil and its function in an image that is, upon close inspection, filled with both overt and oblique pictorial references to it. The sheer lace curtains that frame her head read as a kind of diaphanous veil. Though subtler, the dotted motif of the tablecloth just in front of Camille and the less understated grid of the chair caning inversely mimic the spotted fabric that complicates the terrain of her face. The clustered grapes and discs of potato and sausage, too, further emphasize the stippled pattern of the veil. And the juxtapositions of oil and vinegar cruets at the left of the table and water- and wine-filled bottles on the right remind us of the play of translucency and opacity that defines the formal properties of the veil.

Even the uncovered faces of the maid and the mother figure reference the visitor's veil, albeit antithetically as absence. And the door that is partially opened and through which the maid slips reveals just enough of an enticing glimpse into what is likely a linen closet. These visual facts serve also as potent reminders not just of the circumscribed vision of the woman in black but also of the ways in which our view of her face is mediated. Indeed, as I have argued elsewhere, the veil—as material entity and painted representation—works both ways.[19] The visual experiences of the woman behind it and the person who may look at her from outside are both filtered, though to different degrees, depending on the weave of the fabric. To be sure, the veil is a layered and nuanced object whose physical presence changes the optical and conceptual experience of seeing and being in the world for the wearer and, likewise, limits the viewer's powers to see her face. In this sense, the veil holds within it an articulation not just of the profound complexity of the act of looking, but also of the internal operations of the processes of painting, of the laying down of tangible pigments to represent infinite levels of transparency and intractability. And it is with these ideas in mind that I would like to turn back to the illusive upper part of Camille's visage in *The Beach at Trouville*, where pigment on canvas approximates a veil that reads as being at once a material presence and a shadow, a physical object that declines into its own incorporeal and spectral trace.

---

supports a reading in which Camille posed for two of the figures. Furthermore, given the Monets' unstable finances at the time, it seems unlikely that he would have hired another model and would instead have relied on Camille to sit for both women. Such a practice would not have been unusual for the artist at the time. In other images from around this period, like *Women in Garden* of 1866 (Musée d'Orsay, Paris), he used Camille as the model for at least three of the figures.

18. Building upon Wagner's argument, Hollis Clayson offers a convincing analysis of the empty chair as both welcoming and also denying the viewer "an optical anchor in the picture's space, shutting the viewer out of imaginary participation in the meal" (48).

19. See Kessler 24–25, 29–33.

The Matter of Sand

In this almost fifteen- by a little over eighteen-inch canvas, the small area of muddled paint over Camille's eyes, cheek, and nose is just that—small. And yet it significantly shapes meaning for the image as a whole. Here Monet's touch coincides with and alters Camille's—and our—vision. Although we sense his hand as much in his whipped-up surfaces as in his more flatly abstracted planes, in this seemingly inconsequential stretch of brushwork, we can especially see his thought process, equal measures of hesitation and utter assuredness. He seems to linger at the moment when the medium either becomes something or it does not. Or perhaps, to put it more pointedly, the artist ensures that paint declares its own solid presence even as it pretends to be the very thing that it represents. That this kind of conceptual complexity was on Monet's mind when he worked on this canvas is suggested, even confirmed by the evidence of the painting itself. For he so clearly wanted us to question whether we see skin or fabric and he knew just how far to go to convince us that we simply are not sure and therefore, that we actually perceive both. And all the while, he also makes us aware that what we really observe is paint that performs the work of epitomizing both veil and its shadow on flesh.

Monet allows the viewer to see the push and pull that must occur for illusionistic representation to be successful, but he leaves us hanging by both promising something and then visually undoing it. And this irresolution connects us even more deeply to the fine workings of the painting. But, our entanglement in it is even further heightened by the remarkable—one might even say, fortuitous—fact that countless grains of sand from the beach at Trouville on the very day or days in 1870 when Monet worked on this painting dust the surface of the picture plane (fig. 6.6). Because of the presence of real sand, we feel more sharply the whip of the wind; we hear the distant cries of birds and smell the ocean breeze even more powerfully than we would if all we had was (what suddenly seems like mere) paint and what it can engender. Monet left the sand there, presumably just where it landed as the breeze gusted around him while he stood at his easel, his portable paint box at his side.[20] He made no attempt to blend the sand with the pigment upon which it lighted, even though (or perhaps because) doing this might have disguised the former somewhat, maybe even yielded a beachy kind of texture that would have been congruent with the subject of the composition. Instead, he let the sand exist as itself, pure and simple, concentrated most obviously across the lower quadrant of the canvas—piled upon Monet's rendering of depicted sand between the chair's rungs, settled upon its seat, sunk into the cushions of lush white *matière* across Camille's skirt. It peppers the sky and the beach and it skitters across Camille's upper sleeve. This sediment is memory, for what is sand really but the slow effects of weather and time on rock

---

20. Anthea Callen points out that the contents of such a portable paint box would have been limited and helpfully notes that for *The Beach at Trouville*, Monet's would have contained lead white, cobalt and ultramarine blues, viridian, yellow ochre, vermillion, red-brown ochre, and black (258).

Figure 6.6 A detail from Claude Monet, *The Beach at Trouville*, 1870, oil on canvas, 14.96 x 18.3 in. © The National Gallery, London.

and mineral, their clashing, breaking, rubbing, buffing, moving from here to there on the cusp of water and wind. And here, the sand is lived experience—Monet's and Camille's—bound to the surface of *The Beach at Trouville*.

The real sand's physical presence amplifies the referential quality of the expanse of sand that Monet does paint. For represented sand can only be read as such because of our knowledge of actual sand and here the two are amalgamated. The authentic sand in its infinite varieties—each grain filed to its own unique precision, some winking like bits or silver, others flatly opaque as a sliver of bone—and the paint that stands for sand together inspire a particular type of seeing that coalesces, too, with touch, unleashing a sense of haptic vision in which touch and sight intermingle. We feel and see Monet's sumptuous brushwork and feel and see the granules of sand scattered across the canvas. Indeed, we experience this picture in a particularly phenomenological sense, for our looking at it engages us not only with the spectrum of paint's sumptuous possibilities and patent limitations, but also with the crisp physicality of sand on surface. The words of philosopher Maurice Merleau-Ponty seem useful here: "There is encroachment, infringement, not only between the touched and the touching, but also between the tangible and the visible, which is encrusted in it. . . . There is double and crossed sublation of the visible in the tangible and of the tangible in the visible" (396). Offering a dimension that exceeds a binaristic conceptualization of touch and sight, Merleau-Ponty's ideas help us to understand how Monet's painting uniquely concretizes a form of visual representation that goes beyond a simple merging of the visible and the palpable. For here, authentic sand and the representation of sand do not simply meld on this canvas;

they infringe and encroach upon one another, each encrusted in and by the other. In turn, we become entwined in and with *The Beach at Trouville*. We do not purely see it, but rather we encounter it haptically.

Building upon Merleau-Ponty's theory of phenomenology and late-nineteenth-century art historian Aloïs Riegl's assertion that purely optical vision differs from haptic vision, film theorist Laura U. Marks describes a distinctive way of seeing that she calls "haptic visuality," an experience in which "the eyes themselves function like organs of touch" (162). Marks writes: "While optical perception privileges the representational power of the image, haptic perception privileges the material presence of the image" (163). Marks's words are especially apt ones for describing the singular way in which we become immersed in Monet's painting, in his lavish brushwork, which is by turns thickly rich and densely powdery, in the sand that merges with the picture plane and in so doing, itself becomes *matière*. As our eye sweeps the composition, it falls into beds of thickly worked pigment, glides over flatter chalky patches, and catches on the prickly edges of so many particles of sand, unleashing more than a touch of the anxiety associated with the distant threat of sand blowing into one's eyes, even the desire to scrape it away with the edge of a fingernail and somehow rid the painting of its presence. Our involvement with the whole image is bodily and visceral, our pleasure in it melded with a *soupçon* of uneasiness.

The grains of sand that adhered to wet paint as the breeze blew and the sun tried to peek from behind the downy cover of clouds put us into the image in a phenomenological sense. So much so that we may imagine the actual veil that Camille might have worn on what is not just depicted as, but what the sand substantiates—as much as anything can—was a windy day at Trouville. We may think about the sensation of the fabric as it pulled across her face, or the temperature of the air that enveloped her. Or perhaps we may imagine what Camille might have heard—the muffled sounds of outlying conversations carried along the edge of the wind, the happy cries of children playing in the water. The granules of sand help to make Monet's scene, however non-illusionistic and painterly, somehow also exponentially more evocative and, yes, also more real to us. Its expanse and breath pulsate out from the two-dimensional picture plane, denying, even shattering, the very flatness that we know defines it.

Still, nothing can override the obdurate truth that the image—any image—is always really a representation. But, this one scrambles that actuality because it contains within it something authentic. The sand may have accidentally settled where it did, but it is, to use Jennifer Barker's apposite term, an "extra-textual" (24) artifact that is as much woven into the meaning of the painting as the deliberate strokes of pigment that the artist carefully laid on his canvas.[21] And this is

21. Barker construes this concept based on James Elkins's elegant assessment of a drawing by Pontormo. Elkins writes: "Marks blur and fade into one another, and even the freshest drawing will have uncertain moments where the texture of the paper confounds the sense of a mark, or a group of marks converge into a dark confusion, or a mark moves so lightly across the page that it is not securely visible" (834).

key. Monet allowed what appears to be—the paint that represents two women at the beach—and what is—real sand—to take their places together in his composition, each modulating the other, more powerful in combination than either could be apart. This realization is not just central to our interpretation of the bare facts of *The Beach at Trouville*; it is also critical to our comprehension of the concept of the veil itself. For as an authentic object, the veil also contains within it the unexpected and unintentional shadows that shift and change with every movement, every pitch of light and shade. Even as a painted garment, the veil is always also inscribed with the unanticipated and ineffable qualities we associate with actual veils. They work together, this fabric and its shadow. Whether real or represented, each is imprinted with the trace of the other.

The Shadow in the Veil

Monet communicates this possibility and ambiguity all at once in this small detail of his composition, this precise spot where pigment whispers its presence upon Camille's face. We can certainly see just paint if we want to or we can see only shadow. Or we can choose to look more deeply and if we do, this patch of canvas blooms into a surface and its palimpsestic layers, a seamless blending of lace and shadow. Or perhaps we may question whether Monet depicts the disentanglement of textile from the darkness it casts upon skin, a deconstruction of the object into its component parts. This area of paint thus provides an opportunity to examine the weighty and nuanced sophistication of the work of the late-nineteenth-century French veil. In the image, as in reality, this garment is a quantifiable, structured object that also casts its own illusory and unstructured shadow. It seems to me so clear that this is what Monet captures, whether knowingly or not: the veil *and* its visual effect. The strokes of pigment that partially obscure Camille's face stand not only for themselves—the action of *matière* on canvas—but also for these two disparate yet intimately related things: one tangible and the other not. He fabricates this manifold object in such a way that we both detect and question its presence even as we wonder whether what we see is the veil's or the parasol's shadow. This veil formally and materially does and undoes itself, existing as both thing and not-thing, as both physical substance and the insubstantial absence of light. Monet, thus, represents Camille's veil in this painting as what it is, a paradox, a contradiction. But a contradiction is not necessarily a negation. Indeed, the very fact that the veil—real, represented, and conceptual—contradicts itself only boundlessly adds nuance and depth to our construal of it as both an illusory and an actual object.

Sigmund Freud explored the ways in which the idea of contradiction may be fertile territory for understanding human thought and the unique mechanisms of the unconscious in his 1910 interpretation of philologist Karl Abel's 1884 paper on the historic phenomenon of contranyms, or words that have contradictory meanings. In his study, Freud, heavily citing Abel, compellingly notes that things always also reference their opposite, and that acknowledging this essential condition shades interpretation with depth and richness. He writes:

> Our concepts owe their existence to comparisons. "If it were always light we should not be able to distinguish light from dark, and consequently we should not be able to have either the concept of light or the word for it . . ." "It is clear that everything on this planet is relative and has an independent existence only in so far as it is differentiated in respect of its relations to other things . . ." (157)

If we extrapolate from Freud's development of Abel's ideas, we see even more sharply that the shaded areas throughout Monet's painting are explicable as such because of the places where the artist picked out light, because of the dense white pigment he used to materialize the invisible touch of the rays of the sun as they dispersed across Camille's lap. He rent dark from light and, by doing so, made both all the more potent.

Like most French artists at the time, Monet no doubt knew the perceptive words of Charles Blanc from his widely read *Grammaire des arts du dessin*, first published in 1867, in which he espoused the particular beauty that is created when an artist contrasts light and shadow, or, more precisely, pulls light from shadow. Blanc wrote: "Thus the beauty of the *clair-obscure* [light-shadow] in this painting is nearly sufficient, for it is all that is needed to outline the bodies and contains the poetry of the soul" (*Grammaire* 594).[22] Light and shadow together, for Blanc, are both more extraordinary than either could be alone. And in a painting like *The Beach at Trouville*, in which light and shadow inflect one another so purposefully, we must recognize that the one cannot exist without the other. Where there is light, there is shadow. We appreciate that something falls across the upper portion of Camille's face because Monet varied his brushwork and burnished a deep purple gray into lighter flesh-colored pigment. And with this act, he both merged and separated light from dark, tangible veil from intangible shadow, all the while declaring the contranymic status of the object of his representation.

For Freud, the very concept of the contranym, particularly in its origins in older, what he calls "archaic," languages, has deep significance for the analysis not just of waking life, but also of dreams. As he explains:

> [H]ow frequently the dream-work makes use of a reversal of the representational material for various purposes. . . . In the correspondence between the peculiarity of the dream-work . . . and the practice discovered by philology in the oldest languages, we may see a confirmation of the view we have formed about the regressive, archaic character of the expression of thoughts in dreams. And we psychiatrists cannot escape the suspicion that we should be better at understanding and translating the language of dreams if we knew more about the development of language. (160–61)

---

22. "Ainsi le seul clair-obscur renferme déjà une beauté qui pourrait presque suffire à la peinture, car elle suffit au relief des corps et contient les poésies de l'âme."

So much about these ideas resonates for me as I think about veils in general and specifically about the one Monet imagines and paints in *The Beach at Trouville.* "Representational material," as Freud puts it in relation to dreams, corresponds theoretically on so many levels to represented material on a canvas. For paint is always just paint even as it is a kind of cypher for figuring what it is not. And like the images from our dreams, painted representations screen multivalent—often abstracted and unknowable—significance. One picture, in other words, holds many meanings, some conscious, some not, for both artist and viewer. If the image is of a veil, interpretive reverberations even further abound, since this object always exists as itself even as it marks the many things that it hides. The veil does not just obscure what it causes to be unseen. It also calls to our attention the fact that something *is* unseen.

Freud's theory about screen memories, in which images mean what they overtly denote and also simultaneously signify the many other stories that they mask, even further enriches analysis of the veil as a representation both of itself and of that which it secretes. In fact, the veil, which is literally a physical screen, also screens, a verb that is itself a contranym, since to screen can mean both to show and to conceal. As we look at the veiled face, we may project onto it an ideal of beauty or, to use my own earlier words: "Forced to look even more closely to synthesize all of the parts of the woman's scotomized face, the viewer becomes virtually enmeshed in the viewing system. So, while the veil could, to varying degrees, perform the work of concealing, an outside viewer could decrease that degree of concealment by looking more closely to sharpen the blurred face on the other side" (Kessler 25). This is the enigma of the veil. It simultaneously eclipses and uncovers both the face that it skims and the myriad shadows it engenders. The veil can indeed reveal and hide, entice and seduce, but what is hidden is nevertheless always there, haunting the very fabric that constitutes it.

I would like to think that Monet understood, even wanted to find a way to render this complexity when he tantalizingly blurred a veil of paint over Camille's face, his brushstrokes intersecting to suggest both the filaments of a fine piece of lace and the crosshatching an artist might use to indicate the illusion of shading. Exactly here, *matière* functions as both itself and as that which it indexes, translucent textile and elusive shadow fashioned from an opaque substance. Alchemical magic, really. A sleight of hand. Indeed, Monet exposes the very material essence that is pigment, its resolute facticity, even as he discloses that it, like the veil, cannot be split from what it contains. For, the veil cannot be cleaved from—because it cleaves to—the shadow that it produces.[23] Where there is a veil, there is shadow. Where there is medium, there is that which it represents. Monet gives us just this, all of this, the shifting curve of light, the susurrus of the ocean in the distance, the rustling breeze, a scattering of sand, sea air lifting around two women who sit quietly, as if nothing is really happening.

---

23. Significantly, the verb "to cleave" is also a contranym since it can mean both to split from and to adhere to.

Acknowledgments

It is a pleasure to thank Heidi Brevik-Zender for her invitation to publish this essay and for her gracious and intelligent stewardship of this volume. Linda Nochlin, Susan Hiner, and Abigail Solomon-Godeau offered useful feedback on an early version of this material, as did audiences at the annual Nineteenth-Century French Studies Colloquium and the meetings of the Society of Dix-Nueviémistes. Research for this essay was funded by the Kress Foundation Department of Art History Travel Fund and The Office of International Programs at the University of Kansas. I offer special thanks to Erica Weiss, who told me about Freud's contranym essay in the first place and who inspired me even more than she realizes to revisit the veil. Finally, it is with deep gratitude and love that I dedicate this to the memory of Linda Nochlin, whose support of this essay—and me—seemed as boundless as her love of the beach.

Works Cited

Barker, Jennifer M. *The Tactile Eye: Touch and the Cinematic Experience.* U of California P, 2004.

Baudre, C. de. *Trouville et ses environs: guide du promeneur.* C. de Baudre, 1850.

Blanc, Charles M. *L'Art dans la parure et dans le vêtement.* Librairie Renouard, 1875.

———. *Grammaire des arts du dessin: architecture, sculpture, peinture.* Ve J. Renouard, 1867.

Brettell, Richard R. *Impression: Painting Quickly in France, 1860–1890.* Yale UP, 2000.

Brown, Kathryn. *Women Readers in French Painting 1870–1890: A Space for the Imagination.* Ashgate, 2012.

Callen, Anthea. *The Work of Art: Plein-Air Painting and Artistic Identity in Nineteenth-Century France.* Reaktion, 2015.

Clayson, Hollis. "Invited or Rebuffed? Exploring the Effects of Early Impressionist Foregrounds." *Monet and the Birth of Impressionism*, edited by Felix Krämer. Städel Museum, Prestel, 2015, pp. 46–54.

Elkins, James. "Marks, Traces, *Traits*, Contours, *Orli*, and *Splendores*: Nonsemiotic Elements in Pictures." *Critical Inquiry*, vol. 21, no. 4, 1995, pp. 822–60.

Freud, Sigmund. "The Antithetical Meaning of Primal Words." *The Standard Edition of the Complete Psychological Works of Sigmund Freud*, vol. 11, translated and edited by James Strachey. The Hogarth Press, 1953, pp. 155–61.

Greenberg, Susan D. "The Face of Impressionism in 1870: Claude Monet's *Camille on the Beach at Trouville*." *Yale University Art Gallery Bulletin*, 2001, pp. 66–73.

Hamilton, Vivien. *Boudin at Trouville.* Glasgow Museums, 1992.

Herbert, Robert L. *Monet on the Normandy Coast: Tourism and Painting 1867–1886.* Yale UP, 1994.

Joanne, Adolphe. *Trouville et ses environs.* Hachette, 1907.

Joanne, Paul Bénigne. *Le Havre, Sainte-Adresse, Honfleur, Trouville, Deauville, et leurs environs.* Hachette, 1914.

Kessler, Marni Reva. *Sheer Presence: The Veil in Manet's Paris.* U of Minnesota P, 2006.

Lemonedes, Heather, et al. *Monet in Normandy*. Rizzoli International Publications, 2006.

Marks, Laura U. *The Skin of the Film: Intercultural Cinema, Embodiment, and the Senses*. Duke UP, 2000.

Merleau-Ponty, Maurice. "The Intertwining—The Chiasm." *The Merleau-Ponty Reader*, edited by Ted Toadvine and Leonard Lawlor. Northwestern UP 2007, pp. 393–413.

Nochlin, Linda. "Monet's *Hôtel des Roches Noires*: Anxiety and Perspective at the Seashore." *Bathers, Bodies, Beauty: The Visceral Eye*. Harvard UP, 2006, pp. 153–95.

Rewald, John. "Notes sur deux tableaux de Claude Monet." *Gazette des Beaux-Arts*, vol. 70, no. 6, 1967, pp. 245–48.

Spate, Virginia. *Claude Monet: Life and Work*. Thames and Hudson, 1992.

Wagner, Anne M. "Why Monet Gave Up Figure Painting." *The Art Bulletin*, vol. 76, no. 4, 1994, pp. 612–29.

Wildenstein, Daniel. *Claude Monet: biographie et catalogue raisonné*, vol. 1. La Bibliothèque des arts, 1974.

———. *Monet ou le triomphe de l'impressionisme*, vol. 1. Tachen, Wildenstein Institute, 1996.

CHAPTER 7

STYLE WARS

The Uniform and the Polymorphous in Émile Zola's *La Débâcle*

Nicholas White

> In wartime, individuals changed the clothes of their lives; they put on uniforms; they accepted, however reluctantly, the division between "us" and "them," and knew how to distinguish between the two.
>
> —Jay Winter and Jean-Louis Robert, *Capital Cities at War: Paris, London and Berlin 1914–1919*

> Much more than an anecdotal detail, the uniform is inscribed as an object at the crossroads of the political, social and cultural history of states that impose it on their armies.
>
> —Odile Roynette, "L'uniforme militaire au XIXe siècle: une fabrique du masculin"[1*]

Although military uniforms might, in some sense, seem to represent the very opposite of fashion, with the latter's capacity for individualistic whim and expression, it would be naïve to imagine that they do not exhibit forms of reciprocal influence. To think of nineteenth-century male dress in the terms of John Harvey as "men in black" is to concede that male civilians were already uniformed. Indeed, it is worth reflecting on the verbal play intrinsic—in both English and French—to the very notion of the uniform in its adjectival and then substantive senses, with their implication of homogeneous national identity. The French substantive emerged later, in the seventeenth century, with the appearance of distinctly colored, homogeneous uniforms with a particularly pragmatic purpose, in Odile Roynette's words, "to recognize soldiers in the confusion of a battlefield and to subject each one to better

1. *"Bien plus qu'un détail anecdotique, l'uniforme s'inscrit comme un objet à la croisée de l'histoire politique, social et culturelle des États qui l'imposent à leur armée."

discipline" (*Les mots des soldats* 254).[2] This capacity for uniforms to accentuate national allegiance is implicit but legible in those contrary processes that bracket out the uniform, for instance, the depiction of naked rather than uniformed men in First World War memorials in Alsace. In the words of Audoin-Rouzeau and Becker, "how can one recognize a German from a Frenchman without the uniform?" (230).[3] The pragmatic desire for chromatic distinctiveness in the material fabric used looked ever less practical as the age of modernity unfolded: France adopting in 1829 the bright red *pantalon garance* (in the run-up to Stendhal's novel of 1830, which invokes in its very title the colors of uniforms of different kinds, military and clerical), only for it to be abandoned in 1915 in the face of a different kind of warfare that demanded camouflage. Between these dates lies the humiliation of the Franco-Prussian War of 1870–71, on which this chapter will ultimately focus, using Émile Zola's fiction to bring into focus questions of gender difference and identification that will nuance the models of homosociability and homoeroticism developed in the cultural analyses of Eve Kosofsky Sedgwick and Sharon Marcus, the latter providing a perhaps surprising route for future analyses not only of literary texts on war, but also of the iconography of the uniform. In this vein, I hope to contribute to the discipline known as uniformology and, in particular, to the study of the representation of French military uniforms.[4]

The conservative position on the *pantalon garance* was best expressed, just prior to 1914, by the minister of war, General Étienne:

> To make everything that is color disappear, everything that gives the soldier his cheerful, rousing appearance, and to seek out dull and subdued hues, is to go against both French taste and the demands of the military role. Red trousers convey something of the nation. . . . Red trousers are France. (cited in Roynette, *Les mots des soldats* 125)[5]

---

2. "pour reconnaître les soldats dans la confusion d'un champ de bataille et pour mieux assujetir chacun à une discipline"

3. "comment reconnaître un Allemand d'un Français, sans l'uniforme ?"

4. Odile Roynette refers to "l'uniformologie, cette spécialité, apanage des collectionneurs, que le chercheur en sciences sociales tend encore à considérer avec condescendance, alors qu'elle constitue une base indispensable à toute réflexion plus large" ("uniformology, that specialty, prerogative of collectors that researchers in the social sciences still tend to view with condescension, although it provides a vital basis for any wider reflection") ("L'uniforme militaire au XIXe siècle" 111).

5. "Faire disparaître tout ce qui est couleur, tout ce qui donne au soldat son aspect gai, entraînant, rechercher des nuances ternes et effacées, c'est aller à la fois contre le goût français et contre les exigences de la fonction militaire. Le pantalon rouge a quelque chose de national. . . . Le pantalon rouge, c'est la France." The symbolic force of a soldier's trousers as a marker of male self-respect and honor was played out in the Affaire Bersot of 1915, in which Lucien Bersot was sent to the firing squad by his own commander for refusing to don the blood-stained trousers of a fallen comrade. The Affaire returned to public attention on the publication of Alain Scoff's narrative account *Le pantalon* (1982), which inspired Yves Boisset's film of the same name (1997).

The *bleu-horizon* that the Great War ushered in still marks French institutional memory of 1914–18, as witnessed in the commemorations of its centenary, which began in 2014.[6] As early as 1919, the new Chamber of Deputies, replete with ex-servicemen, was nicknamed the "chambre bleu horizon." Indeed, the 2015 bicentenary of Waterloo bore witness to our desire to refabricate the textures of war through such material detail: as witnessed not only in battle reconstructions *sur place* but also in artistic responses to this pre-photographic event. Opening for the two hundredth anniversary of the Battle of Waterloo, Somerset House (London) presented *Unseen Waterloo: The Conflict Revisited*, a series of portraits by war photographer Sam Faulkner, exploring in posed images taken at these reenactments how we remember the fallen from a time before photography was invented.[7] As we shall see in the case of Émile Zola's *La Débâcle* (1892), narrative fiction too claims to reenact, in mimetically authentic detail, the experience of soldiers at war.

The uniform is a term at odds, it would seem, with the heterogeneity of the *multiforme*, which is related in the Robert dictionary to the inventive possibilities of the *protéiforme* and exemplified there by Chateaubriand's account of Early Modern French history: "This multiform nation was fanatical under Henri IV, seditious under Louis XIII, sober under Louis XIV."[8] In a lexical extension on which Baudelaire plays in his section on "Le militaire" in *Le Peintre de la vie moderne* (1863), the uniform both mimes and fashions (in a Greenblattian sense too) a certain uniformity of expression (or *esprit de corps*, one might say) borne of shared experience:

> Here we can see that uniformity of expression which is created by suffering and obedience endured in common, that resigned air of courage that has been put to the test by long, wearisome fatigue. Trousers tucked into incarcerating gaiters, greatcoats besmirched with dust, stained and discolored—in short, the entire equipment of these men has taken upon itself the special personality of beings who are returning from afar after running the gauntlet of extraordinary adventures. All these men give the appearance of being more solidly backed, more squarely set on their feet, more erect than ordinary mortals can be. (Baudelaire 2: 708–09)[9]

---

6. See, for instance, Chifflet.

7. In the words of the Somerset House publicity material: "Since 2009, Faulkner has travelled to the annual Waterloo re-enactment in Belgium to photograph the 'soldiers' who take part, dressed in the historically accurate uniforms each participant creates with painstaking attention to detail for the event. From his pop-up studio situated on the battlefield, he has made dramatic and painterly portraits which evoke the forgotten faces of Waterloo and re-imagine moments of glory, of hope and defeat." See http://www.unseenwaterloo.co.uk/. Tellingly for our purposes, Faulkner works both on war zones (including Afghanistan) and high fashion (such as Dior and Armani).

8. "Cette nation multiforme [la France] fut fanatique sous Henri IV, factieuse sous Louis XIII, grave sous Louis XIV."

9. "Voilà bien l'uniformité d'expression créée par l'obéissance et les douleurs supportées en commun, l'air résigné du courage éprouvé par les longues fatigues. Les pantalons retroussés et emprisonnés dans les guêtres, les capotes flétries par la poussière, vaguement décolorées,

Their battle-hardened physiognomy is transferred onto their kit and outfit, dulled by combat experience, and shorn of the *astiquage* of the parade ground.

The intensification of military service after the defeat of 1870 played a vital role, according to Odile Roynette's telling phrase, in "the history . . . of a standardization of behavior" (« *Bon pour le service* » 5).[10] Under the Restoration, one in ten Frenchmen spent time, as the phrase goes, *sous l'uniforme*, one in three under the Second Empire, then one in two, and after the Loi Freycinet of July 15th, 1889, six out of ten. By the time Zola wrote his novel, it was very common to see soldiers in uniform traversing ostensibly civilian space. Indeed, such space would become symbolically militarized in the pomp and swagger of parades, which served as the culturally consecrated site of the female heterosexual gaze. In the hypernormative language of the military author, E. Coralys (pseudonym of Ernest-Louis Baussan) writes in *L'Éducation morale du soldat* (1890): "Good males make good soldiers, and girls like good soldiers. . . . A soldier leaves the army with more vigor and masculinity than when he joined up" (cited in Roynette, « *Bon pour le service* » 340).[11] Witness, as an example from literary fiction, the opening of *L'Accident de M. Hébert*, that 1883 novel of wifely adultery by the *petit naturaliste*, Léon Hennique, which pays backhanded homage to the clichéd allure of Ventujol's uniformed male body before the admiring gaze of a local housewife:

> And one afternoon, Ventujol appeared before her, in a sunlit military parade, as banal as the hero of a novel, in uniform, on horseback, responding to the aspirations of her adolescence, the bewilderment of her whimsical mind, and the sickly glamor that a dizzy, bored woman such as this needs. (Hennique 43)[12]

This *éclat* is echoed in the naïve swagger of French troops at the start of *La Débâcle*, "the bright, joyful colors of uniforms against green vines, splashed with sunlight," which contrasts with the "dark uniforms" of the Prussians.[13] If, halfway through the

---

tout l'équipement enfin a pris lui-même l'indestructible physionomie des êtres qui reviennent de loin et qui ont couru d'étranges aventures. On dirait que tous ces hommes sont plus solidement appuyés sur leurs reins, plus carrément installés sur leurs pieds, plus d'aplomb que ne peuvent l'être les autres hommes."

10. "l'histoire . . . d'une uniformisation des comportements."

11. "les bons mâles font les bons soldats et les filles aiment les bons soldats. . . . Le soldat sort plus fort, plus vigoureux, plus mâle de l'armée que lorsqu'il y est entré." As Roynette observes, the alignment of the uniform with a military career is asserted in the French expressions "endosser l'uniforme" and "quitter l'uniforme" (to don and leave the uniform, i.e., to join up and to leave the army).

12. "Et une après-midi, sous le soleil d'une revue, banal comme un héros du roman, en uniforme, à cheval, répondant aux aspirations de son adolescence, à l'ahurissement de son esprit capricieux, au prestige maladif qu'il fallait à ses vapeurs de femme ennuyée, Ventujol lui était apparu."

13. "une gaieté éclatante d'uniformes dans la verdure des pampres éclaboussés de soleil"

first part of the novel, Napoleon III benefits by association with soldiers "attired in luxurious uniforms that were still immaculate," by the end of part 1 this hubris is undermined by Delaherche's account of his dysentery: "all of a sudden, the Emperor comes down from the farm, where he'd stopped to rest and eat. He had an overcoat flung over his general's uniform, even though the sun was very hot. Behind him there was a servant, carrying a camp stool. . . . He didn't look very well, if you ask me, oh no, he stooped, he had a great difficulty walking, his face was all yellow—in short he was a sick man . . ."[14] His cowardice is exemplified through the rumor that he has fled, "leaving one of his lieutenants as a decoy, clothed in his uniform, so like him that it had the army fooled."[15] In the Emperor's fictional version of himself, his uniform functions as a placeholder of rank, a manipulable signifier that allows the individual identity of Napoleon III to slip off into obscurity.[16] In the account of Sedan in the second part of the novel, Delaherche notes by contrast the modesty of the Prussian king, seen through a telescope: "to the fore was a single man, who looked thin and wiry, wearing an undecorated uniform, but whose masterly presence was unmistakable. It was indeed the King of Prussia, hardly taller than half his finger, like one of those miniscule lead toy soldiers."[17]

If military uniforms in the nineteenth century articulated a radically differentiated, indeed opposed, vision of masculinity and femininity, then Zola's novel of the department store, *Au bonheur des dames* (1883), is of course the veritable tale of feminine fashion in Zola's cycle. And the tension between this heterosexual model of normativity and the homoeroticism in the key "buddy" relationship between Jean and Maurice in *La Débâcle* allows Zola to clothe the citizen body of the new Republic in the problematic language of *fraternité*. In chapter 1 of her book *Fashioning Spaces*, entitled "Fashioning the Commune Barricade," Heidi

(Zola 1967, 457). Translations are borrowed from the Oxford World's Classics version by Elinor Dorday (Zola 2000).

14. "un luxe d'uniformes correct encore et resplendissant" (458); "l'empereur, tout d'un coup, est sorti de la ferme, où il était monté faire halte, pour se reposer et déjeuner. Il avait un paletot jeté sur son uniforme de général, bien que le soleil fût très chaud. Derrière lui, un serviteur portait un pliant. . . . Je ne lui ai pas trouvé bonne mine, ah ! non, voûté, la marche pénible, la figure jaune, enfin un homme malade . . ." (550).

15. "laissant, en guise de mannequin, un de ses lieutenants, vêtu de son uniforme, et dont une ressemblance frappante abusait l'armée" (562).

16. Redressing (rather than undressing) demarcates the polite limits of feminine desire in the fantasy life of Hennique's heroine, Mme Hébert: "Ce n'est pas que son imagination déshabille le militaire désiré—tant s'en faut ; c'est plutôt le cas que cette imagination essaie de rhabiller son mari dans l'uniforme de Ventujol, et n'y trouve qu'un clown" ("It's not that her imagination undresses the desired soldier—far from it; it is rather the case that this imagination tries to redress her husband in Ventujol's uniform, only to turn him into a clown") (*L'Accident de M. Hébert* 16). Her fantasy fails because of its comedy.

17. "il y avait un homme seul, l'air sec et mince, à l'uniforme sans éclat, dans lequel pourtant il sentit le maître. C'était bien le roi de Prusse, à peine haut comme la moitié du doigt, un de ces minuscules soldats de plomb des jouets d'enfant" (622–23).

Brevik-Zender reads the staircases of *Au bonheur des dames* "as locations haunted by the specter of the bloody Paris Commune of 1871" and links "Zola's staircases to the stepped barricades erected during this catastrophic civil conflict" (Brevik-Zender 22–23). As such, she brings into focus the scholarship of the likes of Mint, Starr, and Ramazani, which stresses metaphors of violence and war, indeed a "women's war," in the novel. As she argues, "the department store staircase, like the building around it, is a monument to modern fashionable spectacle, yet it equally memorializes a still unfathomable incident from which it originates and which it cannot avoid referencing." In chapter 3, entitled "Waiting for Change: Zola's *Au Bonheur des Dames* and *Nana*," she then examines his use of the antechamber as a form of "dislocation" that stages the tension between the Second Empire depicted and the Third Republic to come, either side of 1870–71, first as Denise waits in the antechambers of Henriette Desforges (just as Zola waits for political and aesthetic change), second in *Nana* (1880):

> By deliberately concluding *Nana* on the verge of the Franco-Prussian War, Zola invites his readers to meditate on the infamous drawn-out wait that subsequently took place in Paris immediately following France's defeat [the Siege of 1870–71]. . . . The dire effect of this period of waiting was the civil war of the Commune, which erupted after almost four long months of rising tensions in the confined and beleaguered capital city. . . . The novel thus concludes as it starts, in anticipation that something imminent will occur. (Brevik-Zender 141–42)

In *La Débâcle*, Zola suppresses this period of waiting by fast-forwarding from Sedan (in part 2 of the novel) through the first (Prussian) Siege of Paris in order to focus in part 3 on the second (Versaillais) Siege of Paris, and thus the Paris Commune itself.

If one googles for images of uniforms, one is immediately bombarded by pictures not only of military uniforms (much of it Nazi memorabilia, it should be noted), but also of school uniforms, girl guide and scout uniforms, cheerleader uniforms, air stewards' uniforms, the uniforms of policemen and policewomen, of nurses, of firefighters, and—in an interesting difference between British and American English—the uniforms of sports teams (which is not a normal usage in British English). What is on display (and often for sale) are not only these uniforms themselves but often also eroticized "fancy dress" versions of these uniforms that play on fantasies of domination and submission in the power politics of the bedroom as well as the nation-state. We should recall, in this context, that the notion of a body for sale is at the etymological origin of the very words "soldier" and *soldat*, not least when we recall that twinning of the death of the prostitute and the start of the Franco-Prussian War on the final pages of Zola's tale of the courtesan, *Nana*, of 1880. Nana is renowned for removing her clothes so as to reveal her body in its full glory, even on the public stage of the theater in the opening chapter of the novel, as an Offenbachian parody of mythology is played out in the kitsch melodramatization of war and love in the forms of Mars and Venus. There are many different readings of the gender politics of this novel's ending, though one such interpretation suggests that the promiscuous female body is blamed in hindsight by Zola's Third Republic tale for the degeneration of the French military body, and thus disposed of in the habitual death ending of the fallen woman while, downstairs, men march down the Parisian street proclaiming their destination, "To Berlin."

This tale of the promiscuous Second Empire woman is followed, in novels ten and eleven, by Zola's archetypal tale of the promiscuous Second Empire man, the philandering Octave Mouret, who arrives in Paris from Provence at the start of *Pot-Bouille* (1882) with plans of developing his career in the fabrics trade, only to be waylaid for four hundred pages by the opportunities for seduction in the "apartment story" (to borrow from the title of Sharon Marcus's first book) on the Rue de Choiseul. By the end of this novel (and thus precisely at the halfway point in Zola's twenty-novel cycle), he has married Caroline Hédouin, the widow-proprietor of the successful but modest store Au Bonheur des Dames, which gives its name to the subsequent novel that inaugurates the second half of the cycle. By the start of this novel, Octave has himself been widowed by the mysterious death of Caroline, who seems to have fallen into a hole in the ground of the building developments by which the store profits from the possibilities of Haussmannization (and thus into the textual lacuna between novels). That very lacuna, at precisely the middle point of the series, exerts untold (literally untold) stress on the naturalistic claims of Zola's narrative technique in the very implausibility of this mysterious death. It is telling, moreover, that precisely at this midpoint do we find the only two consecutive novels in the series to use the same main protagonist, and as such Mouret serves as a bridge or a pivot between each half of the series. Beneath this feat of fictional engineering, however, lies the corpse of his wife. Just as Octave attempts the sexual conquest of women in his first novel, in his second he succeeds in the commercial seduction of women. He himself is vanquished by the shop assistant, Denise Baudu, who resists his attempts at seduction but accepts his proposal of marriage in the final pages of the novel, a marriage that—as Brevik-Zender points out—conjoins capitalism and democracy, whereas the tension between the politics of compromise and radical republicanism symbolized in *La Débâcle* by Jean and Maurice respectively renders impossible the marriage between Jean and Maurice's twin sister, Henriette, as we shall see.

There are, of course, conceptually rich routes into these questions of gender identity and gendered relationships that shape the polymorphous social and sexual interplay of sameness and difference, of the homo and the hetero, that are illuminated through, among other things, military uniforms in Zola's fiction. Two such routes are proffered by Eve Kosofsky Sedgwick and Sharon Marcus. A critical language of the homo and the hetero, and of the social and the sexual, speaks back first to that landmark book, Eve Kosofsky Sedgwick's *Between Men: English Literature and Male Homosocial Desire*, initially published in 1985. In the matrix of permutations made possible by the homo/hetero and social/sexual distinctions, there should be four basic terms: the homosexual and the homosocial (on Sedgwick's repressed continuum), the heterosexual (naturally, or rather, normatively), but also the heterosocial. On the opening pages of the original introduction to her book, Sedgwick writes:

> "Homosocial desire" is a kind of oxymoron. "Homosocial" is a word occasionally used in history and the social sciences, where it describes social bonds between persons of the same sex; it is a neologism, obviously formed by analogy with the "homosexual," and just as obviously meant to be distinguished from "homosexual." To draw the "homosocial" back into the orbit of "desire" is to hypothesize the potential unbrokenness of a continuum between homosocial and homosexual—a continuum whose visibility, for men, in our society, is radically disrupted. . . . My hypothesis of the unbrokenness of this continuum is not a *genetic* one—I do not mean to discuss genital homosexual desire as "at the root of" other forms of male homosociality—but rather a strategy for making generalizations about, and marking historical differences in, the *structure* of men's relations with other men. (1–2)

In the preface written for a subsequent reissuing of this now classic account, Sedgwick makes clear the sexual politics, not least for gay identities, of deconstructing the representational history of what she labels "the available mirror of the atomized, procreative, so-called heterosexual nuclear family of origin" (ix). Indeed, Sedgwick demonstrates the collusion between heterosexual norms and homosocial bonds (not least the homosocial bonds between men that subtend the practices of patriarchy). As she argues, patriarchal homosociability must repress the structural continuum that connects it to homosexual counterculture, and nineteenth-century armies offer one particularly visible instance of such male homosociability. Yet as Brian Martin has shown, the sheer proximity of soldiers at war creates an evocatively ambiguous context that paradoxically conjoins male homoeroticism and a stereotype strong, straight masculinity, both symbolized in their own ways by the stress on dress in military fiction.[18] Military fiction such as Zola's allows nineteenth-century culture not only to soberly commemorate war but also to play wargames on the terrain of such ambiguity, and thus to disrupt the normative disruption of the homo continuum to which Sedgwick refers.

For an account of nineteenth-century homosocial bonds that are not patriarchal and that were widely in circulation in the fashion imagery of Zola's day, we might turn to Sharon Marcus's *Between Women: Friendship, Desire, and Marriage in Victorian England*, whose very title plays knowingly on Sedgwick's, even though Marcus does not stress this connection. Chapter 3, "Dressing Up and Dressing Down the Feminine Plaything," makes much of the homoerotic potential of "hyper-feminine discourses about fashion and dolls," playing on "a theoretical distinction

18. See Martin, in particular 244–54, on Zola's novel.

between the sexual and the erotic in order to show that mainstream femininity was not secretly lesbian, but openly homoerotic. Within the realm of domestic consumer culture, Victorian women were as licensed to objectify women as were Victorian men" (3). To finesse this distinction, Marcus writes:

> Erotic relationships involve intensified affect and sensual pleasure, dynamics of looking and displaying, domination and submission, restraint and eruption, idolization and humiliation. Those erotic dynamics can exist between two people or between a person and an object, image, or text. To say that a woman had an erotic relationship with a woman or an image of a woman does not mean that she wanted to have sex with that woman or masturbated to that image. Erotic dynamics can lead to sexual excitement or activity, but even when they do not, they remain qualitatively different from the more neutral responses people have to the majority of people and things in their environment. A fashion plate is not overtly sexual, but it is designed to evoke erotic feelings in ways that a sewing pattern is not. (114)

To exemplify the homoerotic feminine gaze, Marcus reproduces in this chapter 15 nineteenth-century fashion plates, many of which came originally from France and French artists such as the Toudouze women. As these examples show, and Marcus explains,

> [t]he elaborate color plates that circulated in Victorian fashion magazines and epitomized femininity depict women who solicit and return other women's fascinated, admiring, and probing gazes, who lock eyes, walk arm-in-arm, and stand so close to each other that their hands and dresses overlap. (117)

We might pause to ask whether—in another kind of visual culture—we might find a kind of male homoeroticism paralleling the examples between women studied by Marcus. For I am thinking here of those many nineteenth-century plates not of feminine fashion but of masculine uniforms—which, through Marcus's critical lens, might in hindsight not look so innocent after all. For a tip of this iceberg, see on the Gallica website, for instance, "Le carré par quatre contre la cavalerie bavaroise" in *Guerre de 1870–1871: Infanterie française en tirailleurs* (Pellerin, 1874); Auguste de Moltzheim, *La Nouvelle armée française* (1875), original watercolors, "Intendance militaire" (image 4), "Gendarmerie départementale, à pied" (image 6), and "Marine: officiers de vaisseau" (image 27) (figs. 7.1–7.4). Indeed, the homoeroticism that can be read in these images of uniformed military men might, within nineteenth-century culture, have been more troubling than its feminine variety. For if the erotic refers, in Marcus's terms, to a range of desiring relations that are not simply genital, then it might in some sense be said to sit between the social and the sexual. And yet, as Sedgwick shows, that continuum between the homosocial and the homosexual (where we might want to try to locate the homoerotic) is in fact

FIGURE 7.1 *Guerre de 1870–1871: Infanterie française en tirailleurs* (Paris: Pellerin, 1874). Bibliothèque nationale de France, Paris.

yet more problematic in the world of masculinity (in Sedgwick's terms, cited earlier, "a continuum whose visibility, for men, in our society, is radically disrupted"). For example, the 1870 portrait of the much-famed British army intelligence officer, Frederick Gustavus Burnaby, by the French painter James Tissot, eroticizes the military figure by feminizing his pose (National Portrait Gallery, London) (fig. 7.5). As in Marcus's examples, we see French cultural influence transposed to a British context. Dressed resplendently as a captain in the Royal Horse Guards, Burnaby is

Figure 7.2 "Intendance militaire," Auguste de Moltzheim, *La Nouvelle Armée française* (1875). Bibliothèque nationale de France, Paris.

nevertheless domesticated by his reclining pose, in almost odalisque fashion, the fingertips of his right hand disappearing beyond the books with which he shares the divan. The cigarette, languorously clipped between the second and third fingers of his left hand, points in the direction of the map of the world on the wall, and in particular to its southern oceans. Indeed, by an optical illusion, it seems for a moment almost to prop up the map, even if the cigarette isn't quite straight.

How, then, might we read the Octave Mouret dress-inflected novels as counterpoints to Zola's war novel and in light of Sedgwick's categories of desire and Marcus's analysis of homoerotics in the visual culture of fashion? For both the Mouret novels and *La Débâcle* exert pressure on the homo/hetero, social/sexual matrix, not least through Marcus's category of the erotic. The Mouret novels, which seem (in their stress on adultery and shopping) to promise to underscore the heterosexual norm, end up playing with the heterosocial possibilities of Octave's relationship not only with Denise Baudu in his second novel *Au bonheur des dames*, but already in *Pot-Bouille* with Caroline Hédouin (which casts its force of precedent over the second

FIGURE 7.3 "Gendarmerie départementale, à pied," Auguste de Moltzheim, *La Nouvelle Armée française* (1875). Bibliothèque nationale de France, Paris.

in the form of the painting of Caroline that hangs in Mouret's office). That heterosociability is articulated in these heroines' resistance to Octave's seductions until the final part of each novel, a resistance that affords narrative space for Denise's rhetoric of socially progressive capitalism as she persuades him to improve the lot of his employees, and narrative space for Caroline's career, inscribed in the vestimentary semiotics of her cross-dressing professional "uniform," with a miniature man's tie adorning her black and white dress.

Figure 7.4 "Marine: officiers de vaisseau," Auguste de Moltzheim, *La Nouvelle Armée française* (1875). Bibliothèque nationale de France, Paris.

In *La Débâcle*, the male homosociability of the army is both underpinned and undermined by the homoerotic bond between its heroes, Jean and Maurice, in a series of descriptions and encounters that Henry James, author himself of private homoerotic writings, marked up in pencil in his own personal copy of the novel, which he read while vacationing in France with Paul Bourget and his wife. Whereas heterosexual love ultimately triumphs in the marriages at the end of each Octave Mouret novel, the Versaillais Jean's killing of Maurice on the barricades of the

FIGURE 7.5 James Jacques Tissot, *Frederick Burnaby*, 1870. © National Portrait Gallery, London.

Commune impedes the heterosexual love plot that might have consummated the love between Jean and Maurice's twin sister, Henriette, but in the end, cannot. As we shall see, this is to be read in more than the simple—or *straight*forward—sense of the term as homicide, not only a same-sex killing but a fatal penetration in 1871 of the body and clothing of the man who had worn the same uniform as Jean in the war of 1870. What then of the homoerotic challenge to the homosocial plot of military fiction?

Zola's tripartite novel *La Débâcle* is structured around the relationship between two men, Jean and Maurice, who begin the war in the same uniform, but end up on opposing sides in the civil war of 1871. One of the strangest aspects of the novel, for many readers, has been the physical closeness that Zola repeatedly ascribes to these brothers-in-arms. As Zola writes on page 10 of his *ébauche*: "Not wishing to put women into *La Débâcle*, or rather, not wishing to give an important role to a woman, its novelistic interest will be diminished. I had landed on the idea of depicting a great friendship, all the friendship that can exist between two men."[19] As Robert

19. "Ne voulant pas mettre de femme dans 'la Débâcle,' ou plutôt ne voulant pas donner à une femme de rôle important, l'intérêt romanesque s'y trouvera réduit. Je m'étais arrêté

Lethbridge writes, "as they each represent one part of France, and as their friendship underlines national unity faced with the Prussian invasion, so the fact that they subsequently find themselves on opposite sides images a country divided within itself."[20] This will be key in my reading of one particular episode from, precisely, the halfway point of the novel, namely, the much celebrated defense to the last man, against Bavarian troops, by the *infanterie de la marine*, of a village to the south of Sedan named Bazeilles. For Zola's use of the heterosexual love plot, *malgré tout*, at the heart of this episode, in which Maurice's twin sister, Henriette Weiss, is widowed, is best explained by the novel's own version of *fraternité* and its analogy between the sexual and the political, an analogy that speaks back to Lynn Hunt's groundbreaking study of what she calls "the family romance of the French Revolution."

Zola's novel recounts the troubled tale of Republican *fraternité* through the brothers-in-arms, Jean and Maurice—Jean the proverbial salt of the earth, who has come from the illiterate rural peasantry of Zola's *La Terre* to defend the land he has farmed, leading a small unit of men, including his antithesis, the puny urban bourgeois culture-vulture Maurice, over whom he watches. This colossus of a novel begins with the unit's wild goose chase between Paris, Reims, and eastern France, culminating in its central section in a bravura depiction of the French defeat at Sedan, which triggered the demise of the Second Empire itself. Separated by circumstance, and their conflicting versions of Republican politics, Jean returns to Paris as a Versaillais soldier on behalf of the compromised Third Republic and kills a Communard rebel on the barricades, realizing only too late that this was his beloved Maurice. In the unmistakable political symbolism of this intra-republican death, and its return *to* the repressed conflict at the origin of the new republic, lies a prime motive for a collective amnesia with regard to this novel, making of it a *lieu d'oubli* as much as a *lieu de mémoire*.

One might well argue that war should provide a naturalist novelist such as Zola with the perfect ground on which to prove his ability to describe the excesses of *la bête humaine*. As Henri Mitterand, writes, in a manner that aligns Zola with the greatest nineteenth-century writer on warfare: "There is something of Machiavelli, if not of Clausewitz, in Zola's art of narrative space. He perhaps has Carnot's thermodynamics as a more or less conscious model. But I sometimes wonder whether, no less consciously, he has in mind the models of modern war, as defined by nineteenth century Europe" (87).[21] Peter Brooks's 2005 book *Realist Vision* opens with a yet more general analogy between the mimetic account of characters' lives and the game of playing with toy soldiers (just as Napoleon III and Wilhelm do in their

à l'idée d'y peindre une grande amitié, toute l'amitié qui peut exister entre deux hommes" (1378).

20. Lethbridge, "Introduction" to Zola 2000, xxv.

21. "Il y a quelque chose de Machiavel, sinon de Clausewitz dans cet art zolien de l'espace narratif. Zola a peut-être pour modèle plus ou moins conscient la thermodynamique de Carnot. Je me demande parfois si, non moins inconsciemment, il n'a pas en tête les modèles de la guerre moderne, tels que l'Europe du XIXe siècle les a mis au point."

military planning in *La Débâcle*). In Brooks's words, "The scale model—the *modèle réduit*, as the French call it—allows us to get both our fingers and our minds around objects otherwise alien and imposing" (1). As if realist and naturalist writing were always a wargame. As we have already seen, Delaherche's *lunette* allows him to spy in the manner of a mimetic narrator on the miniature Prussian king despite the latter's camouflage of modest dress, a detail repeated in part 2, chapter 6: "The master figure, the miniscule toy soldier, no taller than half his little finger, whom he thought he recognized as the King of Prussia, was still standing there in his dark uniform."[22]

Indeed, uniforms provide a forum for detail (anyone who has witnessed soldiers' relationship of pride and care to the details of their uniform will know this), which challenges the naturalist eye for detail. And however much care this noncombatant, Zola, took in his soliciting of detail, about Prussian uniforms from his Dutch correspondent, Jacques van Santen Kolff, and about the French army (as shown by the handwritten references on a visiting card from the greatest painter of the war of 1870, Édouard Detaille, to be found in Zola's preparatory dossier for the novel), still, any dubious slip-ups in the military detail of novel were attacked with venom by critics in the press.[23] Unable to find her cousin Dubrueil at the Hermitage, who might accompany her back to Bazeilles so that she could recover her husband's corpse, Henriette ignores the efforts of Jean and Maurice to take cover in the final pages of part 2, chapter 7. She finds ironic compensation in the discovery of a corpse from the same regiment of the Prussian Guard as Cousin Gunther, identifiable thanks to the photograph they had received from him. In the words of the narrator: "The corpse was indeed wearing the uniform of the Guard: dark gray trousers, blue tunic, and white braids, with his overcoat rolled up and slung over his shoulder."[24] She even risks her life in order to distinguish the same red *patte*, or epaulettes, as their cousin's regiment. The clear distinctions of military uniform necessarily misconstrue the complexity of cross-border relations, familial as well as national, in eastern France. When Gunther himself is seen in the distance and Maurice takes vengeful aim, the familial, feminine instinct brings Henriette to her senses and she orders him not to shoot.

In part 3 of the novel, post-Sedan, Prussian mastery is articulated through care for the uniform: "Soldiers were carefully brushing down their uniforms, pegged out on washing lines. Another was finishing a deft repair to his trousers."[25] But the only

22. "Le maître, le minuscule soldat de plomb, haut comme la moitié du petit doigt, dans lequel il croyait avoir reconnu le roi de Prusse, se trouvait toujours debout, avec son uniforme sombre" (686).

23. Mitterand includes both Zola's precise question and Van Santen Kolff's dutiful and detailed answer in his notes. See Zola 1967, 1534.

24. "Et le cadavre portait en effet l'uniforme de la garde : le pantalon gris foncé, la tunique bleue, aux galons blancs, le manteau roulé, noué en bandoulière" (701).

25. "Des soldats brossaient soigneusement leurs uniformes, étendus sur les cordes à sécher le linge. Un autre achevait une habile reprise à son pantalon" (744). For more on this widespread notion of "L'Allemand correct," see Dominé.

way Jean and Maurice can escape as prisoners of war is to renounce their uniform and flee incognito. History will take them down separate roads, but ultimately back together on the streets of the Paris Commune. What Zola's ultimately rather pro-Versaillais account does in its encryption in the Jean-Maurice relationship of the opposed Republican traditions of the conservative Republic and the radical Commune is to remind its French readers of the difficulty in washing away bloodstains and of marrying divergent traditions—literally, in the case of Jean and Maurice's twin sister, Henriette, whose closeness represents the reconciliation that Zola proposes, and yet which can never be consummated before the shared specter of Maurice. When the Versaillais Jean bayonets Maurice on the Communard barricade in the final lines of the novel's penultimate chapter, Jean recognizes Maurice's uniform but not his face, and Maurice only recognizes Jean in the light of the Communard flames a moment after he receives the wound, hence the horror of their tardy mutual recognition: "The fires lit both men up with blinding sharpness."[26]

In the final chapter Jean once again cuts Maurice's uniform, but this time so as to undress and nurse him: "Swiftly he used his knife to slit through the sleeve, and then removed the rest of the uniform. Blood began to flow, and he hurried to bind the arm up firmly, using rags torn off from the lining."[27] In order to take Maurice to safety, Jean dresses him up in the greatcoat and kepi that he has taken from the corpse of a Versaillais comrade, before rowing him along the Seine to relative safety as "Paris by night" burns, so that his wounds can be nursed.[28] Once on dry land, they bump into a company of the 88th Infantry Regiment on the Rue Saint-Florentin. Jean claims to be taking an injured comrade to the field hospital, and as the narrator underlines: "It was the greatcoat flung around his shoulders that saved Maurice."[29] Clothes are also used to try and save Maurice when finally, they reach Henriette, who tears up old shirts to make bandages for her twin brother. And in this, clothes and bandages extend a symbolic chain of cloth and fabric that Zola weaves into the text, in its full etymological amplitude, from the manufacture of sheets in Sedan to the waving of white flags. As Maurice passes away in the final pages of the novel,

---

26. "Les incendies les éclairaient d'une aveuglante clarté" (883).

27. "Vivement, à l'aide de son couteau, il fendit la manche, enleva ensuite l'uniforme entier. Du sang coulait, il se hâta de bander le bras solidement, avec des lambeaux arrachés de la doublure" (890).

28. Jean thus reciprocates the gesture of Maurice who, at the start of part 2, chapter 7, has placed on Jean's injured head the kepi of a dead soldier, so as to make him look the part (689).

29. "La capote, jetée sur les épaules de Maurice, le sauva" (896). The metonymical force of the "capote" and "kepi" combination in designating French soldiers is exemplified in Manet's lithograph *Guerre civile* (1871). See Bass. At the very start of the novel, Jean's amazement at finding himself back in service aged thirty-nine, having returned to civilian life after the Battle of Solferino (1859), is articulated in the same vestimentary terms: "il s'étonnait encore, de se revoir avec la capote aux épaules" ("it still surprised him . . . to see this soldier's cape about his shoulders again") (402).

the narrator reminds us that Henriette is still dressed in her widow's garb, a black thread connecting her husband's death to that of her brother. If the tragedy of the first had subsequently made possible and permissible her nascent feelings for Jean, the tragedy of the second imposes a taboo, and as Jean says his adieu, he can touch neither Henriette nor Maurice.

The work of Zola—sitting uncomfortably between Flaubert and Proust, and to this day embroiled in conflicting accounts of the modernity, even modernism, of his writing and of its literary worth in the face of its manifest cultural and ideological symptomatology—points both inward at the logic of its own compositional imperatives and strategies and outward to the stream of texts and images alongside which it was read. Emblematic in this regard is Zola's account of French courage at Bazeilles near Sedan, to be found in chapter 4 of the eight-chapter central section of *La Débâcle*, and thus at the center of this entire fictional enterprise.

Here Zola fictionalizes the renowned tale of French heroism in the defense of Bazeilles made famous two decades earlier by Alphonse de Neuville's 1873 salon painting, *Les Dernières Cartouches* (fig. 7.6). Given the indulgence of referential illusions (in every sense of that term) in naturalist rhetoric, perhaps the only true historical novel of Zola's *Histoire naturelle et sociale d'une famille sous le second Empire* bears a particular epistemological burden, for the fantasy of Zola and his reading public is that the novel should be both real *and* true—a fantasy much contested in contemporary press responses to the novel and its veracity, or otherwise. The

FIGURE 7.6 Alphonse de Neuville, *Les Dernières Cartouches*, 1873. Musée de la Maison de la Dernière Cartouche, Bazeilles.

episode of Bazeilles, still recalled today in annual commemoration, is such an interesting one for the cultural historian of literature because Zola was himself clearly aware of the saturation of texts and images post-Neuville, which would continue beyond 1892, and in which his own description would swim, or sink. Whether it be in music, in conflicting historical narrative and counternarrative, in theater, in prints, on postcards, or even in a short film from 1897 by one of the fathers of early cinema, George Méliès (*Les Dernières Cartouches* also released as *Bombardement d'une maison*; Star Film Catalogue no. 105). Méliès's short film references Neuville's painting in order to trigger (in more than one sense) a *tableau vivant*, and it performs in visual form the demise of the Imperial army in the collapse of the bombed roof and ceiling of the house in Bazeilles that the French had defended. Méliès finds in the dust of masonry and bombardment a historical referent for his pantomime theatrics of powder usually associated with a countermimetic cinema of fantasy and imagination. Neuville's painting is now to be found in the museum into which this very house in Bazeilles was turned in the years following the war, the name itself of the Musée de la maison de la dernière cartouche bearing witness to the signifying difference generated by Neuville's work of art in the historical imagination. The painting shows a dozen or so uniformed French troops shared between two rooms on the upper floor of the house, the threshold between the fore- and background rooms marked by two wounded soldiers, who are thereby shielded from the ongoing fighting but also symbolically liminal—between rooms, and between life and death. Whereas a nun enters Méliès's film in its final frames so as to nurse a wounded solider, Neuville's painting shows only a dozen or so uniformed men, bound together by heroic purpose, shorn of homoerotic overtones. Zola, in his account of the married couple Weiss and Henriette, will allow a man without uniform and a woman to enter the space of heroism. Subsequently, Henriette, widowed in this scene at Bazeilles, will nurse the wounded Jean, bandaging rather than clothing another heroic body, whose relationship with her brother, Maurice, is yet more eroticized by Zola than their impossible heterosexual love. It is telling that the homoerotically coupled Jean and Maurice are absent from Zola's account of Neuville's representation of this most popular remnant of heroic French masculinity from the war of 1870.

Zola structures the pathos of his account through the rhythm of two simultaneous countdowns: first, the countdown of bullets possessed by these dozen or so Frenchmen until "the last cartridge"; and second, the deaths of those same men. Henry James, who listed *La Débâcle* alongside *L'Assommoir* and *Germinal* as Zola's truly great novels, writes that "it was the fortune, it was in a manner the doom, of *Les Rougon-Macquart* to deal with things always in gregarious form, to be a picture of numbers" (27). But to the homosocial tale of men found in Neuville's painting, Zola adds the shortsighted civilian Weiss (the hero without a uniform), the description of the battle prefaced by the heterosexual suspense of his wife Henriette running to be by his side in Bazeilles against the tide of retreating French troops. In this focus on Weiss, echoed in the image by the Imprimerie Émile Lévy used to advertise

FIGURE 7.7 *Le Radical* publie *La Débâcle* par Emile Zola (1892–93). Bibliothèque nationale de France, Paris.

Le Radical's serialization of the novel (from October 19, 1892, to March 26, 1893) (fig. 7.7), Zola seems to justify his own failure to join up (as the shortsighted only son of a widow) by suggesting that one does not have to wear a uniform to be a patriot, and that one need not have been a soldier to write a patriotic novel on war.

Indeed, so powerful was the patriotic pull of his description of Bazeilles in part 2, chapter 4, that even Émile Faguet, usually intent on a *guerre de plume* with Zola, as one of the founders of the *critique universitaire* that it took Zola so long to penetrate, pours forth praise:

> The finest [of the most conspicuous scenes], which will be a classic tomorrow that you will find everywhere, is the defense of Bazeilles, and in particular of the house of the Alsatian Weiss, this obstinate, furious, battle, boiling over in an intense thirst for death, and for revenge prior to death. This is Mr Emile Zola's version of *The Last Cartridges*. It is one of the finest things written not just by him but by anybody.[30]

30. "Le plus beau [des épisodes qui se détachent en relief] qui sera classique demain et que vous trouverez partout, est la défense de Bazeilles, et particulièrement de la maison de Weiss l'Alsacien, la bataille obstinée, furieuse, enragée, dans une soif ardente de mourir et de se venger avant de mourir. Ce sont « les dernières cartouches » de M. Emile Zola. C'est une des choses les plus belles qu'il ait écrites et qu'on ait écrites." Émile Faguet, review in *Revue politique et littéraire*, June 25th, 1892. Reprinted in Zola 1967, 1433.

In a novel whose aesthetic dilemmas turn on the tension between individual experiences and what Naomi Schor famously refers to as Zola's crowds, the personal and the political meet in a homo prohibition on the hetero, which brings us back to Eve Kosofsky Sedgwick's stress on the radical disruption for men, in our society, of "the potential unbrokenness of a continuum between homosocial and homosexual." For it is Jean (already widowed) who will kill Henriette's brother, Maurice, with his bayonet, the Versaillais soldier killing the Communard rebel as the end of the novel approaches, reinstalling that repressive disruption at the heart of the masculine and imposing a limit on the polymorphous desires of men. In the words of Oscar Wilde's *The Ballad of Reading Gaol*: "Yet each man kills the thing he loves." This imposes an irresolvable taboo on the love shared by Jean and Henriette. How can one love the man who kills one's brother? It is this fracturing of modern France's politics of fraternity in the alternative uniforms of Versaillais and Communard that renders impossible—romantically and politically—any form of ideal union. And this fracture at the heart of republicanism, Zola's novel seems to suggest, is the compromise (in every sense of the term) with which the Third Republic must live.

Works Cited

Audoin-Rouzeau, Stéphane, and Annette Becker. *14–18, retrouver la Guerre*. Gallimard, 2000.

Bass, Jacquelynn. "Edouard Manet and 'Civil War.'" *Art Journal*, vol. 45, 1985, pp. 36–42.

Baudelaire, Charles. *Le Peintre de la vie moderne. Œuvres complètes*. Gallimard, 1976.

Brevik-Zender, Heidi. *Fashioning Spaces:* Mode *and Modernity in Late-Nineteenth-Century Paris*. U of Toronto P, 2015.

Brooks, Peter. *Realist Vision*. Yale UP, 2005.

Chifflet, Nathalie. "1914–2014, un 14-juillet très international." *L'Est républicain*, July 13, 2014, www.estrepublicain.fr/actualite/2014/07/13/1914-2014-un-14-juillet-tres-international.

Dominé, Jean-François. "L'image du Prussien dans la littérature française contemporaine." *Revue historique des armées*, vol. 269, 2012, pp. 11–25.

Harvey, John. *Men in Black*. Reaktion, 1995.

Hennique, Léon. *L'Accident de M. Hébert*. Charpentier, 1884.

James, Henry. *Notes on Novelists*. Dent, 1914.

Marcus, Sharon. *Between Women: Friendship, Desire, and Marriage in Victorian England*. Princeton UP, 2007.

Martin, Brian Joseph. *Napoleonic Friendship*. U of New Hampshire P, 2011.

Mitterand, Henri. "Pour une poétique de l'espace romanesque." *Zola and the Craft of Fiction*, edited by Robert Lethbridge and Terry Keefe. Leicester UP, 1990, pp. 80–88.

Roynette, Odile. *« Bon pour le service » : L'expérience de la caserne en France à la fin du XIXe siècle*. Belin, 2000.

———. *Les mots des soldats*. Belin, 2004.

———. "L'uniforme militaire au XIXe siècle: une fabrique du masculin." *Clio*, vol. 36, 2012, pp. 109–28.

Sedgwick, Eve Kosofsky. *Between Men: English Literature and Male Homosocial Desire*. With a new preface by the author. Columbia UP, 1992 [1985].

Winter, Jay, and Jean-Louis Robert. *Capital Cities at War: Paris, London, Berlin 1914–1919.* Cambridge UP, 1999.

Zola, Émile. *La Débâcle*, vol. 5 of *Les Rougon-Macquart.* Gallimard, 1967.

———. *La Débâcle.* Translated by Elinor Dorday, introduction by Robert Lethbridge. Oxford UP, 2000.

CHAPTER 8

CLIMBING IN PARIS

Stairways, Social Class, and the Sartorial in Proust

Áine Larkin

Marcel Proust's *À la recherche du temps perdu* (1913–27) traces fashions not only in clothing, but in art, politics, and language.[1] The novel is, as Susan Hiner states, "a veritable fashion show of the Belle Époque" (173). Diana Festa-McCormick affirms that "no other novelist in France . . . and probably outside France, has observed, depicted, and analyzed his characters through the optics of clothes as carefully as has Proust" (4). The clothes worn by diverse characters in *À la recherche du temps perdu* serve often to underline tensions between the value system of the dwindling aristocracy, which privileges notions of unchanging continuity, and those of the rising bourgeoisie, for whom newness, endless innovation, and conspicuous consumption are weapons in their struggle for cultural territory—particularly as played out in the streets and salons of fin-de-siècle Paris, as Duncan McColl Chesney notes before providing a neat, accurate summary of the whole gamut of types of salon in Proust's novel (871–72, 879–80). In this novel, intersections of class, race, and sexuality are explored through the evocation of subtleties of dress, adornment, and comportment in social and amorous life. Odette de Crécy and Albertine Simonet are important examples of modern women in this regard, since they learn to exploit fashion to different ends in their dealings with the men who love them; the baron de Charlus is another, as he uses severe masculine tailoring in an attempt to conceal his homosexuality. Garments matter and, as material objects, serve as a great social leveler in this novel, where style is not synonymous with monetary might.

Of interest here, however, will be the exploration of the ways in which Proust represents domestic servants' clothes and general appearance as they perform their duties, particularly within the space of the staircase. One scene from the novel's opening volume involving servants is freighted with complex meanings. It is part

1. *Marcel Proust in Context*, edited by Adam Watt and published in 2013, provides a comprehensive overview of the political, social, and cultural environment that shaped and informed Proust's creative vocation.

of one of the several magnificent society set pieces that populate the novel. An important character in this scene is Charles Swann, a cultured, bourgeois, provincial, Jewish, stockbroker's son, whose wit and social success grant him access to the most exclusive realms of Parisian and British high society. In the first volume of the novel, he becomes deeply infatuated with the relatively artless young courtesan Odette de Crécy (who later becomes one of the most elegant women in the novel). In this emotional state, Swann arrives at a soirée thrown by the aristocratic Mme de Saint-Euverte and there observes the beauty of the grooms and liveried footmen, some of whom wait on that lady's guests, while many others stand to attention "with a stately glitter tempered by common good nature, like saints in their niches" (1: 328).[2] These male servants are, for Swann, "heedful not to fail to carry out the instructions they had been given before being allowed to put on the dazzling livery which they wore only at rare intervals and in which they did not feel very much at ease" (1: 327).[3] Usually engaged in practical domestic tasks, whether as caretaker, butler, or silver cleaner, these men are, on this particular evening, charged with a purely ornamental function, each one is "motionless, statuesque, useless" (1: 326).[4] Of course, as this chapter will aim to show, they are in fact far from useless here. Much of the existing research on clothing in *À la recherche du temps perdu* focuses on the clothes worn by aristocratic and bourgeois women, rather than by servants and working-class characters. The following pages will examine the role of servants' clothing in this and a number of other episodes where the boundaries between past and present, cultural and financial capital, and heteronormative and "aberrant" sexualities are interrogated.[5]

According to Theresa McBride in *The Domestic Revolution* (1976), employing a servant or servants in nineteenth-century France and England was a typical assertion of "the triumph of the middle-class way of life" (14). McBride notes the difficulties involved in defining accurately the terms "servant" or "domestique," since the duties attached to these roles were various and often imprecise (11–13). McBride does note, however, that the terms tended increasingly to be applied to those workers who occupied themselves "exclusively with the personal needs of an employer and of his family in such a way that this occupation established a relationship of

2. "avec un éclat pompeux tempéré de bonhomie populaire, comme des saints dans leur niche" (*À la recherche du temps perdu*, 1: 320). All English translations of Proust are from *In Search of Lost Time*.

3. "attentifs à ne pas manquer aux recommandations qu'on leur avait faites avant de leur laisser endosser la livrée éclatante qu'ils ne revêtaient qu'à de rares intervalles et dans laquelle ils ne se sentaient pas très à leur aise" (1: 319–20).

4. "immobile, sculptural, inutile" (1: 318).

5. Existing research devoted to the representation of clothes in Proust's novel includes Diana Festa-McCormick's *Proustian Optics of Clothes: Mirrors, Masks, Mores* (1984), Anna Favrichon's *Toilettes et silhouettes féminines chez Marcel Proust* (1987), and Eva Maria Stadler's "The Red Dress of Oriane de Guermantes" (1990) and "The Lady in Pink: Dress and the Enigma of Gendered Space in Marcel Proust's Fiction" (2005).

FIGURE 8.1 Charles Bargue, *A Footman Sleeping*, 1871. The Metropolitan Museum of Art, Bequest of Stephen Whitney Phoenix, 1881.

personal dependence on the employer" (11). This nineteenth-century state of increasingly urban affairs contrasted with earlier uses on country estates of the term "servant" or "domestique" for seasonally employed agricultural workers, who were neither housed nor fed (nor indeed clothed) by their employer. Male servants were more expensive than female ones, and therefore more of a status symbol—hence perhaps their proliferation at Mme de Saint-Euverte's party.[6] In well-to-do nineteenth-century French households, it was common practice to employ one woman as both housekeeper and cook—the role played in *À la recherche du temps perdu* by Françoise, to whom we shall return; and the vast majority of middle-class households did not employ more than one or, at most, two servants. At Combray, the unnamed, pregnant "fille de cuisine" who helps Françoise is the only domestic servant mentioned, apart from the gardener; the smocks she wears prompt Swann to refer to her as "Giotto's Charity" (1: 83). These brief examples make it clear that Proust had something of a sociological bent in his depiction of French bourgeois domestic life, as Catherine Bidou-Zachariasen and Cynthia Gamble each confirm.[7] Other servants represented include nannies caring for the children of the well-to-do on outings to the Champs-Elysées gardens, and Jupien the tailor, whose sexual relationship with the baron de Charlus alters to become, first, that of brothel-keeper devoted to satisfying the baron's fantasies and, later, caretaker to an aged and weakened Charlus.

Naturally, the power dynamics of the bourgeois master-domestic servant relationship in late-nineteenth-century France were such that, in principle, the master or mistress had much greater control. The employer is after all free to dismiss an unsatisfactory servant from his or her household, while the servant is dependent on the master or mistress for his or her livelihood, and even for bed and board; existing research using nineteenth-century domestics' own accounts of their positions and treatment testify to the meanness they could and often did routinely suffer—some detailing how old clothes were passed on to servants, whose wages were then docked to pay for these discarded garments.[8] A salient fact with regard to household power dynamics is that nineteenth-century domestic servants "had the same status in the eyes of the law as a child, protected by and subject to the authority of the parent/employer" (McBride 15). Wearing livery while carrying out one's duties as a servant implies, for sociologist Thorstein Veblen, the economic power of the employer who permits this "vicarious consumption of goods" by his employees (49). Together with the provision of "spacious servants' quarters" (49), livery is an unsubtle means through which to demonstrate the extent of the employer's wealth. According to Veblen, it is a mark of dependence, and of "servitude, real or ostensible" (55).[9]

---

6. The increasing feminization of domestic service throughout the nineteenth and into the twentieth century came about as a result of war and increased military service demands.

7. Bidou-Zachariasen, *Proust sociologue*; Gamble, "From Belle Époque to First World War," in *The Cambridge Companion to Proust*, 7–24.

8. Theresa McBride's *The Domestic Revolution* (1976) is a valuable source in this respect.

9. Veblen's extended discussion of servant livery underlines its function as a means of vicarious consumption performed for the benefit of the employer's reputation: "The consumption and leisure executed by these persons for their master or patron represents an investment on his part with a view to an increase of good fame. As regards feasts and largesses this is obvious enough, and the imputation of repute to the host or patron here takes place immediately, on the ground of common notoriety. Where leisure and consumption is performed vicariously by henchmen and retainers, imputation of the resulting repute to the patron is effected by their residing near his person so that it may be plain to all men from what source

Within the domestic sphere, the boundaries between intimate and semi-public space had to be carefully negotiated and patrolled where servants were employed and granted access to all parts of the house, from the threshold spaces of the entrances and hallways, to the semi-public kitchen, sitting and dining rooms, to the private realms of bedroom, bathroom, and wardrobe. "Elaborate rules of etiquette," notes McBride, "regulated the interaction between masters and mistresses and their servants" (21), and the forms of deference were insisted upon.[10] For Proust's often sickly protagonist, however, the power dynamics of the master-servant relationship are neither clear nor straightforward, and his dependence on domestic servants is repeatedly conceived of as absolutely, even frighteningly, abject (1: 4). Edward Hughes affirms that "the boundaries and limit-setting derived from social hierarchy and the extent to which these are accepted, celebrated, and infringed, generate much of the micro-drama of daily life in the opening volume of the novel" (*Class* 45). This first volume (*The Way by Swann's*; *Du côté de chez Swann*) establishes the protagonist's relationships with his family and their servants, and it clarifies his inherited belief in the rigid boundaries separating different social worlds from each other in provincial France and in Paris. Hughes also notes how the new leisure spaces of fin-de-siècle France make the seemingly impermeable boundaries between social classes much more porous as the novel advances (*Class* 45), and certainly we find that, in the final volume (*Time Regained*; *Le Temps retrouvé*), changes in certain characters' social status occur with dizzying frequency and rapidity.

Fashion and style are of course not synonyms; for Proust, the latter quality becomes the more admirable as the protagonist learns to decipher the world and the way people present themselves. Roland Barthes's analysis of what he calls the "fashion system" stresses the way that fashion organizes material signifiers in ways that tell us something about the culture in question.[11] For Theodore Zeldin, nineteenth-century fashion "meant imitation, the opposite of individuality" (436). Nineteenth-century employers of servants were indeed concerned about servants' dress, which externalized that servant's position in the social order—and by extension, the position of their employer; household manuals of the time also show evidence of much resentment of servants whose clothing, in their leisure time, imitated that of their employers (McBride 25).

There are several servant characters in *À la recherche du temps perdu*, and more when one counts as a kind of servant the *demi-mondaines* whose role is to serve male fantasy and give pleasure to the men who pay them, and who permit them to enter their homes at certain, restricted times. Thus, Odette de Crécy, first

---

they draw. As the group whose good esteem is to be secured in this way grows larger, more patent means are required to indicate the imputation of merit for the leisure performed, and to this end uniforms, badges, and liveries come into vogue. The wearing of uniforms or liveries implies a considerable degree of dependence, and may even be said to be a mark of servitude, real or ostensible" (55).

10. In *Fashioning Spaces*, Heidi Brevik-Zender links fashion and servant spaces, underlining the importance of such spaces dedicated to waiting and anticipation (109–42).

11. Barthes, *Système de la mode*.

glimpsed as the young "lady in pink" ("dame en rose"), the protagonist's great-uncle Adolphe's mistress, ascends from shady origins to the pinnacle of Parisian society. Her metamorphoses include being Charles Swann's lover and then wife, and mother of Gilberte; becoming Mme de Forcheville, and finally the mistress of the duc de Guermantes—and the Elstir painting of Odette posing as "Miss Sacripant" implies that she enjoyed cross-dressing in her youth. As Odette de Crécy, she is fashionably but unflatteringly attired, overly slavish in her adherence to the modes of the day; as Mme Swann and Gilberte's mother, her taste becomes assured and refined, abandoning the dictates of passing fashion. In *Le Temps retrouvé*, Mme de Forcheville is unrecognizable to the narrator precisely because her appearance and style remain, with the help of rouge and dye, largely untouched by time: she resembles a "sterilized rose" (6: 258)[12] because of her uncanny lack of signs of age. Odette's *toilettes* are examined at great length; for the protagonist and Swann she represents initially the would-be, budding *bourgeoise*, overly concerned with transient fashion trends and popular chic. As the illicit "dame en rose," the courtesan Odette indeed looks disappointingly demure and conventionally bourgeoise to the young protagonist, who imagines that courtesans' appearance will match their transgressive position in society. When she comments on the boy's resemblance to his mother, however, great-uncle Adolphe dismisses her remark by claiming that the two women have never seen each other. Odette's swift retort points up the fragility of social boundaries in Haussmann's Paris: "I beg your pardon, my dear friend, I passed her on the stairs last year when you were so ill. It's true that I saw her for only a split second and your stairs are quite dark, but that was enough for me to admire her" (1: 78).[13]

The staircase on which the two women cross paths, as each carries out her particular caring role in relation to Adolphe, is a liminal space where different worlds come very close to, and can observe, each other. Here the world of the family as unit of emotional support meets the world of the sex servant. In *Fashioning Spaces:* Mode *and Modernity in Late-Nineteenth-Century Paris*, Heidi Brevik-Zender coins an apt phrase to designate the in-between, not-wholly-public-but-not-yet-private nature of the staircase as a "dislocation of modernity" (5). Removed from the noise and crowds of the street, the staircase is an altogether more intimate intersection, a fact that Odette underlines here. In her determined social ascent, Odette is keenly observant of her social superiors wherever she encounters them, and here she stresses the proximity that Adolphe's illness has brought about between his family and his amorous life, two spheres that he normally takes great pains to keep completely separate. In her demure pink dress, Odette wears the "livery" of the sex servant, which enables her to infiltrate without difficulty the classed space of Adolphe's flat. Sharon

12. "rose stérilisée" (4: 528).

13. "Je vous demande pardon, mon cher ami, je l'ai croisée dans l'escalier l'année dernière quand vous avez été si malade. Il est vrai que je ne l'ai vue que le temps d'un éclair et que votre escalier est bien noir, mais cela m'a suffi pour l'admirer" (1: 75).

Marcus's work shows convincingly the ways in which the public and private, the domestic and urban, intersect in the nineteenth-century Parisian apartment building.[14]

Sitting in great-uncle Adolphe's apartment in her pink dress, Odette de Crécy resembles any well-brought-up young woman, for the crestfallen protagonist at least; though Eva Maria Stadler notes the prevalence of sensual, carnal pinks and reds in the clothes beloved women wear throughout the novel ("Lady" 362). Odette does use her cigarettes astutely to mark her modernity and daring in this scene—these accessories are an important part of her "armature of feminine seduction," in the context of Odette's careful wooing of her lovers.[15] Odette's sartorial savvy shows how successfully she passes herself off as a middle-class lady (and perhaps Adolphe likes her to dress in this carefully conservative way?). Fashionable dress is here an "unreliable indicator of social position," as Susan Hiner notes with regard to post-Revolutionary confusion about clothes (2). Contact between members of different social worlds happens in this scene because of the vagaries of Adolphe's sexual desire, while in fin-de-siècle salons, art is the cause of what Duncan McColl Chesney calls "a preliminary *rapprochement*, a gesture from both directions ('up' from the bourgeoisie and 'down' from the aristocracy)" (880). The interplay of separate social classes, on horizontal and vertical planes of urban existence, is represented both literally and figuratively in *À la recherche du temps perdu* through modern conveniences such as elevators, planes, and cars; and staircases are evoked repeatedly in society scenes, and in domestic and amorous life.

The most important domestic servant of all in *À la recherche du temps perdu* is of course Françoise, the peerless cook whose skills throughout the household make her indispensable to the protagonist's hypochondriac *tante* Léonie at Combray (for whom she is obliged to run up and down stairs all day) and, after *tante* Léonie's death, to the protagonist's own family in Paris. Though transplanted to Paris, Françoise is a "paysanne," and her attachment to her provincial *terroir* is fetishized by the protagonist, particularly as regards her speech, which is rich in regional dialect and shaky in its grasp of standard French. The protagonist conceives of Françoise's peasant status as closely aligned with that of the aristocracy (embodied by the duchesse de Guermantes), which he imagines her forebears to have served for centuries past—that is, he regards her as the embodiment of an unbroken, unchanging peasant tradition that has served the upper echelons of French society, and as such, he endows her with a rich cultural heritage, particularly though not exclusively in the culinary arts: "we had to say to ourselves that in her there was a very old French past, noble and ill understood" (1: 32).[16] She rules absolutely over other domestic servants, notably the pregnant, asthmatic kitchen maid whom she torments by forcing her to

14. Marcus, *Apartment Stories*.

15. Susan Hiner uses this term to describe nineteenth-century women's accoutrements (1). For a more detailed analysis of Odette's provocative use of cigarettes in *À la recherche du temps perdu*, cf. Áine Larkin, "Les objets matériels et le monstre aux yeux verts."

16. "on était obligé de se dire qu'il y avait en elle un passé français très ancien, noble, et mal compris" (1: 28).

prepare asparagus even though she is allergic to it; she also rules over the young protagonist, who both admires and resents the unfamiliar code of conduct governing her actions. Toward the end of the novel, once his procrastination has at last given way to the resolve to complete a literary work of art, the protagonist/narrator underlines how important Françoise's support and influence are to him when he states his determination that, with her help, "pinning a supplementary page in place here and there, I should construct my book, I don't dare say, ambitiously, as if it were a cathedral, but simply as if it were a dress I was making" (6: 343).[17] Thus dressmaking, among all of the domestic arts at which Françoise is skilled, is the source for one of the multiple metaphors used to represent the creative act of writing in which the protagonist finally decides to engage.

Françoise's adroit way with clothes is a mark of her distinction within and for the family she serves. Duncan McColl Chesney neatly defines Bourdieu's term as implying the "evaluative recognition of difference, and its manifestation in signs"; distinction is "performative, negative, and community- or clique-building. It is not about individuals, but groups" (883). This concept troubles what might otherwise appear to be wholly admiring readings of Françoise's clothes in several episodes. For the young protagonist, Françoise is a powerful figure. In his early childhood, accompanying his mother on her annual New Year's Day visit to *tante* Léonie in her Paris home, he first encounters Françoise and describes her headdress carefully:

> Hardly had we arrived in my aunt's dim hall than we would see in the shadows, under the flutes of a dazzling bonnet as stiff and fragile as if it were made of spun sugar, the concentric ripples of an anticipatory smile of gratitude. It was Françoise, standing motionless in the frame of the little door of the corridor like the statue of a saint in its niche. (1: 56)[18]

It is important to note the parallel between this description of Françoise's New Year's Day bonnet and that of the servants' livery at Mme de Saint-Euverte's soirée: in both cases, the event is a special, ritualistic one, and the garments worn are noteworthy precisely because of their deviation from the domestic everyday norm. In both situations, Proust uses the phrase "saint in its niche" to designate these domestic figures now fixed in position, whether for aesthetic worship or devotional thanks. The five-franc piece the protagonist's mother has him pass on to Françoise in this scene suggests the latter, whereas Mme de Saint-Euverte's attendants seem to be choreographed into a purely aesthetic display of power, beauty, and aristocratic

17. "épinglant de-ci de-là un feuillet supplémentaire, je bâtirais mon livre, je n'ose pas dire ambitieusement comme une cathédrale, mais tout simplement comme une robe" (4: 610).

18. "À peine arrivions-nous dans l'obscure antichambre de ma tante que nous apercevions dans l'ombre, sous les tuyaux d'un bonnet éblouissant, raide et fragile comme s'il avait été de sucre filé, les remous concentriques d'un sourire de reconnaissance anticipé. C'était Françoise, immobile et debout dans l'encadrement de la petite porte du corridor comme une statue de saint dans sa niche" (1: 52).

pomp. Margaret Topping notes that, in his handling of religion, "Proust playfully negotiates a fine balance between reverence and irreverence" (138). In both aforementioned situations, clothing effaces the servant's individuality and inserts him or her into an artistic tradition familiar to the cultured, bourgeois onlooker—here, that of religious sculpture; Renaissance art in the Saint-Euverte episode. The description of Françoise's halo-like bonnet here echoes Swann's habit of evoking Giotto's frescoes of the Vices and Virtues when inquiring after the pregnant kitchen maid at Combray (Proust 1: 79–80). Françoise's saintly demeanor is swiftly undercut by the narrator's acknowledgment that she is waiting for her traditional New Year's gift of money; nevertheless, the mockery does not completely dismiss the sense of familial reverence that surrounds Françoise. The whole clan acknowledges her skills, and her contribution to the material comfort of their middle-class family life.

Proust's protagonist/narrator appreciates the power of clothing to convey personal style, and his awareness of this fact means that garments function in *À la recherche du temps perdu* as a democratizing force, since style is something that money cannot really buy. The protagonist's lover Albertine studies other women's clothes carefully because her limited financial resources oblige her to choose judiciously; she dresses increasingly stylishly thanks to advice from the artist Elstir, her own flair, and her lover's tutelage (he likes to think). Odette de Crécy dresses badly in her early years as a courtesan but better as her improving circumstances enable her to afford more expert seamstresses, and her fixed preferences become her personal "brand." But it is Françoise who, in the eyes of the protagonist's family at least, proves most unerring in her taste, when she dresses in bourgeois tante Léonie's cast-off hat and coat for a train journey from Paris with the protagonist and his grandmother. He and his mother remember those garments as hideous on his great-aunt; now, thanks to Françoise's skill, they have been transformed:

> my great-aunt having cast off the coat, Françoise had had it turned and its inside now showed as a fine cloth in a handsome self-colour. . . . And, just as it is sometimes strange to notice refinements which the most deliberate artist might have to strive for, in a popular song or in a white or yellow rose blooming at exactly the right spot on a peasant's house, so with her sound and simple taste Françoise had placed on the hat, which was now a pleasure to behold, the velvet bow and the cluster of ribbon that would have delighted one in a portrait by Chardin or Whistler. (2: 228)[19]

19. "le manteau étant hors d'usage, Françoise l'avait fait retourner et exhibait un envers de drap uni d'un beau ton. . . . Et, de même qu'il est quelquefois troublant de rencontrer les raffinements vers lesquels les artistes les plus conscients s'efforcent, dans une chanson populaire, à la façade de quelque maison de paysan qui fait épanouir au-dessus de la porte une rose blanche ou soufrée juste à la place qu'il fallait—de même le nœud de velours, la coque de ruban qui eussent ravi dans un portrait de Chardin ou de Whistler, Françoise les avait placés avec un goût infaillible et naïf sur le chapeau devenu charmant" (2: 10).

FIGURE 8.2 Jean-Baptiste-Siméon Chardin, *Portrait de Madame Chardin (1707–91) 1775.* © RMN-Grand Palais / Art Resource, NY.

This modest countrywoman "quite devoid of base instincts but 'knowing her place'" (2: 228)[20] shows what her middle-class onlookers consider her impeccable style, in her transformation of coat and hat for this unusual journey on modern public transport, where close contact with strangers makes deciphering social status much less certain than at home. *À la recherche du temps perdu* is an apprenticeship to signs, according to Gilles Deleuze (11), and the signs Françoise emits demonstrate her adherence to principles of good taste that align with those of her employers, reflecting well on them, of course, but which are also regally unaffected by the

20. "qui sait 'tenir son rang et garder sa place'" (2: 10).

transient dictates of the modern nineteenth-century fashion industry.[21] Whereas her starched New Year's Day bonnet was described in terms of spun sugar—a nod to her unparalleled excellence as a cook—here she is promoted to the status of painterly artwork through the evocation of Chardin and Whistler. For Proust, Chardin's importance lies in his rendering of banal and everyday domestic scenes as extraordinary; Whistler's studies, symphonies, harmonies, and variations, in particular colors such as gray, white, flesh tones, and red—which borrow from the abstract language of music for their titles—are sophisticated manipulations and combinations of colors. To evoke his name in relation to Françoise in her traveling suit is to elevate the domestic servant to those cultivated artistic realms, by virtue of her sartorial style alone. Her dexterity is such that a coat and hat declared "hors d'usage" can finally be found handsome by her employers, those critical bourgeois observers.

The passage quoted earlier goes on to state that Françoise "called to mind one of those depictions of Anne of Brittany painted by an old master in a book of hours" (2: 228).[22] So, harking even further back to the Early Modern period here, the middle-class narrator once again obscures the peasant Françoise's individuality in deference to painted representations of a real aristocrat, as opposed to a fictional one: one devoted to her native Duchy of Brittany. The somewhat discomfiting—indeed humorous—implication is that, for her self-satisfied, conventional onlookers, Françoise is so effortlessly, naturally, tasteful that she deserves acknowledgment as a queen of style, reminiscent of Early Modern provincial royalty. Heidi Brevik-Zender observes:

> A paradox of fashion, that it was always changing yet did so by remaining consistent in its seasonal, regular transformations, echoed a contradiction of modernity, which was that a fascination with turmoil and transformation existed in tandem with a longing for consistency and permanence. ("Interstitial" 95)

Here the Proustian Narrator does seem determined to inscribe Françoise firmly within both age-old tradition and transformative modernity. The railway station platform at the modern Gare Saint-Lazare, with its democratically horizontal lines of track laid down to serve all of France's citizens, is the setting where the protagonist and his mother appreciate Françoise's exquisite sartorial taste; Mme de Saint-Euverte's soirée takes place on the (European) first floor of her exclusive Parisian *hôtel particulier*. If the references to Chardin and Whistler with regard to Françoise were admiring in tone, here references to art seem intentionally unflattering. Although she is a marquise, Mme de Saint-Euverte's behavior as hostess is viewed by Swann with a somewhat jaundiced eye. Arriving at her house, he sees the careful arrangement of servants as being "in the foreground of that fictitious summary of their domestic life which hostesses like to offer their guests on ceremonial occasions

21. Nineteenth-century fashion is carefully analyzed in the valuable "Costume" chapter of Anne Green's *Changing France: Literature and Material Culture in the Second Empire*.

22. "faisait penser à quelqu'une de ces images d'Anne de Bretagne peintes dans des livres d'heures par un vieux maître" (2: 10).

FIGURE 8.3 Jean-Baptiste-Siméon Chardin, *Woman Cleaning Turnips*, ca. 1738. Alte Pinakothek, Munich. Photograph credit: bpk | Bayerische Staatsgemäldesammlungen.

and in which they seek to respect accuracy in costume and setting" (1: 325).[23] Phrases such as "au premier plan," "résumé fictive," and the "vérité du costume"

23. "au premier plan de ce résumé fictif de leur vie domestique que les maîtresses de maison prétendent offrir à leurs invités les jours de cérémonie et où elles cherchent à respecter la vérité du costume et celle du décor" (1: 317).

and "du décor," and the use of the verb "prétendre," imply the overt theatricality and falsity of the situation. Swann sees Mme de Saint-Euverte as attempting—without necessarily succeeding, as the phrase "chercher à respecter" ("seek to respect") makes clear—to resurrect status-marking traditions now fallen into disuse. The result for Swann is the spectacle of high society life reduced to a "series of pictures" (1: 326).[24] The clothes the servants wear in the courtyard and on the staircase are relics of a former aristocratic age. Far from functioning as an indicator of rank, pride and belonging, the servant-men's livery sits uncomfortably on their skin, and their uniform arrangement on the staircase steps suggests an allegiance to the household which is directly at odds with the reality of their daily lives, when they work separately as "good people who lived the rest of the week somewhat independent in their domains . . . and by tomorrow would perhaps be in the bourgeois service of a doctor or manufacturer" (1: 327).[25] The economic reality is that their employment is insecure, and their livery a sartorial sign of former Saint-Euverte glory rather than of each servant's identification with that aristocratic family and its territory of origin.

This scene underlines the prevalent nineteenth-century misconception that under the Ancien Régime, servants had been associate family members, models of loyalty who were attached to their employers and accepting of their "place" in society (McBride 16). Even Thorstein Veblen appears to have unquestioningly accepted this idea, when he remarks on the historical shift from the practice of employing armed and liveried servants to the contemporary use of domestic livery:

> In the later development of peaceable industry, the usage of employing an idle corps of uniformed men-at-arms gradually lapses. Vicarious consumption by dependents bearing the insignia of their patron or master narrows down to a corps of liveried menials. In a heightened degree, therefore, the livery comes to be a badge of servitude, or rather servility. Something of an honorific character always attached to the livery of the armed retainer, but this honorific character disappears when the livery becomes the exclusive badge of the menial. The livery becomes obnoxious to nearly all who are required to wear it. (56)

Writing about American sartorial style in the late nineteenth century, Veblen posits a transition (at some undetermined point in time) from employing a proudly defensive servant band to a menial domestic. In fact, as Theresa McBride shows, no such earlier, warlike situation had ever really pertained in French domestic service. What *was* unique to the nineteenth and early twentieth centuries, a period of rapid urban expansion, was the increase in the numbers of domestic servants, for whom such jobs facilitated their transition from rural to urban life.

---

24. "suite de tableaux" (1: 317).

25. "brave gens qui vivaient le reste de la semaine un peu indépendants dans leur domaine, . . . et seraient peut–être demain au service bourgeois d'un médecin ou d'un industriel" (1: 319).

Charles Swann has excellent sartorial taste himself; his circulation among diverse social worlds throughout *À la recherche du temps perdu* means that he "unwittingly shows the relativity of social value," as Edward Hughes notes ("Social Spaces" 156). He sees that Mme de Saint-Euverte's liveried servant men are in borrowed finery, and the inauthenticity of their role is underlined by a drawn-out comparison between two staircases in this scene. In Haussmann's Paris, many buildings are constructed with a service staircase, to be used by domestic staff who might thereby avoid contact with members of the family for whom they worked. These buildings were structured in such a way that the higher up the building one goes, the less prestigious or ostentatious are the uses to which the rooms are put: hence the "chambre de bonne" appellation given to the small attics where maids-of-all-work slept, for example (Ariès and Duby 311). For Swann, as he enters Mme de Saint-Euverte's house, the contrast between its formal staircase and his desire to be with Odette, who is visiting her former dressmaker that very evening, is overwhelming: "Oh, with what joy by contrast would he have gone up the dark, evil-smelling and rickety flights to the little retired dressmaker's" (1: 327).[26] Dressmaking and dressmakers are here relegated to a lowly status both economically and socially, since Swann imagines that she must reside on the fifth floor of her building; his supposition may well be accurate, as Theodore Zeldin notes that in the late nineteenth century, "the average working dressmaker made only 2 francs a day" (436–37). As Swann climbs the stairs, he pictures the staircase Odette may be passing through:

> Whereas in the old dressmaker's pestilential and longed-for staircase, since there was no second, service stair, one saw in the evening in front of each door an empty, dirty milk-can set out in readiness on the mat, on the magnificent and disdained staircase which Swann was mounting at that moment, on either side, at different levels, in front of each anfractuosity formed in the wall by the window of the lodge or the entrance to a set of rooms, representing the domestic service which they directed and paying homage to the guests on their behalf, a concierge, a majordomo, a steward . . . stood under the arcature of their portals with a stately glitter tempered by common good nature, like saints in their niches. (1: 327–28)[27]

26. "Ah! Avec quelle joie au contraire il eût grimpé les étages noirs, malodorants et casse-cou de la petite couturière retirée" (1: 319).

27. "Tandis que dans cet escalier pestilentiel et désiré de l'ancienne couturière, comme il n'y en avait pas un second pour le service, on voyait le soir devant chaque porte une boîte au lait vide et sale préparée sur le paillasson, dans l'escalier magnifique et dédaigné que Swann montait à ce moment, d'un côté et de l'autre, à des hauteurs différentes, devant chaque anfractuosité que faisait dans le mur la fenêtre de la loge ou la porte d'un appartement, représentant le service intérieur qu'ils dirigeaient et en faisant hommage aux invités, un concierge, un majordome, un argentier . . . se tenaient sous l'arcature de leur portail avec un éclat pompeux tempéré de bonhomie populaire, comme des saints dans leur niche" (1: 319).

The modest staircase Swann imagines is described first here, with the result that the subsequent description of Mme de Saint-Euverte's staircase is overlaid on but does not obscure the first, and establishes a parallel between the position of the soiled milk cans on the doormats in the dressmaker's staircase, and that of the footmen at the marquise's party. While this juxtaposition of milk cans and men initially produces a comic effect, there is also a disquieting suggestion that these obliging, working-class domestics are objects as insentient and expendable as milk cans. Theresa McBride affirms that domestic service was indeed for most people a temporary career in nineteenth-century urban environments (9). The passage describing Swann's ascent to and entry into the room where the concert is taking place covers more than three pages, and these three pages contain repeated references to artists whose works depict handsome men, or who are skilled at portraiture—Mantegna, Dürer, Goya, Benvenuto Cellini. Their male beauty is these servants' main purpose, as they pose in their livery in the role of tarnished modern-day "tigers" (1: 325):[28] Proust borrows Balzac's term overtly here.[29] Gender ambiguity characterizes the representation of these stylish men throughout the episode: while their massive stature and musculature are repeatedly stressed, the delicate beauty of their faces and their careful hairstyles troubles the gender performance on display. For Veblen, "there is a marked similarity . . . between the apparel of women and that of domestic servants, especially liveried servants. In both there is a very elaborate show of unnecessary expensiveness, and in both cases there is also a notable disregard of the physical comfort of the wearer" (120). The Proustian Narrator, through Swann's ironical gaze, notes the physical discomfort of Mme de Saint-Euverte's servants. In Volker Schlöndorff's visually lavish adaptation of *Un Amour de Swann* (1984), this scene includes the closeted homosexual baron de Charlus, who discreetly cruises the footmen as he makes his way upstairs. The men's attractiveness underlines the potential of sexual desire to transgress social barriers, which are seemingly impossible to overcome, with all kinds of potentially messy social consequences, as in the mildly awkward exchange between Odette and Adolphe discussed earlier. Veblen goes on to affirm:

> There are of course also free men, and not a few of them, who, in their blind zeal for faultlessly reputable attire, transgress the theoretical line between man's and woman's dress, to the extent of arraying themselves in apparel that is obviously designed to vex the mortal frame; but everyone recognizes without hesitation that such apparel for men is a departure from the normal. We are in the habit of saying that such dress is 'effeminate'; and one sometimes hears the remark that such or such an exquisitely attired gentleman is as well dressed as a footman. (121)

---

28. "tigres" (1: 317).

29. In her 2002 translation of *The Way by Swann's* for Penguin, Lydia Davis translates this phrase as 'Balzac's "tigers"' (1: 325).

Thus, for Veblen, discomfort is characteristic only of women's clothes, and livery carries connotations of "unmanly" excess. Instead of representatives of feudal loyalty, Mme de Saint-Euverte's very numerous domestic servants in livery are embodiments of her conspicuous consumption in the service of her centuries-old family status, and more—they are vicarious consumers of her wealth, displayed purely for the visual pleasure of her guests, irrespective of gender. We find aristocratic privilege here borrowing the unsubtle fashion system of the modern bourgeoisie, in order to shore up a commonly held fallacy about the stability of Ancien Régime life—and to project that life into the present and future. "The disappearance of a legitimate aristocracy did not diminish the appeal of nobility to the imagination of the French ruling and artistic classes" (873), states Duncan McColl Chesney, and in this scene Mme de Saint-Euverte is playing on this imaginative charm of her family background in a carefully staged piece of domestic theater.

In conclusion, it is clear that descriptions in *À la recherche du temps perdu* of clothes and accessories that servants wear point up continued, even fond bourgeois adherence to misconceptions about the past and present constancy of Ancien Régime lifestyles for both the aristocracy and rural-dwelling people, even as the increasingly urbanized bourgeoisie's financial dominance asserted itself ever more emphatically over that of any remaining survivors of the Revolution. The matter of material garments and how servants chose, wore, tweaked, and handled them during the restless fin-de-siècle provide fresh insights into ways modernity was lived through the clothed body. For the ambitious *demi-mondaine* or lower-middle-class girl, mastering middle-class modishness opens doors and enables social ascent through their relationships with heterosexual men, many of whom are shown to be predatory and, in Swann's case, obsessive and jealous.[30] "An article may be useful and wasteful both, and its utility to the consumer may be made up of use and waste in the most varying proportions" (69), observes Veblen, and in the ways in which servants wear clothes and use accessories in *À la recherche du temps perdu*, it is possible to detect a convergence of pleasure, discomfort, self-interest, and social ascension. As invitations not only to cultured appraisal, but also fantasy and even desire, servants' clothing and accessories, however modest, provide valuable material for Proust to manipulate as he takes the measure of his richly populated, status-anxious, and often elegant fictional world.

Works Cited

Ariès, Philippe, and Georges Duby. *Histoire de la vie privée*. 4 vols. Seuil, 1985–87.

Barthes, Roland. *Système de la mode*. Seuil, 1967.

Bidou-Zachariasen, Catherine. *Proust sociologue : de la maison aristocratique au salon bourgeois*. Descartes et Cie, 1997.

30. For detailed analysis of the ways in which jealousy is manifested in Proust's novel, cf. *Cent ans de jalousie proustienne*, edited by Erika Fülöp and Philippe Chardin.

Brevik-Zender, Heidi. *Fashioning Spaces:* Mode *and Modernity in Late-Nineteenth-Century Paris*. University of Toronto Press, 2015.

———. "Interstitial Narratives: Rethinking Feminine Spaces of Modernity in Nineteenth-Century French Fashion Plates." *Nineteenth-Century Contexts*, vol. 36, no. 2, 2014, pp. 91–123.

Chardin, Philippe, and Erika Fülöp, eds. *Cent ans de jalousie proustienne*. Classiques Garnier, 2015.

Deleuze, Gilles. *Proust et les signes*. Presses Universitaires de France, 1964.

Favrichon, Anna. *Toilettes et silhouettes féminines chez Marcel Proust*. Presses Universitaires de Lyon, 1987.

Festa-McCormick, Diana. *Proustian Optics of Clothes: Mirrors, Masks, Mores*. Stanford French and Italian Studies, 29, Anma Libri, 1984.

Gamble, Cynthia. "From Belle Époque to First World War." *The Cambridge Companion to Proust*, edited by Richard Bales, Cambridge UP, 2001, pp. 7–24.

Green, Anne. "Costume." *Changing France: Literature and Material Culture in the Second Empire*, Anthem Press, 2011, pp. 117–45.

Hiner, Susan. *Accessories to Modernity: Fashion and the Feminine in Nineteenth-Century France*. U of Pennsylvania P, 2010.

Hughes, Edward. *Proust, Class and Nation*. Oxford UP, 2012.

Hughes, Edward. "Proust and Social Spaces." *Cambridge Companion to Proust*, edited by Richard Bales. Cambridge UP, 2001, pp. 151–67.

Larkin, Áine. "Les objets matériels et le monstre aux yeux verts." *Cent ans de jalousie proustienne*, edited by Erika Fülöp and Philippe Chardin. Classiques Garnier, 2015, pp. 107–18.

Marcus, Sharon. *Apartment Stories: City and Home in Nineteenth-Century Paris and London*. U of California P, 1999.

McBride, Theresa M. *The Domestic Revolution: The Modernisation of Household Service in England and France 1820–1920*. Croom Helm, 1976.

McColl Chesney, Duncan. "Aristocracy and Modernism: Signs of Aristocracy in Marcel Proust's *À la recherche du temps perdu*." *MLN*, vol. 120, no. 4, French Issue, Sept. 2005, pp. 871–95.

Proust, Marcel. *À la recherche du temps perdu*. 4 vols. Bibliothèque de la Pléiade, 1987–89.

———. *In Search of Lost Time*, 6 vols. Translated by Lydia Davis. Penguin, 2002.

Stadler, Eva Maria. "The Lady in Pink: Dress and the Enigma of Gendered Space in Marcel Proust's Fiction." *Studies in 20th and 21st Century Literature*, vol. 29, no. 2, Summer 2005, pp. 358–80.

———. "The Red Dress of Oriane de Guermantes." *Reading Proust Now*, edited by Mary Ann Caws and Eugene Nicol. Peter Lang, 1990, pp. 255–63.

Topping, Margaret. "Religion." *Marcel Proust in Context*, edited by Adam Watt. Cambridge UP, 2013, pp. 137–44.

Veblen, Thorstein. *Theory of the Leisure Class*. Oxford UP, 2007.

Watt, Adam, editor. *Marcel Proust in Context*. Cambridge UP, 2013.

Zeldin, Theodore. *France 1848–1945: Volume Two: Intellect, Taste, and Anxiety*. Oxford UP, 1977.

CHAPTER 9

EXPANDING CONSUMER LANDSCAPES

Exhibiting French Men's Fashion in the Interwar

John Potvin

The 1925 Exposition internationale des arts décoratifs et industriels modernes in Paris asserted the authority of the Art Deco style within the marketplace as much as it was meant to symbolize the restoration of French supremacy in the decorative and industrial arts. Prestigious cultural industries became impressive and spectacular means of advertising France's unique position within and impact on the global economy, particularly in a period of growing competition from Germany and the United States. Certainly, at the center of these grand claims were women's fashion and the industries of luxury, in particular haute couture, which remained a continuous source of envy and desire. Scholars have long argued for the modern image of Paris as a women's or a feminine city whose landscape was crowded with enticing shop windows, shimmering golden surfaces, and sensory pleasures orienting them toward countless delights, while others have explored how Paris became the capital of modernity through luxury, shopping, and the numerous and varied outcomes of the 1925 Exposition (see: Gronberg, *Designs* and "Paris 1925"; Troy; Weiss; Wilson). Through the art of display and the technologies of modern staging, the Exposition skillfully proclaimed France's entitlement as international arbiter of taste, style, and luxury, with Paris as the pinnacle of unrivaled excellence, the urban locus of distinction. Given its clear financial sway comprising an undeniably significant portion of the national economy totaling nearly 2.5 billion francs by 1924, the role played by women's high fashion within the overall scheme of the Exposition was not insignificant (Gronberg, "Paris 1925" 159).

However impressive and remarkable such statistics may be, the scholarly attention paid to women's haute couture of the period, to the exclusion of men's luxury goods and clothing, has inadvertently painted a rather simplified picture of the intersection of materiality and modernity as much as the role fashion, as a whole, played in France's desire to enlarge its sphere of cultural superiority and hence industrial influence. The picture to date further occludes what is a much more complex set of cultural and national forces at play in the postwar period, in which men's tailored goods emerged as a critical path through which the nation asserted itself in another, as yet untapped, domain. Moreover, what has yet to be explored are the roles played by masculine consumerism and men's fashion in the currently lopsided history of Art Deco, the narrative of postwar restoration, and the return to order that it necessarily engendered. On a purely practical level, men's fashion would not necessarily factor as the most spectacular or luxurious means to enable a nation's phoenix-like rise of rebirth. Nonetheless, despite its reliance on neutral tones and rational idioms, men's luxury tailoring and accessories began to assume a pivotal and expansive role in the propagation of France's sphere of influence in a global landscape already dominated by a centuries-old tradition that placed London's Savile Row at the forefront. Long before the war, London boasted its status as the undisputed epicenter of the fashionable gentleman; it was, after all, the original environment that elicited the birth of the iconic figure of Beau Brummell, the modern dandy whom the French held in such high regard. However, by the early twentieth century, London represented something far more exemplary to the modern and modernist mind alike. Writing in the early years of the new century, Vienna-based architect Adolf Loos claimed London as *the* capital of modernity, an honor it owed almost exclusively to its masculine sartorial excellence. Loos eloquently materialized the twined cultural, economic, and political forces of democracy and capitalism in the form of the gentleman's suit.[1] The "unadorned" Englishman's suit stood four-square as *the* index of modernity—and by extension modernism—precisely because of its stability, sobriety, discretion, and anonymity, and perhaps above all else its rational applications of tailoring. The anonymity of the rational men's suit, to which Loos alludes, seamlessly fit within the new capitalist era. For, as Siegfried Kracauer asserted: "The human figure enlisted in the mass ornament has begun the *exodus* from lush organic splendour and the constitution of individuality toward the realm of anonymity to which it relinquishes itself when it stands in truth and when the knowledge radiating from the basis of man dissolves the contours of nature's visible form" (83).

Metropolitan modernity, fashion, and gender became so inextricably linked that by the time of the 1925 Exposition, it was concluded in the twelve-volume encyclopedia of the Exposition: "If men go to London to find their tailors and shirt makers, there is not a woman who does not dream of being dressed in Paris" (9). Despite this grand proclamation made by the organizers, this chapter seeks to challenge both the exhibition's supposed gendered bias and the long-held exclusive female identity of the fashion capital. In fact, I posit that this geographically determined bifurcated consumer landscape speaks less to purported realities and entrenched traditions, as I initially presumed, than to the emergent desires and intentions of men's tailors and cultural critics that this essay seeks to chart. My ambition to expand the cultural history of postwar commodity culture is premised on the shifting discursive landscape leading up to and as a result of the exposition, as

1. Adolf Loos lived in the French capital from 1923 to 1928.

well as what I see as a pivotal and culminating moment on which all this hangs, the much-neglected Exposition de France à Athènes, which took place three short years later in 1928. The shifting landscape I focus on here hinges on how the reassertion of the elusive and purportedly inherent notion of "French taste" and Parisian chic could be, for the first time in modern history, articulated and jettisoned through men's sartorial choices in an expanding culture of consumption. Men's invitation into this domain, however, in the form of international expositions was conceived of and marketed neither through the supposed frivolous transience of the fashion system nor loftier aspirational registers of elegance as embodied by women's couture, but rather through the unwavering forces of men's rational tailoring as a means to forging a stable and yet diversified industrial force. In short, I seek to explore the ways masculinity, more broadly, and men's fashions, more specifically, were staged, advertised, and discursively constructed as a result of Art Deco's most anticipated and celebrated exhibition and the new directions it quietly promised in establishing a French sense of postwar rational civilization.

If well-heeled French men were compelled for cultural, historical, sartorial, and/or practical reasons to go to London to fulfill their bespoke tailored needs and desires, the tacit implications were that 1) men were dependent on travel to satisfy their consumer itches, and 2) men's fashions were removed from the quotidian fabric of Paris as much as from the national concerns of postwar reconstruction and the balance of payment. In this way, men and their consuming habits (ostensibly through travel to London or importation), at least at first glance, might have seemed unpatriotic. But was this really the case, despite the attention paid to English style and even American taste in contemporary periodicals? The monthly magazine *Monsieur*, for example, reported, "An elegant man, a French man 'comme il faut,' an English 'gentleman' are exemplary results of the species" (Gregh 231). By 1920, men's fashion was defined by way of a triangulated network between New York, London, and Paris, the so-called metropolises of modernity, to tailor a seemingly universal male figure of elegance and civilization. As Europe's first true men's fashion magazine, *Monsieur* was not unlike countless other French periodicals of the period invested in claiming a superior position for Paris when it concerned male fashion, regardless of the origins of the tailor. Founded in 1920 by Swedish impresario Rolf de Maré (1888–1964), the short-lived magazine[2] went to great lengths in applauding and buttressing the various cognate industries that helped to fashion a distinctly (French) postwar dandy, a figure said erroneously to have disappeared with Oscar Wilde's death in 1900. Already equipped with the best that the industries of luxury had to offer, Paris was a seemingly natural milieu in which to stake a claim for the growth of a men's tailoring industry or even the creation of a men's fashion and lifestyle magazine. As I have argued elsewhere, in its discussion of either fashion ensembles or furniture ensembles, *Monsieur* refused any attempt at a reconciliation of fashion's Janus-faced identity, preferring instead to honor its dandy forbearers

2. Under financial duress, de Maré sold the magazine in 1924, which folded in 1925.

by turning to them for leadership and inspiration while also eyeing a future in which men played a critical role in the health and material well-being of national industries through the perceived feminine act of consumption (Potvin, "Housing"). The 1920s, after all, marked an unprecedented moment in the shifting landscape of economic roles; now *both* men and women were engaging in dieting, sunbathing, magazine subscriptions and fashionable attire.

1925: Men's Tailoring on the Horizon

On the occasion of the 1925 Exposition, the glamorous Pavillon d'Élégance has all too often overshadowed the Grand Palais, which was the first space in 1900 to publicly and on such a massive scale exhibit Parisian haute couture outside of the exclusive milieu of the designer salons in the Rue de la Paix. In the Pavillon d'Élégance organized by Jeanne Lanvin, men's fashion was decidedly absent from this luxurious space of femininity steeped in glamour and decorative elegance. However, it was in the Grand Palais where smartly attired male mannequins designed by Pierre Imans stood alongside their female cohorts, together forming general if not slightly unclear groupings in the Garden and Hall d'Hôtel, respectively. Under the glass-roofed Grand Palais, this inaugural, albeit small, inanimate male presence patently performed an auxiliary role to the eye-catching spectacle of women's fashion.

However, it was clear that men's fashions were becoming an important cultural symbol. In an article aptly titled "Les Élégances masculines" from 1925, *L'Art vivant* reasserted the importance of men's fashion, claiming:

> We no longer estimate that costume is a vain thing. When he doesn't put on an odious affectation, when he applies happy and discrete care, an elegant man is surely better seen than a bear. Believe this is big progress, and this is recent progress. Entire generations of French have had on this topic different ideas. They have thought that a man worthy of the name did not concern himself with his clothing because such a concern was not virile. . . . For, on earth, all males of all species are disposed to please and appear in a more magnificent robe than the most tender object of their thoughts. (Marsan 22)

Penned by the celebrated cultural critic and essayist Eugène Marsan, the article declared that France was paying witness to a second "revolution in menswear" (23). The country's decline in menswear and sartorial elegance was supposedly the unfortunate result of a first revolution in 1789 when men turned to England, and no longer to France, the clear result of the renunciation of a decadent, feminized, and debauched monarchy. Within a mere thirty years, the magazine alleged that the "great masculine renunciation" was a *fait accompli*. For the periodical the postwar period, however, marked this prophetic second revolution. *L'Art vivant*, which reported on men's fashion with surprising regularity, was relentless in its positioning of Paris as a new, improved, and directional menswear capital. In 1926 it noted how, "[f]or the first time, since more than a century . . . Paris holds its head equal to London. . . . It was just that fashion took a privileged place among the decorative arts in the Grand Palais. It is essentially an art . . . fashion, like the other arts, interprets nature" ("Londres et Paris" 313). While the magazine might have rightly claimed that the revolution in menswear began prior to the war, I posit that its ascendancy was a result of enthusiastic and determined postwar ambitions, which could be neatly folded into the exposition's organizers' overstated ambitions.

The exhibition represented the first time when the urban landscape and the national best interest were predicated on expanding the consumerist ethos as a means to rebuild a nation at its core infrastructure. Within this novel and unique cosmopolitan landscape of consumption, an architectonic counterbalancing between the horizontality and verticality of the exhibition established and even reinforced clear gendered associations. The feminine horizontality of the purposefully fabricated pathways of the Exposition with its myriad boulevards of consumption were, it must be said, vying equally for attention in a landscape of continuous phallic punctuations. Nocturnal vistas were equally, if not more, stunning than during the day when, for six weeks, famed car manufacturer Citroën helped the cause by transforming the Eiffel Tower into one large, erect shimmering advertisement, both for itself and for Paris's soaring industrial modernity. On the occasion of the Exposition, the multivalent Eiffel Tower stood as a phallic symbol of industrial prowess and decorative marketing. In other words, it stood as a beacon for Paris the Modern.

As an unyielding counterpoint to the haute luxury of Art Deco that dominated the Exposition's French pavilions, Le Corbusier's contentious and minimal "L'Esprit Nouveau" pavilion coupled with his polemical *L'Art décoratif d'aujourd'hui*, published in tandem with the Exposition, was perhaps the event's greatest critique offering a stark modernist agenda set in deep opposition to the perceived decadence of the decorative style. His alternative white-walled program, initially announcing itself as unaffected and untainted by the whims and follies of fashion (see Wigley), was meant to provide a rational antidote to what the architect perceived as rampant decorative and frivolous excess, unrestrained female consumption, and the degenerative, decorative decay of civilization itself. Much has been made of how the Exposition functioned as a women's playground, the site of a hetero-masculinist gaze, and the important moment of Le Corbusier's influential insertion into and redirection of the narrative of French modernism (see, for example, Gronberg, "Paris 1925"); it cannot come as a complete surprise that the role of men's fashion and an alternative masculine presence has largely been oversimplified, or just simply ignored. In turn, this has only served to feed into the erroneous metanarrative of a "great masculine renunciation."

Indebted to Loos's design theories and polemical essays, Le Corbusier took up the Vienna-based architect and designer's notional well-dressed, suited man as the signifier not only of modernity, but also modernism itself, suggesting and symbolically noting how the "bowler hat appeared on the horizon" (Le Corbusier 54). Indeed, a man's hat did appear on the horizon of the Exposition, looming large over

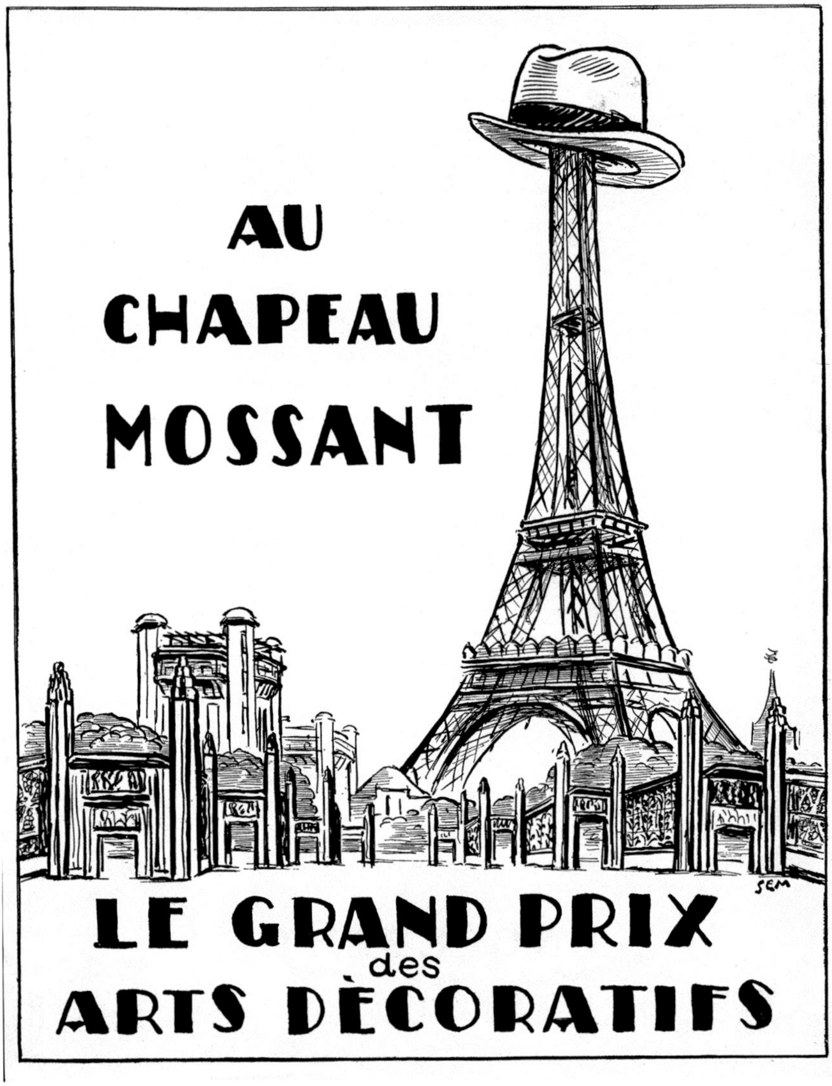

FIGURE 9.1 "Au Chapeau Mossant," advertisement, *L'Illustration*, 23 January 1926. Photograph by John Potvin.

it, thanks in large measure to the advertising campaign of the well-known men's hat maker Mossant (fig. 9.1). Atop the Eiffel Tower, Mossant did not form, in visual terms, part of the intimacy of the boulevard circuit of luxury boutiques, which according to Gronberg "had become almost as important an icon of modernity as the Eiffel Tour" (*Designs* 57), but soared above it. In Mossant's advertisement industrial innovation coheres seamlessly with rational, yet fashionable, tailored goods of distinction. This was not the traditional, formal top hat, however, nor was it the businessman's bowler to which Le Corbusier made reference.[3] Rather, it was a fedora, a novel symbol of fashionable masculine modernity. Although the fedora was first introduced for women in 1889, it was made popular by Britain's Edward, Prince of Wales, in 1924, when he started sporting it in public. While the felt hat was seen to be at once both stylish and practical in its ability to protect men against wind and rain, here it served as a perfect cross-dressed emblem of men's entry into the customarily feminine realm of fashionable consumption. Thus, while the 1925 Exposition built its reputation as a woman's playground, it also clearly announced itself as a salutary gesture to the progressive stance being proposed by French tailors. Stated otherwise, men's entry point into Art Deco's staged topography was enabled and emblematized in the industrially innovative Eiffel Tower of the previous century. Somewhere between the industrial and fashionable, modernity and materiality, innovation and tradition, men's tailored goods, simply and best signified by the fedora, provided a new and unique understanding of luxury somewhere between (feminine) glamour of the Art Deco and the (masculine) ethos of industrial progress.

Whatever glorious terms were used to describe women's haute couture at the 1925 Exposition, such laudatory language devoted to men's wear was exceptional and marked an entirely new territory for national pride and distinction for France. For, unlike in the case of women's wear, the presentation of men's tailored clothing necessarily entered into a competition demarcated along geopolitical lines. As volume 9 of the *Encyclopédie* declared:

> Whatever the English influence on the male costume, Parisian tailors are creating designer originals. Clothes conceived by them distinguish themselves from those realized at the same time by their colleagues in London. Their invention benefits from a favor it has never known and that extends abroad. The advantage of the exchange is not enough to justify the increase of their market outlets. There actually is a French masculine fashion, which expresses our qualities of measure and good taste. It manifests itself all the way into composition of fabric for which English manufacturers do not disdain to welcome the ideas of French tailors, their customers. (15)

The General Catalogue of the Exposition further proclaimed: "this is the work of men who having returned from the war, announced, in peacetime, that a new style is born. This was to be the setting [décor] for the men of the future" (in Gronberg, "Paris 1925" 8). Indeed, setting is everything as we will see in the following section. In the same year as the Exposition, trade publication *Vendre* questioned whether or not French tailors could or should advertise; not surprisingly, the magazine turned

3. By the early twentieth century, the bowler hat had shed its nineteenth-century working-class affiliation and was now being worn by businessmen working the financial district.

to London to answer in the affirmative. At the same time, the monthly magazine also claimed a moral importance for Citroën's unabashed rental of the Eiffel Tower, declaring that "it is not a work of art. . . . It is an affirmation of industrial power, a symbol of the century of iron. . . . At last, this economic force, this incomparable agent of civilization, is at the same time a moral force, for publicity can only place itself in the service of good products, of loyal objects" ("Citroën A Loué La Tour Eiffel," n.p.). For the magazine and Exposition alike, it was the decorative and industrial arts that could pave the way to rebuild national prestige and prosperity.

It was clear that the Exposition's decorative phallic presence, whether in the form of the countless obelisks and sprouting fountains, Mossant's fedora topped or Citroën's glittering Eiffel Tower, gave rise, quite literally, to men's nascent and expanding position within the emerging consumer landscape of the boulevard shopping circuit. In 1926, *L'Art vivant* further commented:

> Was it not on the world map, where France between Italy and Belgium (the three graces, I say with love) had such a beautiful role to play after the armistice? It is only in men's clothing that Paris finally resists, finally opposes the English idea with a better solution. . . . If French tailors are capable, as we hope they are, to support the beauty evident in the execution of their designs, their trial is won. The elegant men of the two hemispheres will turn their eyes toward us. The difference at play is not in the textiles. The debate pertains to cut. But form and the figure (*ligne*) are almost everything in the modern suit. ("Londres et Paris" 313)

The article asserted that the English suit ages its wearer by ten years. Even the great American athlete Talmadge, said to dress in the new English styles, "has a heavy air about him that he did not have before. Those of you who are not Talmadge [in other words not an athlete] you appear like a pot of tobacco. . . . All the real Frenchmen who have read me will refuse with coldness of contempt the new English suits, thickening, aging, disfiguring. They will ask for the new French suits, which are thin and edgy" ("Londres et Paris" 314). However, to which English suits was the magazine alluding? Were they those bespoke goods fashioned in the finest shops in Savile Row to which, the *Encyclopédie* noted, men were flocking? Or, were they the ones turned out by Paris-based tailors like Barclay in the Avenue de l'Opéra or Robert Cumberland in the rue Scribe, which now eclipsed London through the modernity of their cut and aesthetic?

1928: Men's Tailoring, a Classical Ideal

If the 1925 Exposition's Pavillon d'une ambassade Française was meant to display and embody French taste and style in a foreign, diplomatic context, then the 1928 Exposition de France à Athènes set out to take the show on the road. Directed by Edmond Yvan and organized under the auspices of the Comité Français des Expositions and the Comité National des Expositions Coloniales, which were united in 1925, the 1928 iteration set out to establish an industrial as much as symbolic link between French excellence and classical Greek cultural distinction. Unlike in the 1925 international iteration, on this occasion French men's tailoring took center stage, no longer an appendage or footnote to the glamour of women's haute couture or to any other country.[4] Category 86, under which the clothing industry fell, was divided into four discreet subgroups and came under the jurisdiction of Émile Bouton.[5] With this new distinguished presence, men's fashion was worthy of being reported on in widely read weekly periodicals like *L'Illustration* and the newly formed men's fashion magazine *Adam* (founded in 1925). *L'Illustration* noted that the international exposition had become for France, "for its commerce of luxury goods, a flattering triumphant terrain with happy material results. . . . Those of our merchants and industrialists who participate work less for themselves, in truth, than for the renown of France and for the development of the increasing favor, in the world, that French production is witnessing" (Cavaille xxiii). The impact and significance of one of France's most important weekly papers should not, particularly in this context, be underestimated. As Dudley Andrew and Steven Ungar have shown, throughout the interwar period, "*L'Illustration* projected week after week a vision of modernization and transformation; yet, given its nationalist outlook, it also purveyed the proud French tradition, evident in its many photo essays about older architecture and current national events" (264). As with the 1928 Exposition, the weekly journal deployed men's high fashion as *the* register of modernization and transformation, while at the same time suggestively imbuing it with a sense of French tradition.

L'Illustration made clear that within the global arena of French luxury, "a separate space must be made for men's high fashion. It seems, in fact, that hitherto we had not yet seen the latter also clearly aware of the latent power it holds to exercise in his domain, on the world stage . . . to serve as a model, open channels and set the tone. . . . It is a fact of our times that a man with neglected clothes, a man who does not concern himself with a sober elegance, is a fallen man" (Cavaille xxii). The metaphor of the fallen man, burdened by grave postwar insinuations, sees sartorial neglect as akin to moral and national degeneration. However, *L'Illustration*'s position was far from novel, but echoed sentiments expressed in *L'Art vivant* in 1925, which condemned the supposed great masculine renunciation of the nineteenth century as noted in the previous section of this chapter. The art journal was all too eager to stress the important shift taking place in contemporary men's attitudes toward fashion, which sees how "all men at least have the same disgust over a bad suit as they do a vile act" (Marsan 22).

In a different yet related context, Adam C. Stanley has noted the stark differences between the fashion advertisements directed at men and women, respectively, paying particular attention to the fictional environments used to contextualize the goods displayed. While decidedly generalizing in his conclusions, Stanley nevertheless

---

4. Women's fashions were largely not included, save for extravagant and luxurious furs, despite the fact they were consistently referred to in the catalog essay on fashion.

5. Category A: hats for men and women and notions; Category B: men's shirts and accessories; Category C: silk industries; Category D: men's and women's shoes.

FIGURE 9.2 "Ingénieux principe d'exposition—le vêtement présent dans son atmosphère rationnelle," *L'Illustration*, 1928. Photograph by John Potvin.

FIGURE 9.3 "Péristyle de l'église de la Madeleine," *L'Illustration*, 1928. Photograph by John Potvin.

FIGURE 9.4 "Salon d'un grand hôtel du boulevard du même nom," *L'Illustration*, 1928. Photograph by John Potvin.

provides an invaluable assessment for our purposes here. He claims that men populate "public or social settings, while women were generally portrayed without any background image or in a domestic scene" (80). His findings should not come as a complete surprise, given the long-held belief in the ideal divide of the separate spheres that dictated the gendering of public space as masculine, while the domestic was trivialized for its purportedly inherent feminine nature. Such a gendered strategy in fashion advertisements throughout the 1920s is rendered in three-dimensional form in the displays of the 1928 Exposition de France à Athènes (see figs. 9.2–9.4). Indeed, as Stanley asserts, "[s]uch ads defined men as intrinsically rational and calculating about their clothing purchases, interested in clothes for their quality, practicality, and durability" (84), the soaring pillars of industry.

In the Exposition, entire mise-en-scène tableaux situated male mannequins in more specifically identifiable interiors and public contexts. French fashion, translated and transported to the land of Adonis, Hercules, and Apollo, was represented by the best of Parisian tailors, whether English or French, who like Hercules and Adonis in classical times, could transform the shape and contour of the male form through training and sports. In Athens, men's tailored fashion was also to assume the mantle of helping not simply to rebuild, but now expand France's cultural superiority and spheres of influence.[6] What better environment to do so, than in the shadow of the

6. It might be worth noting that in 1924 Paris played host to the summer Olympics, further enhancing its neoclassical pretentions and cultural allusions.

cradle of Western civilization itself, made visibly potent in the advertisement of the Paris-based, English tailor Robert Cumberland whose shop at 3 rue Scribe was renowned for its French and English tailored goods and riding clothes (fig. 9.5). In Cumberland's advertisement for the Exposition's general catalog, a line-drawing of a man in formal, dinner jacket, attire is silhouetted by a blackened Greek figure. The racial ambivalence and ambiguity of Cumberland's twined figures is corrected only by way of the "Antonius" denoted at the presumably sculptural base of the figure. The blackened figure acts in a seemingly duplicitous way. On the one hand, the dark pre-industrial, naked Greek figure is purposefully set in relief to the industrially civilized, sharply attired French man as a means to heighten the latter's modernity and civilization while, on the other, the former conjures a mythical connection between Modern France and Ancient Greece. Richard Dyer argues, "The Aryan/Caucasian myth established a link between Europeans and a venerable culture known to predate Europe's oldest civilisation, ancient Greece. . . . Greece was seen as the cradle of Europe, but something had given birth to Greece, and that had to be compatible with the European sense of self and could not therefore be located in Africa" (21).

The gravitas of the Greek figure does loom large as a historical and connecting presence to the tailor's and by extension the Exposition's ambitions. Proudly announcing its "grand prize" at the 1925 Exposition, the register of cultural and industrial excellence, the Paris-based tailor promotes its well-suited man as if emerging from the shadow of the past and its black, negative impression. The simple and stark black and white figural contrast sets into relief a number of imbricated issues at play in this Exposition: first and foremost is the counterbalancing relationship between (nude) Greek antique sculpture and the modern (tailored) French man, himself equally appearing in representational form. The advertisement figuratively outlines France's pretensions to be the natural inheritor of classical Greek civilization and its well-established and much-celebrated ideals of male beauty, while at the same time marking itself out as a cultured and well-clothed, decidedly modern progression of that idealized material form. While the shadow visibly looms larger than the tuxedo-clad model, Cumberland acknowledges his success, given the 1925 accolades, and the weight of his position in the evolution of elegant masculine civilization.

In the same catalog as Cumberland's advertisement, dandy, cultural commentator, and author André de Fouquières exclaimed: "Men fashions! Frivolous subject matter, some ignorant people would say, but I would wager that the big artists in the vestimentary arts and the thousands of corporate workers will not share this advice and will celebrate the predominance of French taste. Let us repeat that fashion and commerce of luxury are important factors in our radiance in the world" (in Yvan 145). For de Fouquières, men's tailoring was an integral part of the radiance of French luxury around the world; perhaps it is akin to the lasting effects of classical Greek civilization to which Cumberland's advertisement suggests. Contemporary men's fashion was tailored to the needs and gravitas of civilization itself, especially poignant in times of peace and industrial prosperity, short lived though both would prove to be.

Figure 9.5 Robert Cumberland advertisement, Exposition de France à Athènes general catalog, 1928. Photograph by John Potvin.

Paris-based, English tailor Barclay, responsible for the organization of the display of the men's high fashion section of the Exposition,[7] claimed they wanted to give to the "presentation [of men's fashion] the luxury and brilliance that it merited. Thanks to the devoted efforts of the exhibiters, we were able to realize a very novel ensemble, and an indisputable artistic cachet."[8] Various scenes were meant to evoke the racetracks at Deauville, the halls of a grand hotel, the steps and peristyle of La Madeleine, to conjure grand yet rational spaces suitable to a "realistic" representation of bespoke men's fashion and perhaps even masculinity itself (see figs. 9.2–9.4). Within the staged public spaces there is a critical shift that occurs between the two expositions. In the 1928 example, the male mannequins leave behind the cross-sex world of the 1925 Exposition's Grand Palais to indulge in the safe, even if at times ambivalent and ambiguous, realm of a more clearly staged homosociality.[9] The famed glittering, otherworldly mannequins of Stockman and Siegel used for the female mannequins populating the 1925 Pavillon d'Élégance are exchanged here for Imans's realistic wax mannequins similarly used in the Grand Palais. The need for realism and identifiable backgrounds is not without importance within the context of this exposition. Here, these "realistic" male mannequins are meant to define, stand in for, an entire (masculine) industrial system; after all, fashion and tailored goods formed part of the Exposition's industrial arts mandate. In many ways, there was no clearly established language for Parisian tailors to work with; rather, I suggest they borrowed heavily from the rational domain of industry, captivating allure of luxury staging, and the comforting quietude of the mimetic impulse that Imans's non-abstract, nongeometric mannequins offered. Barclay and the organizers' strategy to conjure natural rather than abstract settings kept with the return to order that dominated cultural politics in the aftermath of war,[10] which in the timing and setting of this exposition demanded a controlled, rational approach to objects, bodies, and spatial settings.

In the early 1920s, Art Deco's penchant for zigzags, bursts of color, cubist geometric patterning, and overall fashionable "soft" clothing, which "unsettled even

---

7. High fashion for men included: Barclay, Clément & Brunet, Cumberland F Disslin, Damien, Fislevitz, Fredrik, Harrison, Hase-Pappel, Jamet-Harmaniantz, Jose, Kriegck Balmana & Rabau, and L. Larsen & Company. Men's tailors and luxury shirt makers included: Lenay, Lus & Befve, Manuaté, O'Rossen, Pighinim Portes, Voisin, Yose, Barclay, David, Leinen-Peuch, and Poirier.

8. Barclay, "La Haute Mode Masculine Parisienne," n.p.

9. I am not suggesting in any way women did not participate as visitors, or even that there were not women's fashion included in the Exposition, even if it was limited to a selection of furs. What makes this exposition in Athens unique and distinct from its 1925 predecessor in Paris is the way in which it purposefully staged exclusively male scenarios, leaving open various same-sex desires to materialize.

10. For a detailed discussion of the *retour à l'ordre* found in art in the 1920s, see *Le Retour à l'ordre*; Troy. For a discussion of the *retour à l'ordre* and male fashion's relationship to modern art, see Potvin "Masculinity."

women amazed by this masculine metamorphosis," led to exaggerated styles even if it was their more subdued and refined cousins that were set on display at the 1925 Exposition (Chenoune 148, 151). However, as Farid Chenoune notes, by 1927 the feeling shifted when "[t]he fashion of 'freaks' and 'crazies' seemed like a bad dream to tailors and distinguished gents in London and Paris" (158). One might even go so far as to conclude that the Exposition de France à Athènes served as an antidote to the perceived decadence of the postwar abandon embodied in the then-fashionable gender ambivalence and sartorial ambiguity. For as the 1925 *Encyclopédie* announced: "today the respectable man dresses like an adolescent and the clothing of a young woman is similar to that of her grandmother. There is no longer an age to fashion. This tendency toward uniformity is favored by current economic conditions" (13). In keeping with the times, the *Encyclopédie* proposed a more democratic, barrier-free fashion, devoid of any concerns with gender or age.

L'Illustration described the Exposition's scenes as: "current fashion in its rational milieu" (fig. 9.3). Kriegck's advertisement in the general catalog, for example, is a photograph of two mannequins located from within the Exposition's "Salon d'un grand hôtel du boulevard du même nom" tableau (fig. 9.6). In these staged vignettes, and through advertisements by tailors like Kriegck, repetition and reproduction tacitly emphasize abundance, industrial processes, and modernist mimetic strategies that denoted the return to order espoused by the worlds of art and culture. Rational dress at the Athens exposition appears to have been a reaction to Art Deco and yet borrowed from its consumerist ethos elegantly embodied in the 1925 Exposition. In this way, the 1928 iteration embodies at once the rational Taylorist ideal of standardization through the repetitive images of tailoring while combining them with a budding syncretic model, which sought to incorporate diverging methods and traditions. What emerges is a tension, or perhaps a symbiosis, between the slightly programmatic traditions of tailoring and the modern systems of display, consumption, and staging management embodied by the Art Deco style. Indeed, at the Exposition de France à Athènes the tailors' rational approach to the mise-en-scènes of the male mannequins function as a different sort of mass ornament. As Kracauer remarked one short year prior to the Exposition: "The mass ornament is the aesthetic reflex of the rationality to which the prevailing economic system aspires" (79). The exhibition's "rational" mise-en-scènes constructed especially for the men's tailored sections are premised on a geometric assemblage of inanimate forms confined to a spatial regime that is determined by at once a mimetic drive and rational principles of men's dress.[11] "The ornament, detached from its bearers, must be understood *rationally*. It consists of lines and circles like those found in textbooks of Euclidean geometry" (Kracauer 77–78).

Although several tailors and houses participated, lending their own unique style to the spaces of the event, they nevertheless cooperated toward "a generous

11. By contrast, women's luxury furs were displayed through a simple exhibiting style, devoid of context or identifiable environments.

FIGURE 9.6 Kriegck advertisement, Exposition de France à Athènes general catalog, 1928. Photograph by John Potvin.

ensemble effort . . . that will exalt again, without a doubt, the high ideas, we present abroad, of French taste" (Barclay n.p.). In Athens, the trafficking of men's tailoring became an important part of the national agenda abroad as a means to advertise France's newfound success and marketing acumen. Inspired by London, buoyed by already strong national industries, France's tailors were quickly becoming arbiters of that country's most precious natural resource, luxury; however, Athens and its civilizing force also served as a critical cultural as much as national register for French pretensions. According to the Exposition's catalog: "There exists between the Greek and the French, spiritual brothers, only resemblances, only analogies!" (in Yvan 7). The neoclassical coupling of ancient democracy and contemporary capitalism were made all the more powerful in a discussion of the necessary role played by rationalization in the industrial interests of France, which according to the catalog,

> had renounced the excesses of individualism for which they had been reproached. The magnitude of the difficulties of the war necessitated in France, as everywhere, a sense of a common effort as with a continuous perfecting of their methods. We speak a lot at home of "rationalization" that has become for all European industries, brutally ruined by the war, a sort of, somewhat insistent, "leitmotif." The thing existed before the word, for if it had not existed before, there would no longer be any industry in France. (in Yvan 68)

Within the 1928 Exposition, the common effort achieved through syncretic and Taylorist methods ensured that men's luxury, now located somewhere between the vagaries of the fashion system and the longevity of tradition, was a means toward French industrial progress and success. With the Exposition's emphasis paid to men's wear, the organizers seemed to suggest that, not unlike Ancient Greece, French civilization prevailed, and that the country had regained its health and manpower, belying the devastation wrought by the war a decade earlier. Men should be rationally tailored accordingly.

Conclusion

In his *Reports on the Present Position and Tendencies of the Industrial Arts as Indicated at the International Exhibition of Modern Decorative and Industrial Arts, Paris, 1925*, H. Llewellyn Smith prophetically concluded that the "Paris Exhibition may be regarded in two aspects; as an arena of international rivalry, or as a source of light, inspiration and warning" (37). While he was certainly not referring to men's fashion, but rather to the overall potential driving force of the Exposition, I wish to appropriate Smith's words as a means to conclude what I see as a critical path that men's luxury fashion took following the war and more specifically on the occasion when France aimed to reassert its cultural and industrial superiority. With men's tailoring and accessories, cultural critics, tailors, and government minsters alike saw an opportunity to simultaneously expand France's consumer base both domestically and internationally. After all, Paris in the 1920s was an, if not the most, important destination for the rich and famous, to say nothing of the countless servicemen who remained in the capital. The accelerated prominence of men's tailoring in Paris, whether English or French, served as a means to keep men's bespoke consumer spending in the capital, rather than migrating to London. Paris's desired position in the domain of tailoring was already being heralded by Georges Cécile as early as 1920 in *Monsieur* when he boldly claimed: "If it has not already lost it, London is very nearly losing the supremacy it had in matters of men's fashion. If we are not yet there, at least it is a fact that the English cut is being discussed. . . . Paris is becoming anew the center—which they never ceased being—of Monsieur's fashion. And it is not one of the lesser successes of our journal that dedicates itself to the rebirth of French tradition and taste" (171).

In his short essay on men's fashion featured in the 1928 Exposition's catalog, de Fouquières, France's strongest advocate of men's tailoring throughout the 1920s, concluded by prophetically asking: "Does one have to repeat that fashion and the luxury trade are important factors of our influence in the world?" (in Yvan 145). For de Fouquières it is not women's haute couture that serviced as a new or even modern sphere of influence, but an emerging, revitalized métier that expands an already-existing sense of authority. If any one particular tailor, haberdasher, or hat maker embodied de Fouquières's assertion, it was certainly Mossant (fig. 9.1). For, if as the firm proudly and boldly advertised in 1925, its fedora-topped Eiffel Tower served as a beacon of French industrial and fashionable luxury, by 1928, however, it advertised itself, in *L'Illustration* for example, as the official hat of the globe, declaring: "The entire world is wearing Mossant hats." Mossant's fedora is no longer simply seen as completing the industrial modernity of the Eiffel Tower, but represented as topping the entire globe, a potent signifier of male sartoriality and France's radiating, well-rounded image across all nations.

Works Cited

Andrew, Dudley, and Steven Ungar. *Popular Front Paris and the Poetics of Culture.* The Belknap Press of Harvard UP, 2005.

Ariste. "La Mode Masculine." *L'Art vivant*, 1 January 1925, p. 32.

Barclay. "La Haute Mode masculine parisienne à l'Exposition d'Athènes." *Adam*, 15 April 1928, n.p.

Cavaille, Henri. "La Mode masculine française à l'Exposition d'Athènes." *L'Illustration*, June 1928, p. xxiii.

Cécil, Georges. "Le Vrai chic." *Monsieur*, July 1920, p. 171.

Chenoune, Farid. *A History of Men's Fashion*. Flammarion, 1993.

"Citroën a loué la Tour Eiffel." *Vendre*, vol. 3, no. 23, September 1925, n.p.

Clarisse. "La Mode." *L'Art vivant*, 1 August 1925, pp. 26–30.

Dyer, Richard. *White*. Routledge, 1997.

Exposition internationale des arts décoratifs et industriels modernes: Paris 1925: rapport général. Encyclopédie. Vol. 9, Parure (classes 20 à 24). Librairie Larousse, 1927.

Gregh, Fernand. "L'Élégance et Civilization." *Monsieur*, October 1920, p. 231.

Gronberg, Tag. *Designs on Modernity: Exhibiting the City in 1920s Paris*. Manchester UP, 1998.

———. "Paris 1925: Consuming Modernity." *Art Deco, 1910–1939*, edited by Charlotte Benton, Tim Benton, and Chislaine Wood. V&A Publications, 2003, pp. 156–63.

Kracauer, Seigfried. "The Mass Ornament" [1927]. *The Mass Ornament, Weimar Essays*. Harvard UP, 1995, pp. 75–88.

Le Corbusier. *The Decorative Art of Today* [1925]. MIT P, 1987.

"Londres et Paris," in *L'art vivant*, 1926, p. 313.

Marsan, Eugène. "Les Élégances masculines." *L'Art vivant*, 1925, pp. 22–23.

Potvin, John. "Housing the New Dandy: Designing Lifestyle in *Monsieur* Magazine, 1920–1924." *The Modern French Interior and Mass Media*, edited by Anca Lasc, Georgina Downey, and Mark Taylor. Bloomsbury, 2015, pp. 191–201.

———. "Masculinity, Elegance and Civilization: Art Criticism in Men's Fashion Magazine *Monsieur*, 1920–1924." *Fashion Theory: The Journal of Dress, Body & Culture*, vol. 20, no. 1, February 2016, pp. 1–31.

Le Retour à l'ordre dans les arts plastiques et l'architecture, 1919–1925. Sainte Étienne Centre Interdisciplinaire d'Études et de Recherche sur l'Expression Contemporaine, 1986.

Smith, H. Llewellyn, editor. *Reports on the Present Position and Tendencies of the Industrial Arts as Indicated at the International Exhibition of Modern Decorative and Industrial Arts, Paris, 1925*. Department of Overseas Trade, 1925.

Stanley, Adam C. *Modernizing Tradition: Gender and Consumerism in Interwar France and Germany*. Louisiana State UP, 2008.

Troy, Nancy. *Modernism and the Decorative Arts in France: Art Nouveau to Le Corbusier*. Yale UP, 1991.

Weiss, Andrea. *Paris Was a Woman: Portraits from the Left Bank*. Harper San Francisco, 1995.

Wigley, Mark. *White Walls, Designer Dresses: The Fashioning of Modern Architecture*. MIT P, 2001.

Wilson, Elizabeth. *Adorned in Dreams: Fashion and Modernity*. Rutgers UP, 2003.

Yvan, Edmond, editor. *L'Exposition de France à Athènes, 20 mars–31 mai 1928*. Comité d'Organisation de l'Exposition de France à Athènes, 1928.

CONTRIBUTORS

Heidi Brevik-Zender (Editor) is Associate Professor of French and Comparative Literature at the University of California, Riverside. The author of *Fashioning Spaces:* Mode *and Modernity in Late-Nineteenth-Century Paris* (2015), she has published articles and book chapters on fashion, aesthetics, women's authorship, exile, and the modern urban landscape in French literature, film, art, and visual culture. Her current book project, supported by a Fulbright award, is concerned with architecture and gender in nineteenth-century France.

Anne Green is Emeritus Professor of French at King's College London and was President of the Society of Dix-Neuviémistes from 2011 to 2017. Her books include *Flaubert and the Historical Novel: Salammbô Reassessed* (1982 and 2010); *Changing France: Literature and Material Culture in the Second Empire* (2011); and *Gustave Flaubert* (2017). She is currently writing a book on gloves for Reaktion Books.

Susan Hiner is Professor of French and Francophone Studies on the John Guy Vassar Chair in Modern Languages at Vassar College. She is the author of *Accessories to Modernity: Fashion and the Feminine in Nineteenth-Century France* (2010), as well as numerous articles and essays pertaining to nineteenth-century French culture. With the support of an NEH grant for 2016–17, she is completing a manuscript entitled "Behind the Seams: Women, Fashion, and Work in Nineteenth-Century France."

Cary Hollinshead-Strick is Associate Professor of Comparative Literature and English at the American University of Paris. Her first book, *Staging Publicity: The Fourth Estate at the Fourth Wall in July Monarchy France*, shows how nineteenth-century French popular theater mocked the commercialization of the early mass press, making it impossible for audiences to slide into passive consumption of advertisement-financed news, at least in its early years. Her next monograph, provisionally entitled "The Curved Cliché and the Filtering Net," traces the epistemology of print metaphors in nineteenth-century France. She has published articles on Delphine de Girardin, Alphonse Karr, Victor Hugo, Charles Nodier, and a variety of playwrights whose names have largely been forgotten.

Marni Reva Kessler is Associate Professor in the Kress Foundation Department of Art History at the University of Kansas, where she is also the Director of Graduate Studies. She is the author of *Sheer Presence: The Veil in Manet's Paris*, as well as articles and book chapters on topics related to urbanism, fashion, gender, food, family, and portraiture in French visual culture of the second half of the nineteenth century. Kessler has received numerous grants and fellowships, most recently a New York Public Library Food Studies Fellowship to support research for her current book project, which explores late nineteenth-century French representations of food that, materially and metaphorically, engage with a range of pleasures, anxieties, and unease associated with life in the modern metropolis.

Áine Larkin is Lecturer in French at the University of Aberdeen and author of *Proust Writing Photography* (2011). In 2014 she coedited a special issue of *Romance Studies* on Proust and music, and she is currently editing a special issue of *Forum for Modern Language Studies* on dance in modern and contemporary French culture. She contributed an article on masculinity and disability to a special issue of *L'Esprit Créateur* in 2016 and pursues research in Proust studies, critical disability studies, and dance in the modern novel.

John Potvin is Professor in the Department of Art History at Concordia University, Montreal, where he teaches on the intersections of art, design, and fashion. He is the author of *Material and Visual Cultures Beyond Male Bonding* (2008), *Giorgio Armani: Empire of the Senses* (2013), and, more recently, *Bachelors of a Different Sort: Queer Aesthetics, Material Culture and the Modern Interior in Britain* (2014), winner of the Historians of British Art Book Prize. In addition to being editor of *The Places and Spaces of Fashion* (2009) and *Oriental Interiors: Design, Identity, Space* (2015), he is also coeditor of both *Material Cultures, 1740–1920: The Meanings and Pleasures of Collecting* (2009) and *Fashion, Interior Design and the Contours of Modern Identity* (2010). His current book project, "Deco Dandy: Designing Masculinity in 1920s Paris," explores the fashion, painting, performance, and design cultures of the much-neglected interwar dandy, and in spring 2016 he was awarded a four-year Social Sciences and Humanities Research Council of Canada Grant to explore "Sexuality, Masculinity and Shame in Interior Design: From Professionalization to Queer Theory, 1869–2015."

Pierre Saint-Amand is Benjamin F. Barge Professor of French at Yale University. He writes on the literature and the philosophy of the eighteenth century. Among his books are *The Libertine's Progress: Seduction in the Eighteenth-Century French Novel* (1994) and *The Laws of Hostility: Politics, Violence, and the Enlightenment* (1996). More recently he published *The Pursuit of Laziness: An Idle Interpretation of the Enlightenment* (2011). He has written on the topic of fashion in eighteenth-century culture (in the Goncourt brothers, on Marie-Antoinette).

Nicholas White is Professor of Nineteenth-Century French Literature and Culture in the University of Cambridge and a Fellow of Emmanuel College. He is the author of *The Family in Crisis in Late Nineteenth-Century French Fiction* and *French Divorce Fiction from the Revolution to the First World War*, and he has edited seven volumes of essays and translations, including special numbers on Zola for *Romanic Review* and *Les Cahiers naturalistes*. He was one of the founding editors of the journal *Dix-Neuf* and the Principal Investigator for the United Kingdom's Arts and Humanities Research Council network on "The Art of Friendship in France, 1789 to 1914."

INDEX

Note: Page numbers in *italics* refer to illustrations.